TORTS, EGALITARIANISM AND DISTRIBUTIVE JUSTICE

Torts, Egalitarianism and Distributive Justice

TSACHI KEREN-PAZ
Keele University, UK,
College of Management, Israel

ASHGATE

Published by
Ashgate Publishing Limited
Gower House
Croft Road
Aldershot
Hampshire GU11 3HR
England

Ashgate Publishing Company
Suite 420
101 Cherry Street
Burlington, VT 05401-4405
USA

Ashgate website: http://www.ashgate.com

British Library Cataloguing in Publication Data
Keren-Paz, Tsachi
Torts, egalitarianism and distributive justice
1. Torts 2. Distributive justice 3. Legal polycentricity
4. Sociological jurisprudence
I. Title
346'.03

Library of Congress Cataloging-in-Publication Data
Keren-Paz, Tsachi.
Torts, egalitarianism, and distributive justice / by Tsachi Keren-Paz.
p. cm.
Includes index.
ISBN 978-0-7546-4653-2 (alk. paper)
1. Torts. 2. Negligence. 3. Distributive justice. 4. Law--Methodology. I. Title.

K923.Z9K47 2007
346.03--dc22

2007009691

ISBN: 978-0-7546-4653-2

Printed and bound in Great Britain by Antony Rowe Ltd, Chippenham, Wiltshire.

Contents

Acknowledgements *ix*

1 INTRODUCTION **1**

2 THEORETICAL FRAMEWORK **5**

Introduction 5

I. Distributive Justice 5

A. The Participants 6

B. The Thing Distributed 6

C. Criteria for Distribution 6

II. Egalitarianism 8

A. Concepts of Equality 8

B. 'Progressive', 'Disadvantage' and 'Equality Effect' Defined 12

C. The Level at which Egalitarian Considerations Work 12

III. Tort Law 14

A. Instrumentalism, Pluralism, Contextualism 14

B. A Sketch of Tort Law and its Goals 16

IV. Pulling the Threads Together 17

A. Egalitarian Tort Law in the Context of the Declining Welfare State 17

B. The Limits of the Argument 19

3 NORMATIVE DEFENCE **23**

Introduction 23

I. Illegitimacy 23

A. The Argument 23

B. The Inevitability of the Distributive Effects of Legal Rules and the Political Nature of the Judiciary 24

C. Public Choice 27

D. Ability to Amend 31

E. Substantive versus Procedural Justice 32

II. Randomness 33

A. Redistribution by Tort Law is not Particularly Random 34

B. Random Redistribution is Fairer than the Status Quo 36

III. Excessive Cost 40

A. In General 40

B. Efficiency 42

IV. Ineffectiveness 55
A. Comparative Institutional Inquiry: Will Judicial Egalitarian Commitment Bring About More Egalitarian Results? 55
B. Limited Ability to Achieve Distributive Results by Legal Rules 58
Conclusion 65

4 APPLICATORY FRAMEWORK 67
Introduction 67
I. The Regressive Nature of Existing Tort Law 67
A. The Principle of Restitutio Ad Integrum 67
B. Scope of Responsibility 69
II. Levels of Operation 70
A. Tort Law and Alternative Compensation Schemes 70
B. Choice of Regime 71
C. Desirability of Specific Torts and Doctrines 73
III. Multiplicity of Participants and Entitlements 73
A. Factual and Conceptual Problems 73
B. Identifying those Affected by the Rule 74
C. Conflicting Dimensions of Distribution: Material and Symbolic Goods 76
IV. Direction of Distributive Result 76
A. Expanding Liability 77
B. Limiting Liability 78
C. Unclear Recommendation 78
V. Balancing Egalitarianism with Other Policy Considerations 79
A. Relevance 79
B. Autonomous Nature: Egalitarianism is Broader than Anti-Discrimination 79
C. Lack of Conclusiveness 80
D. Egalitarian Consideration Should Not Serve Merely as a Veto 80
E. Weight 80
F. Conclusion 84

5 STANDARD OF CARE 85
Introduction 85
I. Insights from Other Approaches 85
A. Corrective Justice 86
B. Efficiency 87
C. Loss-Spreading 89
D. Fairness 90
II. Normative Defence 91
A. The Intuition 91
B. Justifications 92
III. Standard or Duty? 101

IV. Reformulating the Standard of Care 103
A. The Role of Egalitarianism in Standard of Care Analysis 103
B. Comparing Disutility: The Difficulties and Guidelines for Courts 105
V. How Does It Work? 113
A. Active Risk Creation 113
B. Failure to Prevent Risk Created by Third Parties 121
VI. Incongruity with Existing Tort Law 125
A. Standard of Care 125
B. Considering Needs and Equality in Tort Law and Private Law 129
Conclusion 131

6 DUTY OF CARE 133
Introduction 133
I. The Effects of Egalitarianism on Duty of Care 133
II. Possible Solutions to the Problem of Maternal Prenatal Duty 136
III. The Egalitarian Case Against Unconditional Duty 138
A. The Arguments 139
B. Egalitarian Framework 141
C. Newborns with Disability as Disadvantaged Plaintiffs? 142
D. General Duty? 144
IV. Conditional Duty 145
A. The Unity of Interests Among Pregnant Women and their Children 145
B. The Tension Between the Practical and Symbolic Results of the Rule 147
C. The Ways Premiums are Collected: Questions of Inter- and Intra-group Justice 148
D. Intra-group Justice: Class and Race 150
E. The Symbolic Aspect of Liability 152
F. Supplementary Comments with Respect to the Suggested Rule 154
G. The Analytical Aspect: Insurance, Standard, and Duty of Care 157
H. The Pragmatic Aspect: Much Ado About Nothing? 158

7 DISCRIMINATION AS NEGLIGENCE 161
Introduction 161
I. Negligence and Alternative Responses to Discrimination 161
II. The Institutional Inquiry 162
A. Advantages 163
B. Disadvantages 166
III. The Conceptual and Normative Inquiries 168
A. Implications of the Choice between Duty and Standard for Denying Liability 168
B. Standard 172
C. Duty 177
D. Damages 180

8 CONCLUSION **181**

Table of Cases *189*
Table of Legislation *193*
Bibliography *195*
Index *207*

Acknowledgements

This study is a culmination of nine years' work. It greatly benefited from the comments of many colleagues and friends who either read parts of the manuscript at different stages, or discussed with me some of the ideas developed in it: Ronen Avraham, Daphne Barak-Erez, Anita Bernstein, Lisa Bernstein, Yishai Blank, Nili Cohen, Tsilly Dagan, Bruce Feldthusen, Martha Fineman, Ruth Fletcher, Daniel Friedmann, Marie Fox, Shelley Gavigan, Joan Gilmour, Yifat Holzman-Gazit, Reg Graycar, Ofer Grosskopf, Duncan Kennedy, Shane Kelleher, Shai Lavi, Risa Lieberwitz, Tali Margalit, Menny Mautner, Michael Mandel, Barak Medina, Catherine O'Sullivan, Frances Raday, Iain Ramsay, Bruce Ryder, Kate Sutherland, Ron Shapira, Sally Sheldon, Yofi Tirosh, Eric Tucker and Omri Yadlin.

I would like to extend special thanks to three people. Hanoch Dagan was the first to expose me to the politics of law and to many of the themes I have pursued in this book, including my interest in the role of distributive justice in tort law. He read parts of the manuscripts and made valuable comments. Ariel Porat taught me much of what I know about tort law, and introduced me to theoretical and pluralist approaches to (tort) law, as well as to the interplay of doctrine and theory. Ariel has read most of the manuscript and his comments significantly improved the final result. Words are not sufficient to express my gratitude to Allan Hutchinson. Allan's help to the development of the ideas advanced in this book, and the way they are represented was invaluable.

I would like to thank Ron Gutman, Daniel Drenger and Julie McCandless for their superb research support, Adam Vital for his linguistic editing, and Alison Kirk of Ashgate for her editorial work.

Several chapters of this book are a reworking of material that appeared in the following articles: 'Private Law Redistribution, Predictability and Liberty', *50 McGill LJ* (2005) 327; 'On Mothers, Babies and Bathwater: Tort Law, Distributive Justice and Prenatal Duties', 14 *Social & Legal Studies* (2005) 179; ' "It Costs Me More": Rejecting the Arguments of Illegitimacy and Excessive Cost Brought against the Promotion of Equality in Private Law', 7 *Haifa ULR* (2004) 541; 'How Does Compensation Law Render the Poor Even Poorer? (And Why Does the Supreme Court Give Inconsistent Interpretation to the Compensation to Victims of Road Accidents Act?)', 28 *Tel-Aviv ULR* (2004) 299; 'Egalitarianism as Justification: Why and How Should Egalitarian Considerations Reshape the Standard of Care in Negligence Law', 4 *Theor Inq L* (2003) 275; 'An Inquiry into the Merits of Redistribution through Tort Law: Rejecting the Claim of Randomness', 16 *Can JL & Jur* (2003) 91. I am grateful to the publishers of these articles for permitting me to make use of them.

For financial support that made the completion of this work possible I acknowledge: Colman Law School, Cornell Law School's Gender, Sexuality and the Family Fellowship, and Keele University's Gender, Sexuality and the Law Fellowship.

Last but not least, I would like to thank my partner, Marie-Andree Jacob, who is my best friend, soulmate, true love and colleague. Marie's sense of justice, thoroughness and patience made this book better. Her love gave me the energy to complete it and a good reason to do so.

This book is dedicated with love and gratitude to my parents. The unconditional love, education, emotional and material support that they have given me thus far are overwhelming. My mother, Dvora, inspired this project with her values and politics. My late father, Avraham, instilled in me the love of learning and the love of books. I wish I could have given him a copy of this one.

Chapter 1

Introduction

Tort law regulates involuntary interactions in private settings, when such interactions harm some, or all participants. As such it raises questions of both social policy and moral theory. William Prosser has observed that '[p]erhaps more than any other branch of the law, the law of torts is a battleground of social theory'.[1] In fact, tort law is a battleground of philosophical theory. The philosophical battleground precedes the social one in the sense that a major battle pertains to the legitimacy of the claim that tort law should be a battleground of social theory. Some dispute the public nature of tort law and ignore its broader social ramifications, both practically and symbolically. Tort law, however, is rife with value judgments concerning the kind of society one would like to live in. It strikes a balance between the values of opposing autonomy-based claims, and between the values of self-reliance and personal responsibility on the one hand and altruism and other-regarding on the other.

The potential reach of tort law is extensive due to the fact that it is based on involuntary interactions which are not mediated by a possible sense of shared community (as might arguably be the case in a contractual setting). These features make tort law an especially interesting philosophical and social battleground. This book endorses a view that is both sensitive to the political stakes of tort law and that is egalitarian; it is committed to advancing the status of disadvantaged members in society. This book tries to show why such a view is commendable and should be endorsed normatively, and how it can be relevant to tort law.

The battle over philosophical and social interpretations of tort law spills over into the question of the goals that tort law should promote. Numerous answers have been given to this question. Although tort scholarship includes some pluralist approaches, it is dominated by two monist approaches: an economic analysis of law, which aims to maximize societal wealth; and corrective justice, which limits itself to meting out justice on a retroactive basis to particular litigants.[2] This book offers another approach to tort law: one that is instrumentalist, pluralist, contextual and progressive.

Instrumentalist (or functionalist) legal approaches are forward-looking. They view law as an instrument which is used to achieve social and moral goals. Pluralist approaches to tort law maintain that tort law should (or does) promote more than one goal. The underlying theme in this study is that in addition to traditional goals, such as deterrence and compensation, tort law should be attentive to its distributive effects; tort law can and should promote equality and in particular the status, power and well-being of the disadvantaged. It will be shown how tort law can promote the status of the disadvantaged, given its structural limitations and its role in promoting other

---

1 William L. Prosser, *Handbook of the Law of Torts* (4th edn, St Paul, 1971), pp. 14–15, s. 3.

2 See Ch. 5.I below.

goals. As will become clear from the discussion in the following chapter, this study dwells on the intersection of doctrine (tort law), conceptual apparatus (distributive justice), and normative commitment (an egalitarian-progressive approach).

This study could be classified as belonging to two streams of scholarship. The first stream attempts to defend the relevance and legitimacy of using private law for (limited) redistributive purposes. The other line of scholarship related to this study is the one trying to employ tort law progressively, with an ambition to be sensitive to the demands of equality and the interests of disadvantaged groups in society.[3]

The book is divided into two parts, theoretical (Chapters 2–3) and practical (Chapters 4–8). Chapter 2 begins by introducing the theoretical framework – an exposition of distributive justice, concepts of equality and a functional approach to law and tort law. The latter will be examined in terms of its function, social impact, goals and normative commitment. It then comments on the relationship between egalitarian tort law and the welfare state, and introduces the limits of the argument advanced in this book. Chapter 3 is devoted to defending the normative claim that tort law can and should promote equality as one of its goals. The discussion attempts to provide answers to critiques from both corrective justice and efficiency-oriented scholars. It responds to the claims that the egalitarian agenda is illegitimate due to the fact that judges are not accountable (illegitimacy), that it is unjust to promote equality by private law since such redistribution is deemed to be partial (randomness), that such an attempt is undesirable since it interferes too much with the attainment of other goals of private law (excessive cost), and that it is likely to be ineffective due to institutional limitations of courts and private law (ineffectiveness). It finds all these charges ultimately unconvincing.

Chapter 4 lays the ground for the application of an egalitarian approach to tort theory. It exposes the inherent regressive bias of existing tort law, explores the ways in which an egalitarian commitment can reshape tort law, presents the difficulties involved in an attempt to assess a rule's equality effect, explains the two possible egalitarian recommendations, and sketches a framework for balancing the dictates of egalitarianism with other competing goals of tort law. Chapter 5 suggests how to formulate an egalitarian standard of care. It defends the adoption of such a standard, while reconciling egalitarianism with other major policy considerations of corrective justice, efficiency, loss spreading and fairness. Chapter 6 explains how a duty of care should take egalitarianism into account. It concentrates on the issue of maternal prenatal duty and concludes, somewhat surprisingly, that a feminist-egalitarian

---

3 Scholars associated with the first stream are Anthony Kronman, Hugh Collins (contract law), Hanoch Dagan (unjust enrichment law), Iain Ramsay, Alan Kruger, and Robert Lee (consumer law). See e.g., Anthony T. Kronman, 'Contract Law and Distributive Justice', 89 *Yale LJ* (1980) 472. Scholars associated with the second stream are Richard Abel, to whom this work owes a lot, Leslie Bender, Kate Sutherland, Elizabeth Handsley, Anita Bernstein, Martha Chamallas, Elizabeth Adjin-Tettey, Bruce Feldthusen, Mayo Moran, Ken Cooper-Stephenson, Ted Decoste, Thomas Koening & Michael Rusted, Chris Sanchiricho, and Duncan Kennedy. See e.g., Richard L. Abel, 'General Damages are Incoherent, Incalculable, Incommensurable, and Inegalitarian (but Otherwise a Great Idea)', 55 *DePaul L Rev* (2006) 253, pp. 323–4; Leslie Bender, 'An Overview of Feminist Torts Scholarship', 78 *Cornell L Rev* (1993) 575.

approach might support a duty that hinges upon the existence of insurance. Chapter 7 maintains that the tort of negligence could and should be used to complement legislation in order to combat discrimination. Chapter 8, after revealing some patterns and lessons emerging from the previous application chapters, concludes by suggesting the contours of a reform to damages law and by flagging a new frontier for egalitarian tort law (which awaits future research) – the fight against human trafficking.

The discussion in the following chapters will revolve around four questions and one theme. An attempt to promote equality and distributive justice by tort law has to inquire what sort of entitlements are distributed by tort law, who is affected by such distribution, what is the price involved in promoting equality, (or engaging in redistribution), and how equality can be promoted effectively and fairly. These questions can be summarized as the 'what', 'to whom', 'at what cost' and 'how' questions. The theme underlying the analysis is the importance of context. Tortious interactions arise in different contexts, and sensitivity to the different variables controlling tortious interactions is warranted in order to develop a normatively attractive legal rule.

With respect to the 'what' question, the analysis calls to attention the fact that tort law distributes different entitlements, that at times a given rule affects positively the distribution of a given entitlement to a certain group, while at the same time affecting negatively the distribution of another entitlement to the same group, and that the analysis should distinguish between issues of redistribution and recognition.

With respect to the 'to whom' question, the analysis distinguishes between issues of inter-group justice and intra-group justice and calls to attention the fact that third parties – those not likely to be litigants – can be affected by the legal rule as well.

With respect to the 'at what cost' question, the analysis maintains that the relative weight that should be given to the goal of promoting equality changes with the context, as is the extent to which tension exists between the goal of promoting equality and other goals. For example, at times the more egalitarian rule is also the more efficient.

With respect to the 'how' question, the analysis suggests the following: (1) The overall distributive result of the rule in question should be examined (as opposed to a Rawlsean approach). (2) Egalitarian commitment may impose a duty on the actor to behave in a certain way; it may also impose a duty on the policymaker to consider adopting a certain rule given the rule's distributive effects. (3) Egalitarian considerations can work in the direction of curtailing liability of disadvantaged groups or enhancing liability toward them. (4) Curtailing liability can at times be based on a rationale of excuse and at others based on a rationale of justification. Given the expressive and symbolic aspects of the law, this distinction is important since egalitarian considerations change the social meaning of the defendant's behaviour. (5) Egalitarian considerations can work both directly and indirectly, by reformulating other policy considerations. (6) The analysis should distinguish between the ability of tort law to redistribute wealth and its ability to redistribute non-material entitlements. (7) In constructing egalitarian rules we can distinguish between rules aiming to help the disadvantaged ('pro-disadvantaged') and rules aiming to deprive the 'haves' of excessive riches (anti-'haves'). (8) In constructing egalitarian rules we can distinguish between rules aiming to reverse inequalities created by the effect of the legal rule, and rules aiming to reverse inequality whose cause is external to the rule in question. (9) Inserting egalitarian sensitivity can be done at numerous levels; the most basic distinction, however, is between rules pertaining to the scope of liability and rules pertaining to the scope of compensation.

This book's ambition is to show that tort law can and should be used progressively, as one mechanism in the ongoing struggle to achieve a more just and egalitarian society. A contextual egalitarian approach to tort law can be squared with other goals that tort law should promote. This book is not a comprehensive descriptive account of existing tort law, but rather a pro-active search for new approaches and conceptual tools to meet the challenges faced by egalitarians. Hopefully, the understanding of tort law offered in this book will bring about better practical results in specific cases, will further the support to the progressive troops in the ongoing philosophical and social battles that take place in the field of tort law as well as elsewhere, and will add another voice – rich, nuanced and sensitive – to the chorus that is tort theory.

Chapter 2

Theoretical Framework

Introduction

This chapter introduces the three concepts which form the theoretical framework and explain the way they interrelate: distributive justice, egalitarian commitment and tort law. Distributive justice deals with distributing benefits and burdens in society in a fair manner according to several criteria. One possible criterion is equality – an attempt to decrease the gaps between the 'haves' and the disadvantaged. Tort law is one area where some kind of burden is distributed – the harm caused by involuntary interactions among individuals. Tort law should develop several criteria to answer the question how to distribute this burden and it has done so. The central claim of this study is that one of these criteria should be equality. After introducing the principles underlying distributive justice, egalitarianism and tort law, in Parts I, II and III respectively, Part IV pulls the threads together and sets the ground for the normative claim and the application of the argument.

I. Distributive Justice

Distributive justice, according to Aristotle's classic definition,[1] is a mechanism to distribute benefits and burdens among the members of a relevant group in proportion to some criterion for distribution, such as merit, needs, equality, status, and so on. Aristotle's formulation is based on a 'geometrical' proportion between two (or more) participants, regarding their possession of the criterion/criteria for distribution and their respective share in the thing distributed (the benefit/burden). For example, if the relevant criterion for distribution is merit, and one person is twice as meritorious as another, the former's share in the good distributed should be double the latter's. It is often noted[2] that Aristotle did not commit himself in his discussion of distributive justice to a particular criterion for distribution, but rather mentioned that such a selection is dependent upon one's political conception of the good. The basic structure of distributive justice, therefore, is comprised of: (1) the participants in the distribution; (2) the thing to be distributed; and (3) the criterion/criteria for distribution.

1 Aristotle, *Nicomachean Ethics* (trans. Martin Ostwald, Book Five, New York, 1962), pp. 117–20.

2 See e.g., Hanoch Dagan, *Unjust Enrichment* (Cambridge, 1997), p. 32.

A. The Participants

Issues of distributive justice are relevant to the distribution of entitlements (goods) between groups consisting of two participants or more. One distinction offered in the literature is between distributions among small groups, and in society at whole.[3] In this respect, the situation in the context of torts is something of a hybrid. From a corrective justice perspective – looking at the specific parties litigating over past interaction – it involves a small number of litigants, usually two. From an instrumentalist perspective – looking at the rule's effects on potential litigants – it includes all the potential litigants affected by the rule, and possibly third parties as well.

An important aspect of the approach presented here is that the examination of the distributive effects of tort rules should be attentive to the group identity of the individuals involved and affected by the distribution. An evaluation of the desirability of the distributive effects of tort rules should therefore be attentive to the ways in which these rules affect different identifiable groups in society. In particular, egalitarian approach requires that we give attention to the ways in which tort rules affect members of disadvantaged groups, such as women, minorities, and the poor.

B. The Thing Distributed

Distributive justice dispenses benefits and burdens among the participants in the distribution. For present purposes it is important to observe three interrelated points. First, the legal rule will also distribute intangible goods. Second, a given legal rule can affect the distribution of more than one good. Third, some goods distributed by the legal rule are derivative of other goods whose distribution by the rule is more evident. The legal rule controlling the distribution of goods (either in regard to persons or property) will distribute more than the rights to the tangible object or its economical value.[4] It also distributes goods such as liberty (both negative and positive), dignity and societal power and status, as well as control, individual security in one's wealth and social responsibility.[5]

C. Criteria for Distribution

Most of the debate in the distributive justice literature is dedicated to the question of which criterion or criteria should control the distribution. Monist approaches emphasize criteria such as entitlement, equality, needs or desert. According to Robert Nozick's libertarian-patterned entitlement theory, individuals are entitled to what they acquired in a procedurally fair manner. Entitlement can be obtained

---

3 See David Miller, 'Distributive Justice: What the People Think', 102 *Ethics* (1992) 555, pp. 556–8, 564; Phillip Brickman *et al.*, 'Microjustice and Macrojustice', in Melvin J. Lerner & Sally C. Lerner (eds), *The Justice Motive in Social Behavior* (New York, 1981), p. 173.

4 See Dagan, *supra* note 2, pp. 3, 23–31, 33; Jules Coleman & Arthur Ripstein, 'Mischief and Misfortune', 41 *McGill LJ* (1995) 91.

5 See Dagan, *supra* note 2, pp. 3, 23–31, 33.

either through a transfer from a rightful prior owner or by a first acquisition. The government has no justification in engaging in redistribution of what was acquired according to the procedural rules, regardless of the desirability of the end-result of the holdings.[6]

Egalitarian programmes all share the idea that the participants in the distribution should get the relevant good according to the concept of equality. What the demands of equality consist of is a hotly debated question briefly commented upon in the next part of this chapter. Nonetheless, egalitarian theories share some commitment to performing the distribution in a way that will diminish existing disparities in holdings among the participants in the relevant entitlement. For example, John Rawls' difference principle demands that, subject to the lexical priority of the equal right to the most liberty compatible with a similar liberty to all, social and economical inequalities should be arranged to the greatest benefit of the least advantaged.[7]

Needs-based programmes 'are premised on the moral priority of supplying individuals with certain basic needs – such as food, shelter and minimal self-respect – over and above the satisfaction of the preferences of any other individual in society, including, according to some theorists, those of the needy themselves.'[8] Needs as a prominent criterion for distribution is embedded in the Marxist (and French socialist) principle of 'to each according to his needs'.[9] The scope of needs-based claims, as well as their origin, is debated in the literature.[10]

Desert-based claims are premised on the idea of giving each person their due.[11] Adherents of desert disagree on the scope, origin and details of desert-based claims. For example, there are different approaches regarding the question whether the proper basis for desert should be effort, talent or outcome.[12] Many view desert as necessarily based on the subject's autonomous decisions.[13]

---

6 Robert Nozick, *Anarchy, State, and Utopia* (New York, 1974), Ch. 7.

7 John Rawls, *A Theory of Justice* (rev. edn, Cambridge, 1999), p. 266. Compare with Kai Neilsen, 'Radical Egalitarian Justice: Justice as Equality', 5 *Soc Theory & Prac* (1979) 209, p. 211 (income and wealth are to be so divided that each person will have a right to an equal share).

8 See Dagan, *supra* note 2, p. 29. For some leading defences of need-based theories see David Braybrooke, *Meeting Needs* (Princeton, 1987); David Wiggins, 'Claims of Need', in Ted Honderich (ed.), *Morality and Objectivity: A Tribute to J.L. Mackie* (London, 1985), p. 149.

9 For a review of Marxist approaches to justice see Bernard Cullen, 'Philosophical Theories of Justice', in Klaus R. Scherer (ed.), *Justice: Interdisciplinary Perspectives* (Cambridge, 1992), p. 15, pp. 39–42.

10 See Dagan, *supra* note 2, p. 30 (distinguishing between a strong version of needs-based distribution premised on some kind of altruism, and a weak version which is premised on commitment to personal liberty).

11 Among the prominent adherents of desert are George Sher, *Desert* (Princeton, 1987) and Wojciech Sadurski, *Giving Desert Its Due: Social Justice and Legal Theory* (Dordrecht, 1985).

12 See Miller, *supra* note 3, p. 563; Robert Young, 'Egalitarianism and Personal Desert', 102 *Ethics* (1992) 319, pp. 332–3.

13 See e.g., Sher, *supra* note 11.

This book endorses a pluralist and contextual approach to the question of determining the relevant criteria for distribution, according to which the selection of the criteria for distribution is contextual and contingent. Pluralist theories of distributive justice are supported by many thinkers including John Lucas, Charles Taylor and Michael Waltzer.[14] According to pluralist approaches there is no one criterion which is preferable to others under all circumstances. The appropriateness of the chosen criterion is at least partially dependent upon the nature of the goods that are to be distributed.[15] Moreover, a given distribution ought not necessarily to be controlled by a single given criterion, but might rather be made according to a synthesis of several criteria.[16]

Egalitarian commitment entails a conclusion that equality and needs are relevant criteria for distribution in the tort context. A pluralist approach entails a conclusion that these criteria should be balanced against other criteria for distribution, including desert, which in the context of tort law roughly parallels the notion of fault. Desert, as a criterion for distribution, can be understood to operate in a way which is sensitive to the demands of equality and needs.[17] An egalitarian reformulation of desert can either view the actions of the disadvantaged who harms others as more justified or excused, or view the actions which harm the disadvantaged or committed by the 'haves' as more culpable.

II. Egalitarianism

A. Concepts of Equality

The goal of this study – inserting an egalitarian sensitivity in tort law – raises four questions: (1) Why should we promote equality at all? (2) What concept of equality would we like to promote and why? (3) Why should tort law be used as a mechanism to enhance equality? (4) How can tort law combine an egalitarian commitment as one of its goals within a pluralist and contextual understanding of tort law? Of these four questions, this study tackles only the last two. The discussion assumes the desirability of equality as a value (and the ethos, albeit not the practice, of Western

---

14 John R. Lucas, *On Justice* (Oxford, 1980), pp. 163–70; Cullen, *supra* note 9, pp. 39–42 (reviewing Lucas, David Miller and David Raphael's pluralist approaches); Michael Walzer, *Spheres of Justice: A Defense of Pluralism and Equality* (Oxford, 1983); Charles Taylor, 'The Nature and Scope of Distributive Justice', in *Philosophy and the Human Sciences* (Cambridge, 1985) 289, pp. 289, 312; Paul Stern, 'Citizenship, Community and Pluralism: The Current Dispute on Distributive Justice', 11 *Praxis-Int'l* (1991) 261, p. 263.

15 See e.g., Lucas, Ibid., pp. 164–6; Walzer, Ibid., p. 21; Cf. Dagan, *supra* note 2, pp. 34–49.

16 See e.g., Norman E. Bowie, *Towards a New Theory of Distributive Justice* (Amherst, 1971), pp. 122–33; Lucas, *supra* note 14, p. 169.

17 Cf. Sadurski, *supra* note 11, p. 169 (meeting basic needs is a precondition for the operation of desert); Richard Delgado, '"Rotten Social Background": Should the Criminal Law Recognize a Defense of Severe Environmental Deprivation?', 3 *L & Ineq J* (1985) 9; See Ch. 5.II.B3 and Ch. 6.IV.D below.

societies endorses equality as a prime value). Of course, those disputing the need to promote equality altogether would oppose a call for a more egalitarian tort law. However, even those committed to the ideal of equality might think that doing so through tort law is unjust, undesirable or impractical. This book responds to those sceptics.

The main dispute regarding the value of equality is centred on the second question – what concept of equality we should adopt. In the discourse of political philosophy, competing political theories are supported by their proponents in the name of equality.[18] A basic distinction in the typology of different approaches to equality is between equality of opportunity and equality of result. The former is concerned with ensuring equality at the starting points of the participants; the latter with ensuring equal end-results. One concept of equality of opportunity is narrow and formal and is limited merely to removing formal barriers to competition between the participants in the distribution. This concept is supported by libertarians. The substantive version of equality of opportunity is concerned with ensuring a *fair* equality of opportunity. The substantive concept takes into account the different starting points of the participants, and focuses on the social construction of disadvantage and history of discrimination. This approach is committed to incorporating an understanding of prior disadvantage and to ensure that all participants have a fair chance in competing for the desired scarce good. Such a concept, however, is not necessarily committed to ensuring equal end-results, and it would usually allow for differences in end-results to be determined by merit.

Equality of result is committed to ensuring that a distributive scheme gives participants the same amount of the entitlement distributed as a final outcome. Different theories exist regarding the question of what is the thing to be distributed equally (the equalisandum). The main dichotomy is between equality of welfare (measured by happiness or preference-satisfaction) and equality of resources (and here, too, different approaches exist regarding the question of which set of resources should be equated).[19]

Another distinction in the equality literature is between formal and substantive concepts of equality.[20] Substantive notion is defined here as one showing sensitivity to the different starting points of the participants, and therefore as being committed to taking this difference into account to a certain extent while distributing the relevant entitlement.

---

18 For one typology see Ronald Dworkin, *Law's Empire* (Cambridge, 1986), pp. 297–301 (reviewing libertarian, welfare-based conceptions of equality, material equality, and resource equality). See also Ronald Dworkin, *Sovereign Virtue: The Theory and Practice of Equality* (Cambridge, 2000), Chs 1–2.

19 See Kyle Logue & Ronen Avraham, 'Redistributing Optimally: of Tax Rules, Legal Rules, and Insurance', 56 *Tax L Rev* (2003) 157, pp. 161–3.

20 Formal equality is traced back to Aristotle. See Aristotle, *Ethica Nicomachea* (trans. William D. Ross, Book V.3, Oxford, 1925), p. 1131a–b. For critique of formal equality see e.g., Martha A. Fineman, *The Illusion of Equality: The Rhetoric and Reality of Divorce Reform* (Chicago, 1991), pp. 20–22. For one definition (out of many and at times incompatible) of substantive equality as equality not of treatment, but rather of conditions or result see Emily L. Sherwin, 'The Limits of Feminism', 9 *J Contemp Leg Issues* (1998) 249, p. 250.

Yet another distinction in the equality literature is the one between redistribution and recognition paradigms. The philosopher Nancy Fraser distinguishes between socio-economic injustice (that is, the unjust distribution of wealth in society) and cultural injustice, which concerns the recognition and status of members of disadvantaged groups in society. The 'socio-economic injustice' paradigm views the unequal distribution of wealth as the main basis of inequality in society; by progressively redistributing wealth the problem of inequality will be solved, so that the membership of individuals in historically disadvantaged groups would become irrelevant. According to such a view, the basic unit of inequality is the individual (despite the relevance of the issue of class), and the main problem (that is, the unequal distribution of wealth) results in a lack of adequate respect for the individual. In contrast, under the 'recognition' paradigm, the main problem is not economic but rather social and symbolic: the problem stems from social bias towards the values and preferences of dominant groups. The basic unit of inequality is the group rather than the individual, and the remedies should focus on legitimizing social divergence and enhancing the status of historically disadvantaged groups.[21]

Another claim made by Fraser is disputed. Fraser argues that the two paradigms are in constant tension with each other, since solving the problem of inequality of wealth distribution (which involves group membership) weakens the collective identity, and its goal is 'to put the group out of the business as a group',[22] while the remedies of the recognition paradigm are meant to affirm the value of group identity. In contrast, Iris Young argues that promoting equality necessarily combines recognition and distribution, and that there is no tension between the two goals.[23] In fact, this debate echoes the difference between symmetrical and asymmetrical approaches to equality and the politics of difference. Asymmetrical models of equality celebrate the differences between members of disadvantaged groups and members of the dominant group. They call for an acceptance of those differences and for their accommodation, rather than for an attempt to eliminate the differences and assimilate the disadvantaged within the archetypical 'have', his values, wishes and needs, which are the basis for comparison.[24] A politics of difference, or intersectionality, maintains that inequality is textured and often compounded by multiple disadvantages, and that (in)equality theories which universalize from the experience of only one disadvantaged group are flawed by their erasure of situated differences.[25]

21 Nancy Fraser, *Justice Interruptus: Critical Reflections on the 'Postsocialist' Condition* (New York, 1997), pp. 13–15.

22 Ibid., p. 19.

23 See Iris M. Young, 'Unruly Categories: A Critique of Nancy Fraser's Dual Systems Theory', 222 *New Left Rev* (1997) 147, p. 159.

24 See Fraser, *supra* note 21, p. 11; Christine A. Littleton, 'Reconstructing Sexual Equality', 75 *Calif L Rev* (1987) 1279; Leon E. Trakman, 'Substantive Equality in Constitutional Jurisprudence: Meaning Within Meaning', 7 *Can JL & Jur* (1994) 27, p. 28.

25 Sheila McIntyre, 'Backlash Against Equality: The "Tyranny" of the "Politically Correct"', 38 *McGill LJ* (1993) 1, p. 3 n.4.

This study merely introduces, rather than fully defends the version of equality it supports. It should also be noted that the argument presented in this study could be supported by competing versions of egalitarian commitment.[26] This is so since tort law can be only one, partial element of a progressive agenda, and it neither can nor should play the main role in advancing the goals of egalitarianism. None of the competing substantive concepts of equality (for example, fair equality of opportunity versus end-result resource equality) can be accomplished by a progressive-minded tort law alone. However, a progressive-egalitarian agenda that is supported by either version of substantive equality could be advanced by tort law as one goal among others.

The essential elements of the approach to equality taken in this book – group-based understanding, and asymmetrical model of equality – have already been explained above. This approach combines a fair equality of opportunity, with a commitment to decreasing (but not necessarily eliminating) gaps in end-result resource allocation. The latter commitment encompasses both ensuring the provision of basic needs at the bottom of the spectrum, and taking some of the wealth accumulated by those in the upper part of the spectrum. Different end-results are allowed (as long as they are not too excessive) by accepting either notions of positive desert or instrumental considerations such as the need to create enough incentives to produce wealth. Matters of recognition and the distribution of non-material entitlements are also taken seriously into account.

While this approach diverges from some egalitarian approaches (most notably Rawls') by allowing desert to play a role, the difference is more apparent than real. First, it shares the view that a desert-based claim, even if not completely arbitrary from a moral perspective, cannot support the subject's demand to the full market value accruing to her due to her natural talents,[27] and therefore justifies redistribution. This approach is also based on the ideas of the diminishing marginal utility of money and the need to promote cohesiveness in society, possibly by encouraging and cultivating some degree of altruism among its members. Secondly, some egalitarian approaches, including Rawls', allow different end-results in practice due to the concept of legitimate expectations (which in turn are based on the need to ensure adequate incentives).[28] Finally, Rawls' theory accepts the relevance of negative desert, which is especially relevant in tort law.[29] This similarity should not obscure the basic disagreements between the concept of equality sketched above and the liberal-Rawlsian concept of equality, which is based on an individualistic (as opposed to group-based), abstract (as opposed to situated), 'neutral' (as opposed to perfectionist), assimilationist (as opposed to accommodating) and decontextual approach.

---

26 Cf. Logue & Avraham, *supra* note 19, pp. 162–3.

27 Cf. Edwin C. Hettinger, 'Justifying Intellectual Property', 18 *Phil & Pub Aff* (1989) 31, pp. 38–9.

28 Rawls, *supra* note 7, p. 274.

29 Ibid., pp. 276–7.

B. *'Progressive', 'Disadvantage' and 'Equality Effect' Defined*

This book advocates the adoption of a progressive approach to tort law that is egalitarian and that takes into account a rule's distributive effect on the disadvantaged. Progressivism, is a political and moral commitment to social change that will empower members of disadvantaged groups in society. Accordingly, the terms 'progressive', and 'egalitarian' (which are used interchangeably), connote a solution or a rule which redistributes benefits from the more to the less advantaged, or burdens from the less to the more advantaged. One can distinguish between strong and weak versions of such a commitment. Proponents of the strong version would insist on using private law rules to narrow gaps in society, while proponents of the weak version would be content with not permitting such gaps to widen as a result of the rule's effect. As for the terms 'disadvantage' and 'the disadvantaged', they should be understood contextually; these terms are related to asymmetrical models of equality and the politics of difference, and are relational and relative.[30] A member of a given group might be disadvantaged when compared to one individual but not when compared to another. Moreover, sometimes we deal with multiple disadvantages. For example, black women in the United States are burdened both on the account of their race and their gender.

An important aspect of the disadvantage is that it is attached to immutable characteristics. These include both traits that are completely immutable such as race, authenticity, sexual orientation and sex (sex operations notwithstanding), and traits that can be changed, if at all, only with much difficulty, such as class. The immutability calls into attention both the strong important group membership aspect of the disadvantage and the injustice ingrained in attaching burdens based on such characteristics.

Viewing the problem of disadvantage through the prism of acceptance models of difference and intersectionality alerts us to the fact that: (1) disadvantage is essentially group-based rather than individual-based, and is systematic; (2) disadvantage almost always has an historical dimension as well, as members of disadvantaged groups do not only face obstacles to their full participation in society in the present, but were discriminated against historically to an ever greater extent than they are today; and (3) the preferred solution might need to be based not on assimilation, but rather on accommodation. Disadvantage is also a relational and relative term.

Equality effect is the rule's overall distributive effect in terms of promoting equality. A rule's equality effect can be either regressive, progressive, neutral or unknown, according to whether it increases, decreases, or leaves unchanged the gap between the 'haves' and the disadvantaged.

C. *The Level at which Egalitarian Considerations Work*

The distributive effects of a given rule can be measured at four levels. (1) A rule or a doctrine can benefit plaintiffs as a group at the expense of defendants as a group or the other way around. (2) Often, potential plaintiffs and defendants can be identified according to their functional capacities – their role in the interaction regulated by the

30 Cf. Trakman, *supra* note 24, p. 28 (substantive equality as a relational term).

rule. The scope of liability will have distributive consequences for these groups.[31] (3) At times, there will be a correlation between the functional capacity of potential litigants and their immutable characteristics. When such correlation exists, the rule's equality effect can be assessed. If it works (on balance) to the benefit of the disadvantaged it is progressive; if it works to their detriment it is regressive. (4) Finally, the rule always has an equality effect with respect to the particular litigants. To illustrate, requiring plaintiffs to establish defendants' duty of care in negligence suits works to the benefit of defendants as a group, since duty serves as liability-curtailing mechanism; a shift from a fault to a no-fault system for road accidents benefits pedestrians at the expense of drivers; if physicians and the average patient are stronger than patients with respect to whom the duty to obtain informed consent has been breached, expanding the scope of liability for such a breach has a progressive equality effect; such an expansive rule can have a regressive effect if in the particular case the patient is a powerful CEO and the physician is young and a member of an ethnic minority group.

One has to decide at which level the rule's equality effect should be assessed, that of the typical or that of the particular litigants?[32] A commitment to instrumentalism suggests that the formulation of rules needs to be strongly influenced by a forward-looking approach. Given an instrumentalist commitment, ignoring the consequences of rules, including their distributive consequences, is nonsensical. In deciding the appropriate level for egalitarian inquiry, and for purposes of resolving the tension between forward- and backward-looking approaches to law, one has to distinguish between two phenomena. First, some of those burdened by the rule will change their behaviour in a way that might thwart the intended distributive consequence. The extent to which an egalitarian rule will produce such a backlash changes with the context, and when backlash is insignificant more weight should be given to the rules *ex post* effects (on both potential and particular litigants). Second, regardless of the problem of backlash, and given issues of over- and under-inclusiveness, a gap might exist between a rule's overall equality effect and its effect in the particular litigation at hand. Any egalitarian-oriented rule that is not *ad hoc* ('decide in favour of the weaker party in the particular litigation') might bring about a regressive result in particular cases, despite the fact that its overall effect is progressive.[33]

Important values, notably predictability and equality before the law, support the evaluation of a rule's equality effect based on the identity of the typical litigants rather than on an *ad hoc* basis. However, we should not exaggerate the risks stemming from an approach which takes the parties' status into account when determining the scope of the mutual obligations of particular parties. More generally, an instrumentalist commitment should not eclipse the importance of an intrinsic perspective and of the need to fairly resolve the dispute with respect to the litigants at hand.

---

31 Rules' distributive effects affect third parties – those not likely to be potential litigants – as well. See Ch. 4.III.B2 below.

32 Where the identity of the litigants according to their functional capacity cannot be established or where there is no correlation between functional capacity and group membership according to immutable characteristics, the rule's overall equality effect cannot be assessed.

33 For the problem and ways to deal with it see Ch. 5.IV.B2(d) below.

III. Tort Law

A. Instrumentalism, Pluralism, Contextualism

The goals of tort law should be understood against the background of a general approach to law which is instrumentalist, pluralist, contextual and progressive. An instrumentalist (or functional) approach to law views law as a vehicle for attaining social goals.[34] According to an instrumental approach, law should be understood as 'a means to social ends and not as an end in itself; so that any part needs constantly to be examined for its purpose, and for its effect, and to be judged in the light of both and of their relation to each other'.[35] Accordingly, the normative evaluation of a given legal rule should be made according to the effects it brings about. By contrast, an opposite approach, allied chiefly with formalism or conceptualism, analyses law according to its concepts rather than its function.[36] Instrumentalists can and do differ on the question of what goal (or goals) the law in general, or a specific legal rule in particular, should promote. The instrumentalist understanding of law, including private law, presents the initial foundation of the argument for promoting egalitarian goals and alleviating distributive concerns through tort law.

An instrumentalist approach can be either monist or pluralist. An instrumentalist-monist approach strives to achieve a single goal. Even if such an approach concedes the legitimacy of other goals, it will nonetheless prioritize the goal it endorses when this goal is at variance with others. Monists may want to promote the same goal across different, and even all, branches of law – the law and economics school is the most notable comprehensive instrumentalist monist theory – or promote different (single) goals by different particular legal rules. By contrast, an instrumentalist-pluralist theory recognizes more than one goal that should be promoted, either by law in general or specific legal rules and branches of law.

Pluralists can and do differ regarding the question of which mix of goals should be promoted by the law.[37] Pluralists can differ regarding the legitimate goals that tort law should promote, as well as the weight that should be accorded to each legitimate goal (either generally or in particular circumstances). Naturally, so long as the goals are not essentially identical, a pluralist cannot usually achieve in full any single goal included in the mix of goals she supports. This is a price one has to pay in order

34 Instrumentalism was espoused and influenced by sociological jurisprudence (e.g., Rosco Pound), philosophical pragmatism (e.g., John Dewey) and legal realism (e.g., Karl Llewellyn), and continues to guide diverse approaches to law such as law and economics, law and society and critical legal studies. See Robert S. Summers, *Instrumentalism and American Legal Theory* (Ithaca, 1982), pp. 19, 22–3; Richard Posner, *Overcoming Law* (Cambridge, 1995), p. 403; Roberto M. Unger, *The Critical Legal Studies Movement* (Cambridge, 1986), pp. 2–4.

35 Karl Llewellyn, 'Some Realism About Realism: Responding to Dean Pound', 44 *Harv L Rev* (1931) 1222, pp. 1233–4.

36 See Ernest J. Weinrib, *The Idea of Private Law* (Cambridge, 1995), pp. 5–6, 19, 21.

37 See e.g., Gary T. Schwartz, 'Mixed Theories of Tort Law: Affirming Both Deterrence And Corrective Justice', 75 *Tex L Rev* (1997) 1801, p. 1819 n.132 (noting the differences between his and Izhak Englard's pluralist theories of tort law).

to try and promote more than one goal.[38] Rather, the pluralist's overall objective is to suggest rules that best promote the mix of goals to be advanced. Therefore, the concept of a trade-off is indispensable to the pluralist. Alternative legal rules would promote different goals to a different degree. However, (presumptively) there would be one suggested rule, which on the whole will best promote the entire mix of goals. The main goal in this study, which is informed by a pluralist approach, is to defend the inclusion of an egalitarian commitment as one of the goals of tort law, and to examine its relations with other goals that tort law should promote.

A pluralist theory may strive to advance either a constant mix of goals under all circumstances or a shifting mix across different contexts. The latter contextual approach disavows any *a priori* mix of goals, and insists instead on a contextual examination, according to which the promotion of certain goals might be undesirable in certain circumstances but imperative in others. More importantly, two or more situations that call for the promotion of the exact same goals may differ with regard to the relative weight that should be given to the relevant goals in balancing them against each other. For example, in certain situations – such as when the potential defendant's negligent activity might risk herself or her family members – less weight should be given to tort law's deterrent role, since the actor already has other strong incentives to be cautious. In a similar vein, a contextual approach accords varying weight to the goal of promoting an egalitarian agenda through tort law. The particular type of tort involved, the identity of the typical litigants, the social background in each culture and the legal background rules within each jurisdiction – all these are relevant for an analysis of the desirable tort rule. Generally, one of tort law's goals should be the promotion of an egalitarian agenda. The exact weight that should be given to distributive concerns should be left to a contextual examination of the circumstances of each relevant case.

A pluralist-contextual approach is susceptible to two kinds of critique. The first touches upon the relative lack of ambition of such an approach. By refusing to provide a grand theory (and by doubting the general validity of grand and abstract theories), it renounces the automatic applicability of the analysis of any specific case study to other doctrinal dilemmas. While this may generally be true, it is not a convincing critique *per se*. As much as the limited availability of a grand theory is disappointing, a good theory with limited applicability is better than a bad theory with ubiquitous applicability. While chemistry is less glamorous than alchemy, experience has shown the former to be a more productive academic pursuit.

The second charge against a pluralist-contextual approach is more cogent. Since a pluralist-contextual approach involves discretionary judgments about values (which goals to promote in any given case and what weight to give to each of the goals chosen), it raises the question of whose discretionary judgment should apply. A pluralist-contextual approach can be accused of being whimsical, unprincipled, unpredictable, subjective and disingenuous. If this critique accuses the supporters of a contextual approach in believing that law is politics to a certain degree,[39] and

38 See Patrick S. Atiyah, *Vicarious Liability in the Law of Torts* (London, 1967), p. 15.

39 For such claims see e.g., Duncan Kennedy, *A Critique of Adjudication: Fin de Siècle* (Cambridge, 1997); Allan C. Hutchinson, *It's All in the Game: A Nonfoundationalist Account*

that judges can, do and should engage in questions of values and morality,[40] I plead guilty to these charges. It is doubted however whether an embrace of a contextual approach is more difficult to justify than an embrace of any other value-committed theory of adjudication. While a contextual approach does seem to be more susceptible to claims of judges' personal biases due to the lack of an 'objective' mechanism to select and prioritize goals, the practical advantage of a contextual approach – reaching more just results – seem to outweigh its problems in terms of procedure and perception of justice. In fact, similar charges to those raised against a contextual approach are equally relevant when raised against equity, as equity is essentially about changing general rules that result in unjust results in particular cases or categories of cases.

Finally, the appropriateness and reasonableness of the choice and weight of the relevant goals can be scrutinized, as are other normative decisions made by judges. The discretion of judges within a contextual-pluralistic framework – their choice of a particular combination of goals to be applied in any given context – is susceptible to scrutiny to the same degree as any other decision judges make. This fact should serve as a safeguard against the apprehension of improper use of judicial discretion.

B. A Sketch of Tort Law and its Goals

Tort law regulates involuntary interactions in private settings, when such interactions harm some, or all participants. It has to balance the interest in freedom of action of potential tortfeasors and the interest in security of potential victims. An important distinction should be drawn between harm caused by conduct deemed undesirable from a social perspective and harm caused by the fact that two activities which are both desirable are incompatible with each other. In both cases society has to determine by means of tort law how to allocate the losses caused by the interaction. With respect to the former category, the criterion of fault suggests itself as a candidate for allocating the loss to the person who caused harm to herself or to others based on either notions of negative desert or on notions of deterrence. However, even in this category, and *a fortiori* when the loss was not caused by anyone's fault, there are other relevant considerations.

Generally, the following considerations should be deemed relevant in allocating the loss: (1) How socially valuable is the defendant's activity that risks and harms others? What was the purpose of the activity, and who stood to benefit from it? (2) How big was the risk imposed, and to what extent it was necessary? (3) How big is the disutility caused to the party who has to bear the loss from the activity? (4) How strong are the relevant parties? The egalitarian consideration, clearly manifested in the fourth question, indirectly affects the answers that should be given to the other questions as well. The social value of the party's activity is determined also by the range of alternatives open to her, and these in turn partially hinge on her social,

---

of Law and Adjudication (Durham, 2000).

40 The last tenet is accepted also by liberal theoreticians. See e.g., Ronald Dworkin, 'Darwin's New Bulldog', 111 *Harv L Rev* (1998) 1718.

cultural and economic status. The question whether the imposition of the risk is necessary, which relates to the costs of precaution, should be determined as well with respect to the range of available options, and of course the disutility of bearing the loss *ex post* (or of having one's autonomy curtailed *ex ante*) is closely affected by one's status, societal power and wealth. Normative considerations reflecting ideas of corrective justice, deterrence, loss spreading and fairness all have their place in tort law. Alongside them there is a place for an egalitarian commitment, and such a commitment should also reformulate the way we understand other considerations.

As one can easily see, these considerations can be translated into criteria for distribution. According to such an approach, tort law is the locus for distributing burdens (and benefits) caused in the process of involuntary interaction in a private setting, and considerations of desert (both positive and negative), merit,[41] needs[42] and equality all serve to help decide how the loss should be allocated, and to whom.

This understanding of tort law ascribes importance to the normativity of law, and the analysis will draw on the expressive aspects of the law. Accordingly, at times one of the goals of tort liability is to convey a moral judgment of the inappropriateness of the defendant's (or the plaintiff's) behaviour. That tort law distributes also non-material goods and has symbolic effects is central to the analysis offered in this study. This symbolic message is important not only within an instrumentalist framework; it also has intrinsic importance.

IV. Pulling the Threads Together

A. Egalitarian Tort Law in the Context of the Declining Welfare State

The idea of using tort law in order to reduce inequality in society can be evaluated against the backdrop of the welfare state – both the ideal and the reality. Much progressive thought in the 1960s and 1970s called for the replacement of tort law with more comprehensive compensation schemes. These schemes would serve the ideal of the welfare state in ensuring security against any debilitating circumstances befalling members of society, regardless of the impossibility of finding another's fault or even human causal responsibility. Such a critique of tort law, based on the haphazard nature of liability and compensation, was offered by Terence Ison and echoed (with some variations) by many other scholars, such as Richard Abel and Allan Hutchinson.[43] (It

41 Examples of considerations of merit in the tort context are, for instance, the inquiry into the social value of the defendant's activity and the purpose of imposing the risk. The idea of fairness, that one should bear the costs of any activity that one stands to benefit from, calls attention to the different moral evaluation of self-serving as opposed to altruistic behaviour.

42 One manifestation of need is the idea of loss spreading. Since losses cause disutility, spreading the loss will preserve one's basic needs and prevent a significant loss of utility.

43 Terence G. Ison, *The Forensic Lottery: A Critique on Tort Liability as a System of Personal Injury Compensation* (London, 1967); Richard L. Abel, 'A Critique of Torts', 37 *UCLA L Rev* (1990) 785; Allan C. Hutchinson, 'Beyond Non-Fault', 73 *Cal L Rev* (1985) 755.

was also offered by many others, not all of whom are committed to the ideal of the welfare state.[44])

Such criticism seemingly casts doubt on the significance and desirability of inserting egalitarian commitment to tort law in two ways. First, if indeed tort law ought to be dispensed with for progressive reasons, and all the more so if it is already fading away, there is no apparent use in trying to insert progressive notions into it. Secondly, striving to achieve progressive results by tort law might not only be less than ideal, due to the limited reach of the solution, but also unwarranted, since the appearance of the progressive (but partial) solution would take the pressure away from achieving a more comprehensive and radical solution. Stephen Sugarman has dubbed this problem as the good being the enemy of the best.[45]

This criticism is unconvincing on both levels, and for several reasons. To begin with, as was noted by Iain Ramsay, '[T]he argument made in the 1960s that much of private law, such as tort law, would fade away in the administrative state seems currently to have been hopelessly utopian.'[46] Tort law has been remarkably resilient and does not appear to be fading away; rather it is the welfare state which is under siege. In this state of affairs, it does not seem that an attempt to use tort law in a progressive way is a cause for the decline of the welfare state; instead, it might be its effect.

Moreover, the relationship between tort law and the ideal of the welfare state is more complex than might be thought on first reflection. While a true commitment to a comprehensive welfare structure seems to obviate the need for tort law (or the bulk of it anyway), the Scandinavian experience shows the opposite. During the 1970s and 1980s Finland moved toward a welfare state model. During these same decades, there was a tendency to move towards need-orientation in the Finnish law of obligations, including tort law.[47] We see therefore that in Finland there was a positive correlation between a use of tort in order to achieve progressive results and an increase in state welfarism. 'The need-oriented elements are elements of the law in a welfare state',[48] or at least they *can* be, as the Finnish experience teaches us, rather than a progressive-agenda for tort being a (poor) substitute for the state's dissociation from the ideal of a welfare state.

Nonetheless, it seems that inserting egalitarian sensitivity into tort law might be even more crucial and laudable in a political climate hostile to the ideal of the welfare state, although of course the judiciary might be less likely to insert progressive-attentiveness into tort law in such a political climate. The lesson we should learn from the Finnish experience is that, contrary to claims of some critics

---

44 See e.g., Stephen D. Sugarman, 'Doing Away with Tort Law', 73 *Cal L Rev* (1985) 555, pp. 592–6; Patrick S. Atiyah, *The Damages Lottery* (Oxford, 1997); Jeffrey O'Connell, *The Lawsuit Lottery: Only the Lawyers Win* (New York, 1979).

45 Sugarman, Ibid., p. 592.

46 Iain Ramsay, 'Consumer Credit Law, Distributive Justice and the Welfare State', 15 *Oxford JL Stud* (1995) 177, p. 196.

47 See Thomas Wilhelmsson, *Critical Studies in Private Law* (Dordrecht, 1992), pp. 111–25, 147.

48 Ibid., p. 147.

on the left, the agenda promoted here will not necessarily hinder the struggle for a more comprehensive shift toward the welfare state ideal.[49]

As for Sugarman's argument that the good is the enemy of the best, there are two points to be made. First, the phenomena of the general resilience of tort law and the retrenchment of the welfare state seem to be rooted in sociological, political and cultural currents which run much deeper than any general progressive shift that tort law may be assumed to be undergoing. Secondly, to the extent that the critique is more narrow, and holds only that a specific progressive tort law rule will prevent a more comprehensive (but localized) response by the state to the problem regulated by the rule, it must be recognized that this is a contingent and empirical claim. Chapter 3 below raises some doubts about its cogency, based on institutional considerations and public choice insights.

A major theme underlying this study is animosity to the status quo, and the belief that it harms much more than protects the interests of the disadvantaged. To those who share this animosity, a policy of abstaining from a small change in the positive direction in order not to jeopardize the chances for a major change in the positive direction seems a non-starter. In short, the approach taken here is informed by pragmatism preferring evolution to an anticipated (but doubtful) revolution. Accordingly, the current study could be viewed as part of a trend of progressive-minded scholars, who believe in the ability of private law to bring about limited progressive change. However, it should not be understood as a defence of the tort system as we currently know it, either generally or for its potentially useful role in promoting a progressive agenda. Rather, it should be understood as the claim that, given the institution of tort law and its resilience, we should and can try to use it progressively.

B. The Limits of the Argument

This study is concerned with the area in which distributive justice, egalitarianism and tort law overlap, namely understanding tort law as one tool for promoting equality, while understanding that in doing so tort law serves as one tool for promoting distributive justice – the just distribution of losses caused by incompatible involuntary human interactions in private settings. The limits of the inquiry and scope of argument should be clear: first, an egalitarian agenda can and should be promoted by means other than tort law. Tort law does not have a conclusive or even major role in the promotion of equality. Similarly, tort law is only one (and in some respects a limited) instrument for the promotion of distributive justice. Second, we should not exaggerate tort law's capacity to promote equality. However, it has a role which is far from trivial. Third, distributive justice in general, and the distribution of burdens with which tort law deals in particular, should use several criteria, and not merely a commitment to equality. Indeed, tort law should promote goals other than the empowerment of the disadvantaged in society and the latter goal should

49 For a view of tort law as protecting the disadvantaged (mainly unorganized consumers) against the 'haves' (mainly corporate greed) see Thomas H. Koening & Michael L. Rusted, *In Defense of Tort Law* (New York, 2001).

not take precedence over other goals. This study neither defends the claim that tort law should promote other distributive goals (such as loss spreading or fairness) nor examines in detail the way in which it can do so. Fourth, some of the arguments mounted against an attempt to promote equality by tort law can similarly be raised against attempts to achieve other distributive goals.[50] While it might well be the case that the responses offered in the next chapter in the context of promoting equality are applicable in other distributive contexts as well, such a general claim is not made. However, the discussion in the next chapter can serve as a useful framework and starting point in analysing tort law's legitimacy and effectiveness in promoting other distributive goals.

Fifth, while the application part of this book concentrates on tort law (mainly, in fact, on the tort of negligence), the normative argument advanced in the next chapter basically applies to the promotion of equality in private law. While some important distinctions exist between different branches of the law of obligations – mainly between contract law's obligations, which are consensual, and tort law's obligations, which are not – these distinctions should not always change the analysis, and when they do change it this fact will be noted. Accordingly, the argument put forward in Chapter 3 could be understood as a general claim that equality should be promoted by private law rules.

Sixth, this book does not delve into the contentious and elusive, but not unuseful dichotomy between public and private. This should be understood neither as a call for the abolition of this dichotomy, nor as a support for the view that one's duty to treat another equally is the same in private and public settings. In fact, the scope of the duty to promote equality changes even within different contexts in private and public law. With the exception of the discussion in Chapter 7, which deals with the duty not to discriminate, the rest of the applicatory part of this book deals with the duty of rule-makers to design tort rules with an egalitarian sensitivity in mind. Nor is much space devoted to the interesting issue of the public authority's tort liability. A useful starting point would be that the weight of egalitarian considerations in this context should be more significant, but this application requires more detailed and refined analysis. While there are obvious differences between the meaning of the requirement for equality in public law and the meaning of egalitarian commitment as defended in this book, nevertheless, public authorities should take into account the egalitarian concern to a greater extent, given the role of the government according to (non-libertarian) common and diverse political theories.

Seventh, no claim is made to having exhausted the discussion of the role of egalitarian sensitivity in tort law. The project is still in its infancy. Finally, the argument made in this book is normative, not descriptive. The study does not try to establish (or refute) the claim that egalitarian sensitivity is currently understood by the courts to be one of tort law's goals (although this may be true to some extent) and if so, how significant that commitment is. Descriptive claims merit suspicion for two reasons. One reason is that reality is so rich and complex that bodies of law can hardly be expected to be reduced to one explanatory principle. In other words,

50 See e.g., Richard A. Epstein, 'The Social Consequences of Common Law Rules', 95 *Harv L Rev* (1982) 1717.

law makers (or at least most of them) are pluralist and contextual. The other reason for being suspicious of descriptive claims is that they seem to reflect a researcher's bias. There is a frequent positive correlation between the researcher's normative commitment and his descriptive account of the law – Posner and Weinrib's conflicting descriptions of tort law as reflecting, respectively, efficiency and corrective justice is a good example of this phenomenon. Descriptive theorists, it seems, are searching for the lost doctrinal coin under their own theory's streetlight.

Chapter 3

Normative Defence

Introduction

The purpose of this chapter is to defend from a normative standpoint the promotion of equality, in the sense defined above, as one of the goals of private law. While the discussion concentrates on tort law, the argument is broader in scope. Arguably, even given a commitment by society to promote equality, there are several reasons for preferring the exclusive use of public law for the promotion of equality, mainly (within the context of wealth distribution) by means of the tax and transfer system. According to this view, there are four arguments against promoting equality by means of private law: illegitimacy, randomness, excessive cost and ineffectiveness.[1]

These arguments fail to convince that private law rules should not or cannot be employed in an attempt to narrow (or at least to prevent the widening of) gaps between the 'haves' and the disadvantaged. While the role of private law in the Sisyphean struggle for equality is limited, it is an important one. One major conclusion from the analysis is that both the extent to which it is justified to attempt to promote equality by private law and the likelihood that such an attempt will be successful are more significant in certain interactions than in others. Therefore, a contextual analysis is always needed.

The analysis distinguishes between different versions of the arguments that can support an egalitarian reformulation of legal rules to different extents. The more limited (and hence easier to defend) version of the argument that is defended here is that an egalitarian agenda which is pro-disadvantaged, rather than anti-'haves', that deals with inequality that is not wealth-based or that attempts to rectify existing regressive effects created by the rule in question, is especially justified. However, a case is also made for an agenda which is not so limited.

I. Illegitimacy

A. The Argument

The decision how to distribute resources in society is political by nature. Therefore, it has been argued that such activity should be made by the accountable branches rather than by the judiciary.[2] Indeed, this view is expressed both by scholars such

---

1 These arguments partially overlap, and the suggested classification is made for purposes of analytical clarity.

2 For a recent claim that promoting distributional (as opposed to political) equality in private law is illegitimate since distributional equality should be the domain of accountable

as Ernest Weinrib who flatly reject instrumental approaches to private law, and by economic analysis of law scholars such as Alan Schwartz.

Weinrib argues that choosing a certain distribution among several alternatives necessitates consideration of a collective goal which is external to the structure of corrective justice, and as such is political. A specific distributive decision should be made by elected institutions since it affects the interests of many individuals. Judges, who are not elected and who are institutionally constrained by the limitations of the judicial process, are not appropriately situated to select a certain distribution among possible distributions.[3]

Alan Schwartz argues that while a wealth-maximization goal is a neutral and apolitical goal, distributive decisions are political by nature, and therefore, as a matter of course, should not be taken by the judiciary. Distributive rules can only be chosen, rather than being derived from the underlying distributive goals that we would like to promote. This is due to the fact that distributive considerations are more value-laden than non-distributive considerations; therefore, there are more alternative distributive rules to choose from than there are general (non-distributive) rules.[4]

The illegitimacy claim is unpersuasive for four reasons. First, the characterization of the decision to avoid redistribution as neutral and apolitical is unconvincing. Rather, the political nature of judicial rule-making is inevitable. Second, even as a matter of procedural justice, judicial engagement in redistribution might be justified. Third, the legislature's ability to amend and react to court-made tort rules adequately resolves any possible difficulty caused by lack of judicial accountability. Finally, the possible deficiency of court-made distribution from the perspective of procedural justice might be offset by the possible superiority of the distributive result from the perspective of substantive justice.

B. The Inevitability of the Distributive Effects of Legal Rules and the Political Nature of the Judiciary

The first response is informed by the inevitability of distributive effects of court-made rules and draws heavily on the insights of the legal realists. Tort rules, like any other legal rules, have inevitable distributive effects. Intended or not, tort law distributes wealth, liberty and other primary goods. To illustrate: denying a duty of care improves the condition of potential tortfeasors at the expense of potential victims. Allowing estranged wives to continue with the fertilization process without the

---

branches, see Yoav Dotan, 'The "Public", the "Private" and the Legal Norm of Equality', 20 *Can JL & Soc* (2005) 207, pp. 216–21.

3 Ernest J. Weinrib, *The Idea of Private Law* (Cambridge, 1995), p. 211. Weinrib argues that by contrast, corrective justice involves no decision as to the selection of a collective purpose. Ibid., pp. 211–12.

4 Alan Schwartz, 'Products Liability and Judicial Wealth Redistributions', 51 *Ind LJ* (1976) 558, p. 564. The vivid debates among law and economics scholars about the efficiency of competing legal rules regarding fundamental questions reveals Schwartz's claim on the ability to 'derive' an efficient legal rule to be overly optimistic. See Part III.B1 and n.70 below.

continuous consent of their husbands improves the lot of the former at the expense of the latter.[5] Moreover, as a matter of course public law litigation has clear distributive effects, and these effects lie at times at the heart of the litigation; and yet no one seriously disputes the legitimacy of courts in dealing with these issues. Consider for example the *Brown* integration decision.[6] Once the relationship between equality and distributive justice is understood, it is hard to understand why the rulings of courts in public law litigation which is based (in part) on considerations of equality is deemed legitimate, while similar rulings in the context of private law litigation are not. Consider disputes over frozen ova, for example. Such disputes can arise in a private law context, as a claim in contracts, torts, or property. Alternatively, they can arise in a public law context, for example as a challenge to the constitutionality or legality of the state's regulation of the procedure, under which implantation requires the husband's consent. Whatever the legal framework involved, the interests that have to be balanced are essentially identical, and the ruling has clear distributive effects which have to be taken into account. Clearly, an approach according to which courts, while resolving disputes over frozen ova, are allowed (and indeed required) to take into account considerations regarding gender equality in public law litigation and yet are forbidden to take these considerations into account in the private law litigation is absurd.

To the insight that tort law has inevitable distributive results we should add the insight offered by the legal realists: the state's failure to intervene in interactions among individuals is just another form of regulation and intervention by the state. Such regulation is as political, value-laden and non-neutral as any other possible form of regulation. Robert Hale and Morris Cohen convincingly revealed the fallacy of the public/private dichotomy, and the state's pretence of neutrality in abstaining from regulation.[7] Hale and Cohen show that in protecting property rights the state affects the distribution of income and the direction of economic activities,[8] and determines the future distribution of goods that are not yet in existence.[9] It follows that the decision not to 'intervene' is in fact a politically value-laden decision, one which takes sides in the struggle between different groups in society, and is heavily biased in favour of the status quo and the 'haves' and against the disadvantaged.

The libertarian ideal of the night-watchman state is not apolitical. The shift from the Hobbsian natural condition towards a social contract enables but does not entail a *laissez faire* political arrangement. Without private law being structured in the way it was, certain individuals would not have been able to accumulate their wealth and power. There is nothing natural or immanent about the existing pattern of holdings, including its significant inegalitarian nature. The existing regulation of interactions between private actors and their respective rights is only one possible form of

---

5 See Ch. 5.V.A, Example 7 below.

6 *Brown v Board of Education*, 349 US 483 (1954).

7 See Morris R. Cohen, 'Property and Sovereignty', 13 *Cornell LQ* (1927) 8; Robert L. Hale, 'Coercion and Distribution in a Supposedly Non-coercive State', 38 *Pol Sci Q* (1923) 470.

8 Hale, ibid., p. 470.

9 Cohen, *supra* note 7, p. 13.

regulation out of many. More importantly, it *is* a form of regulation and intervention as much as any other alternative mode of regulation.

So far two insights were presented. One concerns the inevitability of some distributive results of tort law; the other reveals that a decision to perpetuate the status quo is as political in nature as a decision to deviate from it. It follows that the use of political considerations by the judiciary while creating court-made law is inevitable. Judges do make value judgements, they cannot but make value judgements – political judgements in the broad sense – and they ought to make political judgements. It is therefore desirable to be candid about the discretion judges have and the political nature of their enterprise.[10] Since there is broad room for discretion, which necessitates a value judgement, and it is the judge's duty to reach a just decision, a just decision cannot be defined without taking political considerations into account. Furthermore, since non-interference is nothing if not taking sides, judges cannot exempt themselves from deciding an issue on the ground that it is political. A decision to abstain from intervention is as political as a decision to intervene, since it protects a certain distribution which is only possible with the law's assent. Judges make tort rules. Tort rules have inevitable distributive results. A decision to avoid any change from the status quo in terms of the equality effects of tort rules is as political as a decision to bring about a change. What is therefore the basis for accusing judges of making impermissible political decisions if they deviate from the status quo but not if they perpetuate it?

The only possible justification for judicial deference is dependent upon the implausible conclusion that the status quo reflects a conscious, informed and legitimate decision by the legislature opposing the decision that the court is asked to make (by a litigant striving to achieve social change). If we can safely conclude that the legislature, as the accountable branch, believes that the status quo perfectly reflects the ideal distribution, then, subject to the constitutional question regarding courts' judicial review powers, courts should respect this decision by the accountable branch and refrain from any attempt to promote distributive goals. Even then, given the inevitability of distribution by court-made rules, it is not clear how any new rule, which presumably brings some change to the status quo, is defensible. It might be then, that taking this inherently implausible approach to its logical extreme would prevent courts from developing new tort rules at all.

In any event, the assumption that the legislature sanctifies the status quo is irredeemably flawed for several reasons. First, as a matter of constitutional law, common wisdom holds that there is no legislation by omission. While, in some instances, one can deduce from the legislature's silence a purpose to limit the regulation exclusively to whatever was included in it explicitly, courts cannot, should not and do not assume from the absence of regulation of a certain area that the legislature is satisfied with the situation as it is. This is especially true in areas which historically are the domain of the common law. Indeed, the opposite approach will prevent any court-made law. More specifically in the context of distributive justice, we know that legislatures redistribute primary goods all the

10 Cf. Allan C. Hutchinson, *It's All in the Game: A Nonfoundationalist Account of Law and Adjudication* (Durham, 2000), p. 323.

time. Therefore, we cannot assume that they are satisfied with the status quo at any given point.

Furthermore, the fact that the legislature did not enact the rule which the court is now contemplating to adopt could be explained by many alternative explanations, other than the assumption that the status quo is sanctified and approved of by the legislature. The legislature may not have anticipated the situation being litigated in court nor its undesirable distributive effects, or it may have deferred to the court because the issue was within the courts' traditional purview. The legislature may be interested in making the change now made by the court, but is prevented from doing so due to its own institutional constraints.[11] An additional reason for the feebleness of the assumption that the legislature is sanctifying the status quo by acquiescence is but an aspect of the third response: the power of the legislature to change in subsequent legislation a court-made law only renders the categorical rejection of judicial intervention less plausible. To sum up the first response: however troubling the lack of accountability of the courts may be, it can provide no support for an argument against involvement in redistribution, since preserving the status quo (which is only ostensibly neutral) is as political as engaging in progressive redistribution.

C. Public Choice

1. In General The illegitimacy charge is based on an assumption that from a procedural justice perspective the fact that judges decide issues of resource distribution is problematic, since judges are not elected and their decisions do not necessarily reflect the preference of the majority. Indeed, responses such as the one presented previously, that such a result is inevitable, or the one presented in the next section, that the court-made rule can be amended by the legislature – assume that from a procedural justice perspective court-based redistribution is inferior to legislated redistribution.

Political philosophers distinguish between just results and just procedure.[12] Substantive justice evaluates the result according to substantive criteria derived from one's values, morality and ethics. The desirability of the result is measured according to the extent to which the rule abides by the substantive requirements of justice. For such purposes, the fact that the rule may have been adopted in a problematic way is irrelevant. By contrast, procedural justice evaluates the desirability of a rule merely according to the way in which it was adopted. The question of whether the content of the rule is desirable according to substantive criteria is irrelevant.[13]

Any given number of rules can be compared according to the different and unrelated dimensions of substantive and procedural justice. In the political realm,

---

11 For this contingency see Section C below.

12 See e.g., John Rawls, *A Theory of Justice* (rev. edn, Cambridge, 1999), pp. 74–5 (distinguishing between perfect, imperfect and pure procedural justice).

13 According to Rawls, ibid., in the case of either perfect or imperfect procedural justice, the fairness of the result can be evaluated according to a criterion which is external to and independent of the procedure. In the case of pure procedural justice, there is no independent criterion for the right result other than adherence to the procedure.

and given the plurality of opinions regarding what conforms with the demands of substantive justice, the major criterion for evaluating legislation as valid is procedural. Generally speaking, if a given legal rule was created in accordance with the demands of procedural justice, it is considered to be valid, regardless of one's doubts regarding its substantive merit. In this respect, in democracies the principal criterion for procedural justice is majoritarianism. If a rule was adopted by legislators who represent the majority of the voters, then the rule is valid. Majoritarianism – which represents an egalitarian ideal of its own, that of 'one person one vote' – challenges the legitimacy of judicial review and judicial crafting of legal norms, since both practices entrust an unaccountable body with the power to overrule the majority's decisions or preferences. The illegitimacy charge, therefore, is rooted in notions of the inferiority, from procedural justice perspective, of judicial redistribution. This section disputes the correctness of this assumed inferiority, on the basis of insights derived from the public choice literature.

2. Superiority of the Judiciary? Two preliminary points are in order. First, a full examination of the correctness of the public law claim necessitates a contextual examination which is jurisdictional and time-specific. In particular, public choice analysis is sensitive to the political structure that affects the incentives given to legislators, regulators and judges. This study, as one providing a general defence of distributive-egalitarian considerations in tort law, will not delve into the particularities of interest groups in any given jurisdiction. The relative susceptibility of the judiciary, compared to the other two branches, to pressure from interest groups is likely to vary in different jurisdictions. It would depend, among other things, on the way in which judges are nominated or elected, the constitutional structure in each jurisdiction and similar factors. This notwithstanding, the gist of the argument presented here – that it is easier for interest groups to block progressive legislation than to promote regressive legislation – should hold true, to a great extent, across different jurisdictions with different kinds of pressures by interest groups. The second point is that one should distinguish between the questions of legitimacy and effectiveness. This section deals with the normative question whether the attempt by courts to engage in redistribution is legitimate from a procedural justice perspective. Part IV below examines whether judicial intervention is likely to bring about progressive results.

An important theme within public choice theory is the superiority of the judiciary over other government institutions in terms of being relatively immune to undue pressures of interest groups. Mancur Olson's collective action theory suggests that, due to problems of free-riding and rational ignorance, smaller groups are better able than larger groups to organize collectively and to combine their resources.[14] Accordingly, accountable branches of government are likely to be susceptible to interest group pressure and to make decisions based not on the public good, but rather on the selfish interests of interest groups, government officials, and legislators. Such

14 Mancur Olson, *The Logic of Collective Action: Public Goods and the Theory of Groups* (Cambridge, 1965).

a phenomenon is also problematic in terms of procedural justice, for two reasons.[15] First, it gives the 'haves' – the interest groups – power and influence exceeding their electoral weight. By this, the majoritarian justification for legislation is undermined. Arguably, a rule may have been passed or derailed not because the majority of the voters wanted this to happen, but because of the interests of the powerful few. If the majoritarian argument stands as the basis of the assumed preference for legislative, as opposed to judicial, rule-making, the power possessed by interest groups casts a serious doubt on such preference.

More importantly, if legislators legislate or abstain from legislating based on their expectation of reaping benefits from powerful interest groups, the rules they enact are tainted with favouritism, or, worse, conflict of interest. According to one view, the process of legislation is the selling and buying of preferable laws in which legislators seek perks, campaign contributions and other re-election advantages.[16] Conceptually, therefore, we are talking about something akin to a bribe: the legislators sacrifice the public interest and receive personal benefits in exchange for furthering the agendas of interest groups. Such a phenomenon is undoubtedly a gross violation of procedural justice. Arguably, the judiciary is less susceptible to the promotion of selfish interests, due to, among other reasons, a lack of accountability. This has been suggested as a major justification for judicial review.[17]

Many scholars dispute the proposition that interest group theory establishes the institutional superiority of the judiciary and provides justification for judicial review.[18] It was noted, probably correctly, that a public choice analysis is associated with conservative and right-wing politics,[19] and that it overestimates the influence of interest groups and underestimates legislators' counter-incentives.[20] Furthermore, Frank Cross has argued that due to institutional limitations, such as the availability of resources, the standing requirement and precedent-chasing, the judicial process is more susceptible to manipulation by narrow interests than the more democratic

15 Obviously, it is problematic in terms of producing a result which is substantively inferior to the one that could have been achieved had interest group pressure been not exercised.

16 See e.g., William N. Eskridge, Jr. & Philip P. Frickey, 'Statutory Interpretation as Practical Reasoning', 42 *Stan L Rev* (1990) 321, p. 344.

17 See e.g., Cass R. Sunstein, 'Interest Groups in American Public Law', 38 *Stan L Rev* (1985) 29; Erwin Chemerinsky, 'The Supreme Court, 1988 Term-Foreword: The Vanishing Constitution', 103 *Harv L Rev* (1989) 43, pp. 46–7, 78, 80–81.

18 See e.g., Frank B. Cross, 'The Judiciary and Public Choice', 50 *Hastings LJ* (1999) 355; Einer R. Elhauge, 'Does Interest Group Theory Justify More Intrusive Judicial Review?', 101 *Yale LJ* (1991) 31.

19 See e.g., Cross, ibid., p. 358. For the broader claim associating judicial review with conservative politics see Michael Mandel, 'A Brief History of the New Constitutionalism, or "How We Changed Everything So That Everything Would Remain the Same" ', 32 *Isr LR* (1998) 250.

20 See e.g., Cross, *supra* note 18, pp. 368–9; Benjamin I. Page & Robert Y. Shapiro, 'Effects of Public Opinion on Policy', 77 *Am J Pol Sci* (1983) 75. For an intermediate approach stressing both material incentives and social norms see Hanoch Dagan, 'Just Compensation, Interests and Social Meanings', 99 *Mich L Rev* (2000) 134.

branches of government, and that expanding judicial review of the actions of those branches would increase rather than decrease the influence of narrow special interest groups over public policy.[21]

3. The Relevance to the Development of Private Law of the 'Easier to Block' Phenomenon The claim that generally the judiciary has relative priority in terms of procedural justice compared to other branches is therefore contested. Still, two observations are in order. First, at the general level, since the question of relative priority is contested, it is far from clear that the court's involvement in policy-making is deficient merely because of the court's lack of accountability. Secondly, and more importantly, one should distinguish between judicial review and the creation and development of tort law (including the promotion of distributive goals through it).[22] Kay Schlozman and John Tierney found that interest groups are more effective in blocking legislation undesirable to them than in advancing favourable legislation (the 'easier to block' phenomenon). The effectiveness increased when the issues had relatively low visibility, when the group had substantial support from other groups and public officials and when the group was able to select a favourable forum.[23] These findings are accepted by both proponents and opponents of interest group theory as a justification for judicial activism.[24] While Cross argues that these features characterize most judicial action,[25] both the 'easier to block' phenomenon and the distinction between judicial review and the creation of tort rules support a contrary conclusion.

According to the findings of Schlozman and Tierney, the 'haves' are likely to be able to block legislation engaging in progressive redistribution. However, if the court produces a progressive rule, the 'haves' will find it more difficult to trigger legislation overruling the judicial decision. While '[j]udicial review functionally gives the factions another bite at the apple',[26] tort rules do not. If the rule reached by the judiciary is flawed on its merits, the legislature will not face special opposition to changing it. If the judicial rule results in excessive progressive redistribution, the 'haves' will not block legislation intended to amend the court-made rule, because they will support the legislation and the disadvantaged will probably not succeed in blocking it because they do not have the requisite political muscle. If, on the other hand, the rule is progressive but not progressive enough, this is hardly a convincing

21 Cross, ibid. Many law and society scholars have noted the systemic advantages that the better-off possess in relation to litigation. See e.g., Marc Galantar, 'Why the "Haves" Come Out Ahead: Speculations on the Limits of Social Change', 9 *Law & Soc'y Rev* (1974) 95; Kevin T. McGuire, 'Repeat Players in the Supreme Court: The Role of Experienced Lawyers in Litigation Success', 57 *J Pol* (1995) 187.

22 Cf. William J. Fenrich, 'Common Law Protection of Individuals' Rights in Personal Information', 65 *Fordham L Rev* (1996) 951, pp. 978–85 (public choice insights support courts' creativity and activism in developing tort law).

23 Kay L. Schlozman & John T. Tierney, *Organized Interests and American Democracy* (New York, 1986), pp. 314–16, 395–8.

24 See Fenrich, *supra* note 22, pp. 979–80; Cross, *supra* note 18, p. 373.

25 Cross, ibid.

26 Ibid., p. 372.

reason to oppose judicial activity. A partial solution is better than none at all,[27] and the assumption is that the legislature would not have done anything, had the court not come up with the progressive rule, given the blocking powers of the 'haves' in the legislative body. Therefore, only if there is reason to believe that judicial activity will result in *regressive* distribution, might interest group theory suggest that courts should not try to achieve distributive goals. As the discussion below demonstrates, such a result is unlikely.[28]

D. *Ability to Amend*

Even if it were true that the lack of accountability of the courts presents a real challenge to their legitimacy in pursuing distributive goals, the ability of the legislature to react to courts' rulings by either amending or complementing them, should provide an adequate response to this concern.[29] In fact, even in the context of judicial review, in which majoritarianism poses a greater challenge to courts' activism, it was suggested that the legislature's ability to react to judicial review by new legislation responds to the majoritarian concern. According to such an approach, courts and legislatures engage in a dialogue; such a discourse provides an adequate defence to the practice of judicial review from the majoritarian charge.[30] This response is even more convincing when courts create legal rules under common law principles. In such case, courts 'are always ultimately accountable to the electorate because anything they do is subject to legislative reconsideration or veto',[31] and judicial creativity should be viewed as 'an entirely appropriate part of a joint lawmaking responsibility'.[32]

Granted, game theory teaches us that, given institutional limitations, a legislature cannot always change a decision that is not to its liking.[33] However, this observation weakens rather than supports the lack of judicial legitimacy claim. Game theory insights with respect to the constraints operating on legislators reveal the weakness of the majoritarian justification of legislature-made norms. If, for example, the agenda setter (who controls the order of voting) can influence the content of the act through 'cycling',[34] or if gatekeepers can affect the chances that legislation will

---

27 See Part II.B below.

28 See Part II.A3; Part IV.A below.

29 Fenrich, *supra* note 22, p. 982.

30 See e.g., Peter W. Hogg & Allison A. Bushell, 'The Charter Dialogue Between Courts and Legislatures', 35 *Osgoode Hall LJ* (1997) 75.

31 Cornelius J. Peck, 'The Role of the Courts and Legislatures in the Reform of Tort Law', 48 *Minn L Rev* (1963) 265, pp. 281–2, 286, 293–4.

32 See Edmund Ursin, 'Judicial Creativity and Tort Law', 49 *Geo Wash L Rev* (1981) 229, p. 256.

33 See e.g., Daniel A. Farber & Philip P. Frickey, *Law and Public Choice: A Critical Introduction* (Chicago, 1991), pp. 38–42; Jeffrey A. Segal, 'Separation-of-Powers Games in the Positive Theory of Congress and Courts', 91 *Am Pol Sci Rev* (1997) 28; Omri Yadlin, 'Judicial Activism and Judicial Discretion as a Strategic Game', 19 *Bar Ilan University L Rev* (2002) 665, pp. 671–87.

34 In a heterogenic voting body the majority might, under certain conditions, prefer option A to option B, option B to option C, and option C to option B. In such a case, the result

pass,[35] it means that neither the legislature nor the judiciary enjoys a majoritarian justification, and it is unclear whether from procedural perspective legislature- rather than court-made norms should be preferred. Alternatively, it may be argued that a sufficient response to the legitimacy concern is that the legislature has theoretical or formal ability to amend the court-made rule. The fact that the proponents of such a move could not muster a majority proves that the court did not act contrary to the view of the majority so that its decision is legitimate.

Two differences between developing common law doctrines and exercising judicial review make the former practice much less susceptible to charges of illegitimacy. First, in the former case the court does not necessarily contradict a majoritarian preference. The fact that the legislature has not already created an equivalent rule does not support a conclusion that the court's rule contradicts a majoritarian preference. Secondly, and more importantly, in using its judicial review capacities, the supreme court of each jurisdiction usually has the final word.[36] Its ruling either cannot be overruled at all, or it can with significant difficulty. This near-finality of the court's decision requires much carefulness and a degree of deference by the courts, lest the majoritarian principle be too easily sidestepped. By contrast, when the court creates a tort rule, the legislature can easily overrule it. The prospect of legislative intervention, then, adequately responds to the arguable deficiency of court-made redistribution from the perspective of procedural justice.

E. Substantive versus Procedural Justice

As mentioned in Section C above, due to the disagreement within democratic societies regarding the conception of the good, it is well accepted that the validity of legal norms (mainly legislation) is determined by procedural justice. Legislation passed by the votes of those representing the majority of voters is valid. However, in most democracies the commitment to procedural justice alone is not absolute. It is generally accepted that legislation, even when backed by the majority, should conform to some basic threshold of substantive justice. In constitutional discourse, the tension between procedural and substantive justice has been dubbed 'democracy of means' versus 'democracy of ends'.[37] Constitutional judicial review of legislation, therefore, is partially based on the trade-off between procedural justice and substantive justice. In terms of procedural justice, a court-created rule which invalidates a given statute is inferior to a legislature-created rule, due to courts' lack of accountability. Nonetheless, the court is endowed with the power to invalidate the statute, because from a substantive justice perspective the judicial rule is preferable to the legislative rule.

---

might reflect the preference of the agenda setter rather than that of the majority. See Farber & Frickey, ibid.

35 Gatekeepers are elements in the legislative process whose consent is essential for promoting it. See Yadlin, *supra* note 33, pp. 701–4; Segal, *supra* note 33, pp. 29–30.

36 But see Hogg & Bushell, *supra* note 30, for qualification of this point.

37 See Michael Mandel, 'Democracy and the New Constitutionalism in Israel', 33 *Isr L Rev* (1999) 259, pp. 286–7 (Democracy in Israel).

We can see, therefore, that situations exist in which substantive justice is accorded precedence over procedural justice. Judicial redistribution through tort law might be another situation in which we should be willing to trade procedural justice for substantive justice. This argument will be referred to as the 'trade-off argument'. The trade-off argument maintains that even if courts' engagement in advancing distributive goals is problematic from a procedural justice perspective, it can still be justified provided such engagement brings about results which are significantly superior from a substantive justice perspective.[38]

The distinction between judicial review of legislation and the development of court-made law is relevant to the trade-off argument as well. The less problematic the intervention of the court from the perspective of procedural justice, the more leeway the court can take in creating new tort rules in order to attain a better result (compared to the status quo) in terms of substantive justice. Since the gist of the three responses presented in the previous sections is that courts' intervention is not procedurally problematic despite its lack of accountability, courts are free to pursue changes that bring about even small improvements in substantive justice. (By contrast, when courts' intervention is problematic procedurally, as is the case with judicial review, intervention is justified only when the improvement in terms of substantive justice is appreciable.)

Note that the trade-off argument builds on the assumption that courts' engagement in redistribution is problematic from a procedural justice perspective; this point is not conceded. Indeed, all the other three responses dispute the claim that the fact that judges are not accountable renders judicial engagement in distribution illegitimate. The argument presented in this section, therefore, should be understood merely as a fallback position.

The relevant question then becomes whether courts' sensitivity to distributive concerns is likely to bring about a more egalitarian result than that achieved when legislatures are acting alone to promote progressive redistribution. Needless to say, evaluating the results from a substantive justice perspective requires an agreed upon criterion against which the results can be judged. Once such a criterion – for the purposes of this book, egalitarianism – is accepted, the relative competence of courts in advancing it, and the results of the interaction between courts' engagement in redistribution and such engagement by other branches should be assessed. This is done below.[39]

II. Randomness

Assuming the overall desirability of comprehensive progressive redistribution in society, the discussion attempts to respond to those who reject the use of tort law, or, more generally, private law, as an appropriate mechanism for redistribution on the grounds of randomness. The charge of randomness is twofold: partiality of participants and crudeness of results. The first aspect reflects the problem that

---

38 Cf. Ronald M. Dworkin, *Law's Empire* (Cambridge, 1986), pp. 144–7.

39 Parts II.A3 and IV.A below, especially the discussion concluding Section A1.

only some of those who should participate in the ideal comprehensive progressive redistribution that society envisions are likely to do so under redistributive tort rules. The second aspect reflects the problem that the share of the entitlement either taken away from or given to those few who participate in tort redistribution are unlikely to correspond to the share due to those same participants under the ideal (and comprehensive) distributive scheme. In fact, for a reason to be explained below, tort law necessarily fails to bring both parties to their ideal distributive results.

Notwithstanding these difficulties, random redistribution, provided it is progressive, is desirable, and progressive redistribution should be regarded as one of the goals of tort law, despite the possibility that such redistribution will be random. The charge of randomness rests on three claims, of which two are factual and one normative. First, there is the assumption that existing tort law is not redistributive in nature. The discussion in the next chapter proves this to wrong.[40] Second, there is the assumption that a redistributive tort rule is especially susceptible to the charge of randomness. This is challenged in Section A. Third, there is the claim that because of the deficiencies of redistribution through tort law, the perpetuation of the status quo should be preferred to random progressive redistribution. This is critically examined in section B.

A. Redistribution by Tort Law is not Particularly Random

There seems to be broad consensus that redistribution through private law is more narrow and selective than redistribution through the tax and transfer system. For example, Ernest Weinrib comments that the idea of loss spreading 'should lead not to the adjudication of tortious claims but to social insurance of accident losses and, more generally, to a redistribution of wealth through progressive taxation'.[41]

Each of the following four arguments questions to a different degree the assertion that distribution through tort law is random, either absolutely or in comparison to alternative distributive mechanisms.

1. The Thesis of Localized Distributive Justice On its face, tort law as a mechanism for redistribution appears to suffer from the problem of the limited extent of participation in such redistribution. Seemingly, the egalitarian concern fails to single out those participating in the tort interaction as the only ones who should participate in progressive redistribution. Based on the model of distributive justice presented above and Stephen Perry's thesis of localized distributive justice,[42] a possible answer to this criticism is to view those involved in the underlying tort interaction as a distinct group whose members ought to bear, among themselves alone, the burden of the *particular* loss. Once the participants are so identified (based on the idea of

40 Ch. 4.I below. See also Part I.B above.

41 Weinrib, *supra* note 3, p. 37 (citing Calabresi). See also ibid., pp. 74–5.

42 See Stephen R. Perry, 'The Moral Foundations of Tort Law', 77 *Iowa L Rev* (1992) 449.

outcome-responsibility), distributive considerations, including egalitarianism, can influence the decision how to distribute the loss among the involved parties.[43]

2. Broad Participation through Insurance Insurance works as a loss-spreading mechanism. Many individuals pay a premium over time that reflects their loss expectancy. By using this mechanism, instead of a few individuals suffering large, unexpected one-time losses, many individuals suffer small and predictable losses over time. Insurance as a mechanism for participation in losses solves, or at least considerably attenuates, the problem of the partialness of participation. The identity of those who participate in the tort law interaction is, indeed, random. However, the loss those participants suffer is not. Other potential litigants share the costs of the redistribution, since they belong to the same pool of insured.

The existence of insurance responds to the demands of intra-group justice at the giving-end of the redistribution.[44] In terms of inter-group justice, progressive compensation rules at times merely attenuate the effects of regressive cross-subsidy.[45] While we are still left with the problem of intra-group justice at the receiving end – the rule would result also in redistribution of wealth from uninjured poor insured to poor victims – a progressive rule would not exacerbate this problem. Under the current regime, the insured poor subsidize rich victims. Overall, then, combining a progressive tort rule with a wealth-blind premium collection would be superior, from a distributive perspective, to a non-redistributive tort rule coupled with a wealth-blind premium collection, both in terms of inter- and intra-group justice.

3. The Complement Thesis[46] Under the complement thesis, the availability of complementary measures (mainly through public law mechanisms) for achieving redistributive goals provides the basis for an argument for, rather than against, the use of tort law to promote wealth redistribution. According to the complement thesis, not only may injustice that is created by random distribution be corrected by the legislature, but random tort law redistribution may *increase* the likelihood that legislatures will engage in comprehensive progressive redistribution. Random progressive redistribution by the courts would trigger a new distributive equilibrium, shifting from the status quo to a more complete progressive redistribution. Such random progressive redistribution would create an intermediate unstable equilibrium under which the random redistribution would more likely be complemented progressively than abolished. This argument is in line with claims associated with the dispute-centred tradition in law and society scholarship.[47] The argument is based

---

43 For elaboration see Tsachi Keren-Paz, 'An Inquiry into the Merits of Redistribution through Tort Law: Rejecting the Claim of Randomness', 16 *Can JL & Jur* (2003) 91, pp. 96–8.

44 For the concepts of intra- and inter-group justice see Section B below.

45 See note 59 below and accompanying text.

46 The discussion in this subsection summarizes Randomness, *supra* note 43, pp. 100–104.

47 See Michael W. McCann, 'Reform Litigation on Trial', 17 *Law & Soc Inq* (1992) 715, pp. 730–35.

on the 'easier to block' phenomenon[48] – the finding that strong interest groups find it is easier to block legislation undesirable to them than to ensure that desirable legislation is passed. It is also based on the assumptions that for accountable officials, the cost of endorsing naked discrimination is very high[49] and that inequalities are easier to maintain, perpetuate, and justify when they are hidden, latent, or entrenched in the status quo.

Random progressive redistribution through tort law would place pressure on the legislature to complement random redistribution with comprehensive progressive redistribution. The decision will expose the initial injustice of the previous regressive distribution, will endorse the claim of the disadvantaged for a progressive change, and will create pressure to make the distribution more just from the perspective of the disadvantaged who do not benefit from the redistributive judicial rule and the 'haves' who did participate. From the perspective of the 'haves', the opposition to complementary progressive redistribution will decrease, since for them there is less at stake – some of their excess was already taken away by the judicial rule. Moreover, the ability of the 'haves' to procure legislation overruling the judicial decision is limited, due to the political cost to legislators of endorsing inegalitarian rules. This conclusion is supported by the easier-to-block phenomenon.

4. No Comparative Randomness The last challenge to the randomness assumption is comparative in nature. It concedes that tort law redistribution is random. However, it disputes the assumption that tort law is especially susceptible to the randomness charge. Under this view, all methods of redistribution are random by nature; all achieve and can achieve only part of the comprehensive redistribution necessary to bring us to, or closer to, the ideal distributive result. All of the methods therefore need to be complemented by other mechanisms. Indeed, when examining distributive patterns of the tax and transfer system, one can only conclude that such redistribution is random on both sides of the equation – collection and transfer.[50]

B. Random Redistribution is Fairer than the Status Quo

This section responds to the normative claim that the status quo is more just than partial progressive redistribution. Arguably, the interest of participants in the redistribution not to be singled-out randomly, that is, their interest in horizontal equality, supersedes the desirability of the partial redistribution on its merits – the attainment of vertical equality. Robert Goodin has presented the argument as follows: 'In the same way redistributivists think it unjust for some people to get rich by sheer luck, so too must

48 See Part I.C3 above.

49 See e.g., Peter Westen, 'The Empty Idea of Equality', 95 *Harv L Rev* (1982) 537, p. 594 (using equality rhetoric, when the concept of equality is superfluous, is probably done in order to place conservatives in the uncomfortable position of having to argue against equality). See also Part IV.A1 below.

50 See e.g., Douglas A. Kahn & Jefferey S. Lehman, 'Tax Expenditure Budgets: A Critical View', 54 *Tax Notes* (1992) 1661; Boris I. Bittker, 'A "Comprehensive Tax Base" as a Goal of Income Tax Reform', 80 *Harv L Rev* (1967) 925.

they agree that it would be unjust for some but not others to be relieved of their undeserved riches by the sheer bad luck of their being the uncompensated victims of accidents or injuries.'[51] Section 1 introduces a methodology for answering this criticism and then, Sections 2 and 3, examine and reject the claims that random progressive redistribution is less fair than the status quo, due to the problems of partiality of participants and crudeness of results.

1. Methodology: The Ideal Distributive Scheme as a Reference Point The two possible distributions – that achieved under tort law which does not attempt to achieve redistributive goals (the status quo), and that achieved under a redistributive tort rule – should be compared to the ideal distributive scheme. That scheme is the one envisioned by society as the appropriate distribution of benefits and burdens in society, and it uses diverse mechanisms – tort law is one such possible mechanism – in order to achieve the ideal distribution. The deviation of the two actual distributions from the ideal should be compared, so that the one closer to the ideal distribution is preferred. Two parameters are relevant: the magnitude of the deviation and its direction. Magnitude simply examines the gap in absolute value between the actual and ideal holdings of the participants in the distribution. According to such an examination, it is equally wrong to have too much or too little. Direction examines whether the distribution increases or decreases the gap between the 'haves' and the disadvantaged, and whether it reverses the direction of injustice: whether it gives too much to individuals who previously had too little, or vice versa. Finally, in evaluating the desirability of the possible distributions, one should examine three dimensions. One is the issue of inter-group justice between the 'haves' (the 'Hs') and the 'disadvantaged' (the 'Ds'); the second is the issue of intra-group justice among the Hs – the claim of a participating H against other Hs who did not participate in the redistribution at the giving-end of the redistribution; the third is the issue of intra-group justice among the Ds – the claim of non-participating Ds against a participating D at the receiving end of the redistribution.

2. Limited Participation in Redistribution In the weak sense of the concept of randomness, redistribution is random if the participants in the redistribution do not comprise all those who would participate in the comprehensive redistribution under the ideal scheme of distribution. However, each random participant is stripped of, or receives, the same amount she should have given or received under the ideal distributive scheme. This why-me claim is weak, since in absolute terms, those who participate in the actual distribution are no better off or worse off than they would be under the ideal comprehensive distribution. The limited participation claim is based on the fact that the random participant is treated differently from the other members of her group.

Such a begrudging sentiment, however, is a poor basis for opposing partial redistribution. As for H, his complaint against the differential treatment he receives in comparison to other Hs should not absolve him from his obligation to bear the

51 Robert E. Goodin, 'Compensation and Redistribution', in John W. Chapman (ed.), *Compensatory Justice Nomos XXXIII* (New York, 1991) 143, p.162.

burden he would bear under the ideal distribution. *Accepting such a claim would merely widen the gap between the actual and ideal distributions.* The partial redistribution is closer to the ideal distribution and therefore preferable to the status quo. H's claim should be limited to a demand to impose equivalent burdens on other Hs. What is needed is more just results, not fewer, such as the prevention of progressive redistribution.

Similarly, the fact that some Ds do not receive the fair share that they would receive under the ideal distributive scheme should not be considered a valid reason for depriving a particular D of the benefit conferred upon her randomly. Non-participating Ds should have no claim against the D who receives a benefit, but, rather, against the Hs who would bear the burden under the ideal distributive scheme of handing over undeserved riches and against the authorities who do not implement that scheme. Allowing Ds to prevent the participating D from keeping what she receives from H in the litigation would merely widen the gap between the ideal distribution and the existing status quo.

3. Crudeness of Results The typical tort law redistribution involves another kind of randomness, which leads to a stronger claim of unfairness. This strong claim also involves the discrepancy between the practical outcome and the sought-for result under the ideal distributive scheme. If the burden H bears under the redistributive tort rule is greater than his fair share under the ideal distributive scheme, his claim of being treated unfairly relative to the non-participating Hs seems stronger, since in a sense he is subsidizing them. Similarly, if D receives from the tort redistribution more than her fair share, in a sense she deprives non-participating Ds from their fair share.

Finally, if the redistribution is random in this respect, there is no longer any guarantee that it is preferable on grounds of inter-group justice between H (or Hs) and D (or Ds). To make matters worse, due to general institutional limitations of tort law and of courts, the tort distribution will almost never be able to bring both participants to their ideal distributive holdings. As there are more Ds than Hs, and assuming we seek to treat equally members of the same group, then, on average, the amount taken from any given H should be divided and distributed amongst several Ds. If this is in fact the case, tort law seems to suffer from a fundamental institutional deficiency. Since paradigmatically the amount taken from the defendant is equal to that given to the plaintiff, at least one of the parties will pay or receive an amount that is either more or less than the amount that should be taken or given to her under the ideal distributive scheme.[52] Indeed, this is one of Ernest Weinrib's claims: the bipolar structure of tort law undermines the attainment of distributive goals.[53] It is also possible that the rule will err in both directions, so that D receives more than her fair share and H is stripped of more than his fair share.

52 A possible solution to this difficulty will be to deviate from the bipolar nature of private law rules. The H will pay the amount he owes according to ideal distribution, the D will receive the amount due to her, and the difference will be distributed to other Ds.

53 Weinrib, *supra* note 3, pp. 63–4, 71–2, 74–5.

(a) Inter-group justice. From an inter-group justice perspective, the problem of crudeness of result is that the distribution under a redistributive tort rule might be further from the ideal distribution than the one under the status quo. There are two responses to this concern. The non-radical response maintains that as long as courts craft a redistributive rule which is pro-D, rather than anti-H, the result will be closer to the ideal distribution than is the status quo. On average, the amount that should be taken from any H is greater than the amount that should be given to any D (due to existing patterns of holdings and the attempt to achieve intra-group justice). Therefore, adopting a rule which aims at bringing Ds who participate in the interaction as close as possible to their lot according to the ideal distribution will bring them close to that distribution, while bringing the participating Hs closer to their ideal distribution relative to the status quo. While participating Hs still have more than they should, the gap is smaller than the one under the status quo. As a prescription, then, courts should try and adopt rules which are D-oriented, rather than H-oriented, and there is reason to believe that this intuition in fact underlies the activity of courts.

The radical response maintains that reversing the direction of the injustice in holdings is desirable. According to such an approach, random injustice is better than systemic injustice. Accordingly, even if the magnitude of the deviation under a redistributive rule is likely to be greater than that under the status quo (an unlikely result), the fact that now the identities of the Hs and Ds have been reversed (so that those who had previously too much now have too little, and vice versa) is desirable. If we are doomed to live in a society in which some individuals have too much and others too little, it is fairer that those who have too much and those with too little shift positions from time to time. This result would be fairer than one where inequality in holdings is attached to membership in disadvantaged groups, which is based mainly on such immutable and fundamental characteristics as sex, race, and class.

(b) Intra-group justice among Hs. As long as participating H pays no more than his share according to the ideal-distributive scheme, his claim about horizontal justice should not be heard. The intra-group justice claim should be subordinated to the inter-group justice claim. An appropriate analogy is viewing Hs as joint and several debtors. Hs owe Ds a debt according to the demands of the ideal distribution. The participating debtor cannot defend against the claim of the creditor by claiming that other debtors have not paid. Recall, that the redistributive rule is a step which brings society closer to the ideal distribution.

(c) Intra-group justice among Ds. A fairness concern, based on the fact that random D has received more than her ideal fair share, is not a valid reason for opposing random redistribution through tort law. There are two lines of argument to support this position. The first argument holds that the other disadvantaged are more likely to benefit from the windfall to lucky D than from maintaining the initial distribution. First, based on public choice insights, Ds have a better chance of triggering legislative action to redistribute benefits held in excess by certain other Ds than of triggering redistribution from the Hs to the Ds. Second, other Ds are more likely to enjoy a surplus held by another D than a surplus held by an H. This would be so for several reasons, including: physical proximity; relations between the disadvantaged (including kinship and friendship); and a higher likelihood that D, rather than H,

will show compassion, solidarity, commitment, and altruistic tendencies towards her fellow Ds. Third, there are some non-pecuniary benefits from a redistributive tort law rule that all members of the group enjoy because D is unable to exclude other Ds, even if she wants to. For example, the law's symbolic effects with respect to the importance of egalitarianism is shared by all Ds. Moreover, at times, awarding some Ds preferential treatment is instrumentally justified in order to protect the interests of the rest of the Ds, who do not participate in the particular random redistribution. For example, adopting a rule of compensating victims according to average damage (rather than individual damage) which seemingly gives injured Ds a windfall, in fact improves the lot of all Ds, since it eliminates the incentive to channel the risk towards them under the full compensation rule (*restitutio ad integrum* or RAI).[54] Finally, since under a random tort law redistribution rule, any D might end up with a windfall, we should not underestimate the value of hope.

The second line of argument maintains that even if those benefits do not trickle down, the tort distribution is still fairer overall than the initial distribution under the status quo. First, we should not encourage a politics of envy between the disadvantaged. We should seek to promote the least advantaged and not hold back the slightly-less disadvantaged. Moreover, on its merits, it seems that somewhat narrowing the gap between several individual Ds and Hs outweighs the injustice in creating a new gap between the D who received more than her ideal share and her fellow Ds.[55] Finally, random redistribution is important merely by virtue of its challenge to the status quo.

III. Excessive Cost

A. In General

Many critics of an egalitarian approach to private law would concede that private law can be used to promote equality to *some* degree. Some might also agree that partial promotion of equality is better than no promotion whatsoever. However, they argue that an attempt to promote equality inevitably hampers private law's ability to promote its classic goals.[56] These goals include the common aspiration of liberals and utilitarians to adopt clear and predictable rules, the liberal aspiration to minimally encroach upon individuals' liberty, and the aspiration of law and economics scholars to achieve efficiency. Given the potential of public law generally, tax law in particular, and other alternative means to promote equality more effectively than private law, critics argue that the promotion of equality should be left to these mechanisms, whereas private law should continue to promote its more traditional goals. Viewed this way, the excessive cost argument is a formulation of the 'lack of proportionality' argument: private law is not the least restrictive means by which to promote equality, and should therefore not be the mechanism of choice.

---

54 See Chs 4.I.A, 8 below.

55 For an application see Ch. 6.III.C1 below.

56 Elizabeth Anderson, 'Compensation Within the Limits of Reliance Alone', in John W. Chapman (ed.), *Compensatory Justice Nomos XXXIII* (New York, 1991) 178, pp. 182–3.

This section will summarize the response I gave elsewhere to the concerns about predictability and liberty.[57] Section B will introduce the response to the concern for efficiency. As will be seen, there is a great degree of similarity between the responses to the liberty and efficiency claims. An initial response to the excessive cost argument is to expose the monistic and hierarchical predilections of its supporters. From a legally monistic view, lexical priority is given to promoting the chosen goal over other goals. In contrast, any attempt to pursue multiple goals, with the intent of achieving an optimal 'mix', requires relinquishing the overriding aspiration to promote any particular goal optimally. Only those committed to a monistic approach (such as some advocates of corrective justice and wealth maximization) will see the mere attempt to sacrifice the attainment of one goal for the promotion of another as problematic in itself. If it is accepted that we must deal with trade-offs and balancing, one must then ask whether a given balancing of goals is reasonable. This question cannot be answered *a priori*, but must instead be examined in a given factual context.

Concerns with respect to predictability revolve around both the uncertainty whether one will participate in redistribution affected by an interaction regulated by private law rule and the timing and extent of the participation.[58] The prevalence of insurance answers both difficulties and allows the relatively simple actuarial calculation of the value of the redistributive component and the pricing of this component in the premium. This makes all insured participate in the redistribution and respects the interest in predictability. Furthermore, the effect of combining a progressive legal rule with liability insurance will result in a progressive cross-subsidy which will partially offset the prevalence of regressive cross-subsidy.[59] While the extent to which redistributive legal rules will produce a predictable redistribution will vary, there is no reason to believe that clear rules cannot be formed as the examples throughout the book and elsewhere demonstrate.[60]

Concerns with respect to liberty are based on the assumption that there is a qualitative difference, in terms of the degree of intrusion in one's affairs, between redistribution effected by taxation and redistribution effected by private law mechanisms. Both methods negatively affect positive liberty simply by virtue of taking away amounts of money. In addition, redistribution by legal rules affects negative liberty by either curtailing some possible courses of action or by obliging the actor to take a certain course of action.[61]

---

57 Tsachi Keren-Paz, 'Private Law Redistribution, Predictability and Liberty', 50 *McGill LJ* (2005) 327 (Predictability & Liberty).

58 Goodin, *supra* note 51, p. 157; Schwartz, *supra* note 4, p. 572.

59 Predictability & Liberty, *supra* note 57, p. 339. For regressive cross subsidy see ibid., pp. 337–8; Ch. 4.I.A below. For applications of progressive cross subsidy see Chs 6.IV.C, 5, Example 4 below; Kyle Logue & Ronen Avraham, 'Redistributing Optimally: of Tax Rules, Legal Rules, and Insurance', 56 *Tax L Rev* (2003) 157, p. 214.

60 See e.g., Part IV.B below; Chs 5, Examples 4 and 7, 6.IV.F below; Predictability & Liberty, Ibid., pp. 341–3; Keren-Paz, *supra* note 43, pp. 121–6; Logue & Avraham, ibid., pp. 207–252.

61 Charles Fried, *Right and Wrong* (Cambridge, 1978), pp. 143–50; John Rawls, 'The Basic Structure as Subject', in Alvin I. Goldman & Jaegwon Kim (eds), *Values and Morals*

There are three responses to this criticism. First, it assumes that both methods of redistribution – tax and transfer and legal rules – are equally effective in promoting the desirable redistribution, but that tax redistribution is less intrusive. However, when one recalls that legal rules redistribute more than wealth alone and when one takes into account the symbolic aspect of legal rules, this assumption can no longer be defended. At times, legal rules will be more effective in achieving redistribution and therefore we should be willing to pay more in the currency of liberty. Second, it assumes that redistribution through legal rules is more intrusive than redistribution through legal rules. This too is contested. A common shortcoming in the liberty analysis is that it ignores the liberty effects of the participation in the redistribution on those participating from the receiving end. Private law redistribution, while possibly more intrusive than its alternative from the perspective of the 'haves', might increase the liberty of the disadvantaged to a greater degree than would tax-based redistribution.[62] One version of the argument would collapse it to the first response – that we are dealing with a desirable trade-off of liberty for equality. Another version might concede that total liberty in society might decrease as a result of the redistributive tort rule (since the loss to the 'haves' outweighs in absolute terms the gain of the disadvantaged) yet insist that such a result is desirable in itself since it leads to a more egalitarian distribution of liberty in society. According to such view, liberty is an entitlement which itself has to be distributed in a more egalitarian way. Yet another version holds that total liberty itself will increase in society through private law redistribution, since the increase in the liberty of the disadvantaged will outweigh the decrease of the liberty of the 'haves'. Finally, if the supposedly superior method for redistribution (tax) is not likely to be used, redistributing through private law rules is better than the status quo. These three responses roughly correspond with the ones offered below in Sections B3, B2 and B5 respectively regarding the efficiency-based critique.

B. *Efficiency*

Louis Kaplow and Steven Shavell ('K&S') have argued that any attempt to effect redistribution, if it is to be done at all, should be made solely by the tax and transfer system, and not by private law rules.[63] Their basic claim is that using legal rules in order to promote progressive redistribution of wealth is inefficient. Because of disincentive effects and high administrative costs, using private law for redistribution results in a greater loss of wealth than the loss resulting from the use of tax and transfer for the same goal. For this reason, the former

---

(Dordrecht, 1978), pp. 47, 65; Michael J. Trebilcock, *The Limits of Freedom of Contract* (Cambridge, 1993), pp. 100–101. This argument is the equivalent of the double distortion argument made by Kaplow and Shavell and discussed in Section B below.

62 As is shown in Predictability & Liberty, *supra* note 57, pp. 346–7, 353 the analysis should distinguish between the contract paradigm in which seemingly the regulation thwarts both participants' liberty interests and the tort paradigm in which one party's liberty loss involves the other party's liberty gain.

63 Louis Kaplow & Steven Shavell, 'Why the Legal System is Less Efficient than the Income Tax in Redistributing Income', 23 *J Leg Stud* (1994) 667 (K&S I).

method of redistribution is deficient. K&S's basic claim is that using legal rules 'to redistribute income distorts work incentives fully as much as the income tax system – because of the distortion caused by the redistribution itself – and also creates inefficiencies in the activities regulated by the legal rule'.[64] The latter loss is caused by choosing a rule which, due to its distributive effect, is not efficient (wealth maximizing). K&S's claim that the tax system is more efficient than the legal system in redistributing wealth is disputed in the economic-legal literature. Among those who specifically dispute K&S's argument are Sanchirico, Jolls, Logue, Fortus and Avraham.[65] This section joins this critical camp, offering five lines of critique. K&S's model is based on five assumptions, which will all be challenged.

1. Attainability of Efficiency A basic premise of K&S's model is that private law rules are indeed able to bring about efficient results when they are not tainted by an attempt to promote distributive goals. Under such a premise, an attempt to promote distributive goals will bring about a significant efficiency loss, which will outweigh the benefit gained in the promotion of the distributive goal. Contesting the accuracy of this assumption will weaken K&S's argument. In fact, if the response is founded, it warrants generally much more scepticism regarding the relevance of the normative claim of economic analysis of law. As such, its scope is broader than the argument presented in this book. The doubts regarding the accuracy of the attainability of efficient legal rules are valid across the different branches of private law doctrine, albeit, supposedly, to differing degrees. Recently, for example, Eric Posner, in evaluating the contribution of law and economics to contract law, has concluded that economic analysis of contract law has failed both to explain existing contract doctrine and to criticize it normatively. The models offered are either too simple, and therefore determinate but wrong (since they ignore relevant variables) or too sophisticated but unpredictable (since they hinge on variables that are not verifiable).[66]

Similarly, an examination of tort law raises serious doubts regarding its ability to achieve efficiency. A major reason for this is the frequent availability of liability insurance, which strongly erodes the deterrent effect of tort law, all the more so given the limited ability of insurers to collect premiums based on the individual

---

64 Ibid., p. 668.

65 See Christine Jolls, 'Behavioral Economics Analysis of Redistributive Legal Rules', 51 *Vand L Rev* (1998) 1653; Chris W. Sanchirico, 'Should Legal Rules be Used to Redistribute Wealth? Taxes Versus Legal Rules as Instruments for Equity: A More Equitable View', 29 *J Leg Stud* (2000) 797; Ronen Avraham, David Fortus & Kyle Logue, 'Revisiting the Roles of Legal Rules and Tax Rules in Income Redistribution: A Response to Kaplow & Shavell', 89 *Iowa L Rev* (2004) 1125; Logue & Avraham, *supra* note 59. See also Louis Kaplow & Steven Shavell, 'Should Legal Rules Favor the Poor? Clarifying the Role of Legal Rules and the Income Tax in Redistributing Income', 29 *J Leg. Stud.* (2000) 821 (K&S II); Chris W. Sanchirico, 'Deconstructing the New Efficiency Rationale', 86 *Cornell L Rev* (2001) 1003 (Sanchirico 2).

66 Eric A. Posner, 'Economic Analysis of Contract Law After Three Decades: Success or Failure?', 112 *Yale LJ* (2003) 829.

level of risk posed by the insured.[67] Other reasons include problems of myopia, bounded rationality, rational ignorance and strategic behaviour.[68] Indeed, as Stephen Sugarman noted, empirical research has found that the liability threat of tort law is considered as background noise by firm managers and does not affect their decisions.[69] More generally, the ongoing debates between leading law and economic scholars with respect to the question what is the efficient rule in many fundamental issues, casts serious doubt on the ability of courts to craft efficient rules.[70]

If private law rules are ill-equipped to promote wealth maximization, adding a distributive goal cannot significantly compromise the goal of efficiency. It might be argued that the fact that we face a problem in achieving efficiency is not a good reason to exacerbate the problem. However, one should remember that a pluralistic approach requires a trade-off between the better attainment of one goal and the lesser attainment of another. Even given the desire to advance efficiency by private law rules, the inherently limited ability to achieve this goal causes the marginal loss of efficiency from pursuing a distributive goal to be small. Therefore, given some effectiveness in advancing the distributive goal, the result of the balancing between efficiency and distribution will tend to justify redistributive intervention by private law rules more than the model of K&S suggests. The more sceptical one is regarding the possibility of crafting efficient rules, the less costly in terms of lost efficiency becomes an attempt to achieve redistributive goals. Of course, the extent to which legal rules can achieve either efficiency or progressive redistribution, or both, varies with the context,[71] as does the extent to which there is a tension between promoting the two goals.[72] Therefore, there is no need for an all-or-nothing approach. As will be discussed below, in situations in which we have reason to doubt the guiding-behaviour potential of legal rules, redistributive rules are not likely to come at the cost of efficiency loss.

2. Equal Distortion of Incentive to Work K&S's model is based on the assumption that an equal amount redistributed away under both methods of redistribution equally distorts the incentive to work.[73] This basic assumption is disputed by both Chris Sanchirico and Christine Jolls. Sanchirico argues that K&S's equal distortion thesis is correct only when the redistributive component of the rule is

---

67 See e.g., Stephen D. Sugarman, 'Doing Away with Tort Law', 73 *Cal L Rev* (1985) 555, pp. 573–81.

68 Sugarman, ibid., pp. 564–73; Don Dewees, David Duff & Michael Trebilcock, *Exploring the Domain of Accident Law: Taking the Facts Seriously* (New York, 1996), pp. 15–26, 414–21.

69 Sugarman, ibid., p. 566.

70 See e.g., *Jordan v Duff & Phelps, Inc.*, 815 F 2d 429 (7th Cir 1987) (contract interpretation, J Posner and Easterbrook disagreeing on the efficient rule). Similar disputes exist with respect to many issues such as the case for and against damages for pain and suffering, contributory versus comparative negligence, and property versus liability rules.

71 See Part IV.B below.

72 See Section B4 below.

73 K&S I, *supra* note 63, p. 669.

a function of the parties' income, while it is possible to craft redistributive rules that are not income-dependent.[74] More generally, Sanchirico argues that K&S's model is based on the assumption that the redistributive rule affects equally all its addressees, while in fact redistributive rules affect different individuals differently; for this reason, it is possible to achieve distributive goals without efficiency loss.[75] K&S, in response to Sanchirico's argument, dispute his claim that their model is limited with regard to its assumptions and argue that it has general scope.[76] They mention that while Sanchirico's analysis is not inconsistent with theirs, they believe his interpretation – that private law rules could be used extensively to reduce the gap between the poor and the rich – is misleading.[77] While they further qualify their general claim, they still believe that the redistributive role of private law is negligible, and that it works differently from the manner that they suspect most legal academics have in mind when they talk about adjusting legal rules to favour the poor (mainly as rectifying the distortion of the incentive to work caused by tax-based redistribution).[78] Further contribution to the debate was made by Avraham, Fortus and Logue.[79] They criticize K&S's double distortion argument for assuming that the distortion to work would be the same under the two mechanisms for redistribution. Under a redistributive legal rule the 'haves' can change their work effort, their regulated activity or both. Given the fact that individuals are heterogeneous with respect to their preferences, accident-proneness, and so on, administrative and information costs make impossible a tax and transfer system that will achieve the same redistributive result in a more efficient way. Logue & Avraham however argue that Sanchirico's case for frequent use of legal rules to redistribute *income* is overstated.[80]

Further challenge to the equal distortion assumption comes from the work of Christine Jolls.[81] Based on a behavioural law and economics approach, Jolls argues that the distortion to work incentives might actually be lesser under redistributive legal rules than under taxation. One reason for this result is a cognitive bias manifested by unrealistic optimism regarding the probability that a bad event would occur to the subject. Such bias will cause lesser distortion of the incentive to work when redistribution is affected by private law rules. Another reason for this result is the 'mental accounting' phenomenon. According to this phenomenon redistribution through private law might be viewed as expenditures out of income, and not as expenditures against income. Therefore, it would create a lesser distortion to work.

Logue & Avraham qualify the significance of Jolls' critique given the prevalence of insurance. With respect to the probabilistic tax argument, they mention that the existence of insurance is likely to erode the difference in incentives (since it converts

74 Sanchirico, *supra* note 65, pp. 799–800.
75 Ibid., pp. 805–7.
76 K&S II, *supra* note 65, p. 825 n.7.
77 Ibid., pp. 822–3, 829–32.
78 Ibid., pp. 827–35.
79 Avraham, Fortus & Logue, *supra* note 65.
80 Logue & Avraham, *supra* note 59, pp. 201–6.
81 Jolls, *supra* note 65.

a probabilistic tax into a definite increase in premiums) so that the case for private law redistribution may hinge on the question of the advantage of insurers' competition in collecting taxes;[82] with respect to her mental accounting argument, they mention that the effect of insurance is less obvious and it might depend on how insurers design their premium statements (an issue of framing).[83]

The upshot of the discussion is that it is far from clear that private law redistribution distorts work incentives to the same degree that tax distribution does.

3. Equal Effectiveness A major assumption in K&S's model is that the two competing redistributive mechanisms are equally effective in achieving the desired redistributive result of the relevant entitlement, while the cost of advancing the redistributive goal, in terms of efficiency loss, is higher in private law redistribution.[84] This assumption will be referred to as the equal effectiveness assumption. To the extent that this assumption is purported to be of general scope it is mistaken. If private law is more effective in achieving egalitarian results than tax law, it follows that even if it were true that private law redistribution costs more in terms of efficiency losses than tax-based redistribution, this still does not support the proposition that one should use *only* tax law for redistributive purposes. Private law redistribution might be more costly, but it might also give better results than exclusively using tax law for redistribution.

Private law redistribution might be more effective than tax-based redistribution for two reasons: (1) legal rules redistribute entitlements other than wealth, and they can redistribute these entitlements more effectively than the tax system; (2) even with respect to wealth, the social meaning of the redistribution changes under the two alternative distributive mechanisms. Private law redistribution might be deemed more empowering to the disadvantaged, and more just (and hence also more likely to be accepted as legitimate) at least in so far as it aims to rectify regressive redistribution of wealth caused by the private law rules themselves. Accordingly, a strong case for a redistributive role for private law rules can be made when the rule involves redistribution of entitlements other than wealth *or* when the rule is trying to offset a regressive redistribution of wealth caused by the interaction itself which is being regulated by the legal rule.[85]

(a) Redistribution of other entitlements. Private law rules have inevitable distributive consequences. A crucial aspect of the argument made in this book is the plurality of the entitlements distributed by private law rules. These rules distribute not merely wealth but also liberty, security, status, power, dignity, and notoriety. Some of the entitlements distributed by private law – such as security and liberty – are the result of the coercive aspect of the law. For example, a tort rule defining a given activity as non-negligent, increases the liberty of those engaging in this activity and decreases the liberty and security interests of its potential victims. Other entitlements are distributed by private law due to its normative aspect and

82 Ibid., pp. 199–200.
83 Ibid., pp. 200–201.
84 K&S I, *supra* note 63, p. 669.
85 For an important application see Ch. 5.II.B3(b) below.

its capacity to create social meanings, and more particularly to stigmatize. For example, a finding by a court that the defendant acted negligently or that he did not act in good faith, might trigger (or exacerbate) non-legal sanctions and market deterrence.

With respect to the law's normativity or its expressive aspects, it has been argued that the content of legal rules affects the way individuals perceive themselves and the way they are perceived by others.[86] Legal rules may change the normative preferences of individuals, and can have symbolic and educative messages regarding what society conceives as appropriate and normative. Breaching legal norms might trigger the imposition of non-legal sanctions by other individuals, while conforming with legal norms might confer prestige and certain benefits.[87]

Note that private law's effectiveness in redistributing different entitlements varies. While there are entitlements (such as wealth) whose distribution is more difficult to affect by changing private law rules (or some of them), private law rules might be an important, and at times even central mechanism for redistributing other entitlements, such as liberty, dignity and social status. According to this approach, private law can respond better than the tax and transfer system to some issues of distributive justice, such as cultural injustice and recognition, which are broader than the question of wealth-distribution. With respect to these issues, the law's coercion – and especially the law's normativity – make redistribution through private law especially effective.

Consider for example a rule prohibiting the owner of a restaurant from discriminating on racial grounds.[88] Even if the result of such a rule is efficiency loss (and this is debatable), it is clear that the ability of such a rule to advance equality and prevent humiliation and loss of dignity, is far more significant than the ability of tax law to achieve these results. In fact, it is clear that in this example, the egalitarian motivation of such a rule is not to redistribute wealth from the rich to the poor or from the members of the racial majority to racial minorities, but rather to deal with issues of recognition, social status and self respect. One can, of course, think of other examples in which an egalitarian change to legal rules is desirable despite the fact that the change's effect on the distribution of wealth in society is insignificant, at least in the short run. In such situations the change is desirable due to its transformative potential – its ability to change over time the status of the disadvantaged and the way in which they and others perceive their proper role in society. The arguments with respect to the proper scope of maternal prenatal duty[89] and parental liability

86 See e.g., Richard H. McAdams, 'The Origin, Development, and Regulation of Norms', 96 *Mich L Rev* (1997) 338; Eric A. Posner, *Law and Social Norms* (Cambridge, 2000); Cass R. Sunstein, 'On the Expressive Function of Law', 144 *U Pa LR* (1996) 2021. Such approaches are based on Hart's internal understanding of the law. See H.L.A. Hart, *The Concept of Law* (2nd edn, Oxford, 1994), pp. 79–91.

87 See e.g., Lisa Bernstein, 'Private Commercial Law in the Cotton Industry: Creating Cooperation through Rules, Norms, and Institutions', 99 *Mich L Rev* (2001) 1724; Julie Barker Pape, 'Physician Data Banks: The Public's Right To Know Versus The Physician's Right To Privacy', 66 *Fordham LR* (1997) 975.

88 See also Ch. 7 below.

89 Ch. 6 below.

for negligent supervision[90] are based on such an approach which emphasizes the status of women relative to men and perceptions of women's role in society. In these cases, the progressive redistribution of wealth affected by these rules is likely to be insignificant due to the common phenomenon of joint finances within the family unit.

The effects of legal rules described above – normative, symbolic, expressive, educational – might be (according to the weak version of this argument), and perhaps are even likely to be (according to the strong version) more significant relative to the tax system, for several reasons. First, the potential of legal norms to bring about these results turns in part on their visibility and resonance, and in many instances legal rules will be more visible than tax rules. Second, in many instances the distributive character and effect of a legal (redistributive) rule will be clearer than a list of changes in the tax and transfer system. Third, and most importantly, the normative justification for the redistribution might be different under the two alternative mechanisms for redistribution, so that redistribution through the legal system might be considered as more justified and more empowering to the disadvantaged. Since this reason is relevant also to wealth redistribution, it will be explored separately.

(b) The social meaning of the redistribution: private law redistribution as more empowering. Redistribution effected by the tax system is often portrayed by its opponents as an act of charity and benevolence bestowed by the productive in society on the unproductive.[91] However, it is often forgotten that private law rules often can and do systematically redistribute wealth from the poor to the rich.[92] Provided that the current regressive nature of private law is well understood, a 'direct' adjustment of private law rules in order to reduce or eliminate this regressive result should meet with greater support than an indirect adjustment through the tax system. Such direct adjustment will be justified as a proper response to the unjust redistributive result effected by existing regressive private law rules. In contrast, the link between a change in tax law and the underlying unjust redistributive result is less noticeable and, for that reason, less likely to attract support. Private law redistribution therefore could enjoy four advantages in comparison to tax-based redistribution.

First, it is more empowering to the disadvantaged. The change of existing regressive effects is more likely to be perceived as a right of the disadvantaged supported by the requirement of justice than as a charitable act. This stands in sharp contrast to transfer payments from the 'haves' to the disadvantaged through the tax and transfer system.[93]

Second, it is more likely to enjoy legitimacy and consensus. In fact, a limited redistributive role to private law as rectifying existing regressive effects should be accepted, at least in part, even by libertarians. A libertarian approach sanctifies the status quo and is inimical to involuntary wealth redistribution. If private law rules

90 Section B4, Part IV.B1 below.

91 See generally, Michael B. Katz, *The Undeserving Poor: From the War on Poverty to the War on Welfare* (New York, 1989).

92 See Ch. 4.I below.

93 Cf. Posner, *supra* note 86, pp. 179–84.

systematically redistribute wealth involuntarily from the poor to the rich, a libertarian should support the reformulation of the rules to rectify this redistribution.

Third, to the extent that the change in private rules reduces the accumulation of wealth by the 'haves' private law redistribution is less destructive to the well-being of the 'haves'. The endowment effect teaches us that taking away what was already accumulated affects more negatively one's well-being than preventing that person from accumulating what is going to be taken away.[94] Fourth, for all of these reasons, private law redistribution is more likely to happen, since it will be perceived as more just and will trigger less opposition. It could also be that direct adjustment of private law rules will raise fewer objections than redistribution effected by the tax system simply because the former method of redistribution is less visible than the latter.[95]

Two tort examples will clarify the inability of tax-based redistribution to achieve the distributive results achieved by legal rules.

The restitutio ad integrum rule. This rule harms the disadvantaged by disproportionately exposing them to risk.[96] An attempt to compensate the poor by adjusting transfer payments (which is never done) is problematic for several reasons. First, it involves formidable administrative costs. The tax authorities will have to evaluate the degree of excessive exposure to risk and the resulting harm. There is reason to believe that the courts are better equipped than the tax authorities to do this job.[97] Second, even if it were feasible for the tax authorities to fully compensate the poor for their excessive exposure to risk, and to do so at reasonable administrative cost, such a system would merely compensate *ex post* for the regressive exposure to risk, rather than prevent the *ex ante* inegalitarian exposure to risk and injury, with its practical and ideological consequences. Third, such a transfer payment is more likely to submit the poor to attacks that they are lazy, unproductive and a burden on hard-working taxpayers. By contrast, it should be clear that a direct change of compensation rules in the direction of standardization of awards – which results with decreasing the gap between the rich and the poor – is not a benevolent act made by society towards the disadvantaged. Rather, it is merely a manifestation of the substantive notion of equality before the law according to which it is unacceptable to systematically expose the poor to higher risks.

---

94 See Daniel Kahneman, Jack L. Knetsch & Richard H. Thaler, 'Anomalies: The Endowment Effect, Loss Aversion, and Status Quo Bias', 5 *J Econ Persp* (1991) 193. Cf. Jolls, *supra* note 65. Note that this advantage is more relevant for the development of property and contract rules dealing with the creation of entitlements and is somewhat less relevant to the development of tort rules which are more focused on the preservation of already existing entitlements. This distinction however is not so clear-cut. The tort of negligence, for example, deals also with the creation of entitlements and not only with protecting existing entitlements.

95 See Jolls, ibid., p. 1656. Note that this assumption at first glance is inconsistent with a previous assumption that the visibility of legal rules and their distributive effects might be more significant than that of tax rules. Each assumption might be correct under different circumstances.

96 See Ch. 4.I below.

97 Cf. Logue & Avraham, *supra* note 59, pp. 230–32.

Wealth-dependent standard of care. Chapter 5 develops reformulation of the standard of care so that the evaluation of whether the defendant was negligent would take into account her means as well as that of potential plaintiffs. Such an approach is based on the theory that the means of the parties are morally relevant for the evaluation of whether the defendant properly balanced his interests against those of others. For present purposes it is important to observe that according to this approach, when the defendant is found not liable it is because we think that she acted properly (a justification rationale), and *not* because we believe that, despite the fact that she acted improperly, we absolve her from liability since she is poor (an excuse rationale).

This justification-excuse distinction explains why the same distributive result could not have been reached by tax and transfer. Presumably, an alternative solution would be to find the defendant liable whenever taking precaution is cost-effective and to make a transfer payment to compensate her for her costs. This solution (which is in essence the one suggested by K&S) is inadequate. First, it is unclear how in practice the tax and transfer system could be modified to compensate the poor tortfeasor for her liability or for her precaution costs. Second, liability entails results (financial and other) over and above the obligation to pay damages to the plaintiff. Stigmatizing the defendant as negligent might trigger non-legal sanctions against her with material and non-material consequences. Should a transfer payment compensate the tortfeasor for these costs? If the answer is negative, it is proof that private law redistribution is more effective. If the answer is affirmative (assuming such costs can at all be quantified), then substantively, the tax system tracks the change that should have been done by private law. Even then the question remains whether incorporating such changes in the tax system would not generate greater efficiency losses than a change in tort rules. Finally, we are still left with the problem of incommensurability of values and money. The evaluation of the defendant as negligent is value-laden and it stigmatizes the defendant. If it is true that the proper normative evaluation is that the defendant was not negligent, the ensuing stigmatization following a finding of liability is improper even if financial compensation for it is provided.

(c) Four concluding remarks. First, to be fair to K&S's argument, the line of criticism offered above does not go to the accuracy of their model but rather to its practical relevance. Strictly speaking, the authors seem to argue merely that private law is an inferior mechanism to tax law in terms of redistributing *wealth*. If, however, it is true that accurate reading of K&S is that they make an implicit broader claim that private law should not be used to advance equality in society, then their model is lacking. It ignores the fact that egalitarianism exceeds wealth redistribution, and the limited nature of their claim should be acknowledged and understood.[98] This would mean that at best (and ignoring the other challenges raised in this section) K&S's claim explains why private law rules should not be used (or used extensively)

98 For a similar claim see ibid. (maintaining that with respect to wealth redistribution the tax system enjoys superiority over legal rules, but nevertheless legal rules might have some limited room for complementary wealth redistribution and that they have significant role in redistributing other entitlements).

to redistribute wealth. It does not provide a cogent reason to oppose using private law rules in order to advance an egalitarian agenda – that of redistributing power, liberty and status in society. Moreover, even with respect to the redistribution of wealth, private law redistribution might be more effective from the perspective of the disadvantaged, due to its different social meaning.

Second, the argument builds considerably on the expressive aspect of the law. The significance of this aspect is contested.[99] In any event, the law's normative and symbolic message has intrinsic value, regardless of its attitude-modification potential. Third, the argument does not advocate replacing tax redistribution by private law redistribution but merely complementing it. Therefore, there is no need to defend the strong claim that private law redistribution is generally likely to be more effective than tax-based redistribution. It is sufficient to show that a change of several rules in private law could bring about redistributive results which cannot be achieved as effectively by tax and transfer. The examples given support this claim.

Finally, the analysis leads to the conclusion that from a normative perspective it is easier to defend an egalitarian approach which aims merely to prevent a regressive result stemming directly from the rule in question, than an approach willing to redistribute through private law rules in order to correct inequalities which are external to the rule in question. While the latter, broader approach is supported here, one does not have to agree with it in its entirety. Even if the latter approach is deemed undesirable, it is important to observe how considerable is the room left for the redistributive role of legal rules according to the former approach, and how uncontroversial is the case for crafting legal rules which will not excessively burden the disadvantaged.

4. Efficiency/Distribution Trade-off K&S's model assumes (yet does not necessitate) a tension between the efficient and the egalitarian rule. Hence, a shift from the egalitarian to the efficient rule would save money that could be distributed by the tax system. While at times promoting distributive goals would result in an efficiency loss, at other times it is not clear that such a loss would exist, while at other times still it seems that the egalitarian rule would be the efficient one. Especially when a proper understanding of efficiency is adopted – one that takes into account wealth effects – it becomes clear that egalitarianism and efficiency sometimes overlap.

At first glance, a good example of a trade-off between efficiency and redistribution is a shift from the *restitutio ad integrum* rule to some version of standardized compensation. Since it is cheaper to risk and harm the poor, individualized compensation is regressive. When measured in absolute terms, such a rule is efficient, since the decrease in value of what is already of low value causes a lesser loss than the decrease in value of what was of high value prior to the accident. Moreover, a shift toward standardized awards (based, say, on the average loss of

99 See e.g., Stewart Macaulay, 'Law and Behavioral Sciences: Is There Any There There?', 6 *Law & Pol'y* (1984) 149, p. 168; Robert E. Scott, 'The Legal Construction of Norms: The Limits of Behavioral Theories of Law and Social Norms', 86 *Va L Rev* (2000) 1603.

accident victims) seemingly will create a moral hazard problem in the case of poor victims who receive more than their real loss if injured.

But even in this example it is not clear that a shift toward standardized awards is inefficient.[100] First, as long as the average amount is set correctly, defendants' incentives to take care do not diminish. Second, administrative costs would be significantly reduced under a rule which does not necessitate individual evaluation of damages. Third, divorcing the amount of damages from proof of the harm caused to the individual plaintiff does not give plaintiffs a negative incentive to rehabilitate before the trial has ended. Fourth, while poor victims are given a worse incentive to take precautions compared to the existing rule, rich victims are given a better incentive. It might be, then, that the under-compensation to the rich alleviates the problem of the victim's moral hazard in the segment where it counts most. Finally, given wealth effects and diminishing marginal utility of money, and given the fact that tort law generally under-compensates, removing the incentive to risk the poor under the existing rule might decrease the incidence of injury to the poor, which causes them significant disutility.

The following examples demonstrate that the egalitarian rule is efficient. The common law rule regarding negligent parental supervision of minor children who harm third parties insists that the liability is individual and that one parent's negligence is not imputed to the other.[101] Such a rule is problematic, since it is likely to burden women disproportionately, given their role as primary care takers and as primary custodians in single-parent families.[102] This results in (insignificant) regressive distribution of wealth between women and men and in problematic symbolic messages (mainly that taking care of children is a woman's role). A more egalitarian rule would hold both parents jointly and severely liable and would give the parent who actually paid a right to contribution for half of the amount, without considerations of fault, based on the theory that parenthood should be viewed as a partnership. The suggested rule is also likely to be more efficient. To the extent that efficiency considerations are relevant here at all, namely under the controversial assumption that the content of the legal rule can affect at all the degree of parental care, the individualistic common law rule is inefficient. Under the assumption that the quality of care declines the longer the duration of the supervision, the relative absence of fathers from the picture of supervision, which lengthens the

100 Recently, the Israeli Supreme Court – while deciding that the compensation for loss of minor's earning capacity should be calculated upon neutral indexes which should not take into account the plaintiff's sex and ethnic origin – mentioned that such result was supported by both considerations of distributive justice and efficiency. CA 10064/02 *Migdal v Abu Hanna*, Takdin-Elyon, 2005(03) 3932 (Israel), paras 38–42. See especially ibid., para. 41.

101 See Restatement (Second) of the Law of Torts § 316 (1965); *Cashman v Reider's Stop-N-Shop Supermarket*, 504 NE 2d 487 (Ohio Ct App 1986). For other aspects of the doctrine see Ch. 5.V.B below. A more detailed analysis of this issue can be found in Tsachi Keren-Paz, *Limits of Private Law* (D.Jur. dissertation, York University, 2000), pp. 429–70.

102 A case exemplifying the problem caused by the current rule (although one might fairly argue that it was wrongly decided even according to the inner logic of that rule) is *Bruttig v Olsen*, 453 NW 2d 153 (Wis Ct App 1989) in which *neither* parent was present and yet the parents were ascribed different degrees of comparative fault.

duration of mothers' supervision, will increase the potential for momentary lapses of concentration by mothers while supervising their children. Accordingly, giving a legal incentive to fathers to supervise their children more effectively is likely to increase the quality of supervision by both parents.

Similarly, the rule defended in Chapter 6 below with respect to the scope of maternal prenatal duty is desirable from an egalitarian perspective and is not inferior to its alternative from an efficiency perspective. The suggested rule hinges the duty upon the existence in fact of liability insurance. In the absence of insurance, liability will harm women's status without improving women's incentives to take care.[103] In a similar vein, it has been argued that compensation for pain and suffering and the adoption of a subjective standard of care are supported by both notions of progressive redistribution and efficiency.[104] Similar claims have been made in the context of contract and property law.[105]

5. Likelihood that Superior Redistributive Mechanism will be Used In order to justify, on efficiency grounds, judicial deference with respect to redistributive policy, it is not enough to show that there is an alternative redistributive mechanism which is theoretically superior. Rather, the question is whether such mechanism is likely to be used. K&S, fully aware of this issue, are quick to mention that the wealth saved through using taxation for redistribution can be used to the benefit of those disadvantaged who are on the receiving end of redistributive efforts.[106] They concede, however, that in practice, redistribution through the taxation of income would not literally make everyone better off.[107] The theoretical advantage of the taxation system remains hollow if we have a reason to believe, as we do, that the legislature will not engage in progressive redistribution. Therefore, the lower the likelihood that the theoretically superior alternative will be used, the less judicial

103 Ch. 6.III.C1 below.

104 Logue & Avraham, *supra* note 59, pp. 228–32, 237–42. Note, however, that the efficiency-based justification to pain and suffering damages is contested. See ibid., p. 229.

105 See Tsachi Keren-Paz, ' "It Costs Me More": Rejecting the Arguments of Illegitimacy and Excessive Cost Brought against the Promotion of Equality in Private Law', 7 *Haifa ULR* (2004) 541, pp. 617–20 (analysing Israeli's contract law doctrine which softens formal requirements and tends to give effect to preliminary agreements. Such tendency negatively affects unrepresented weaker parties who find themselves bound by contract contrary to their expectations, so that they lose their ownership in their parcels to developers. It is also inefficient, since the rule creates uncertainty and increases litigation costs); Lisa Bernstein, 'Understanding the Limits of Court-Connected ADR: A Critique of Federal Court-Annexed Arbitration Programs', 141 *U Pa LR* (1993) 2169 (uncertainty of results in arbitration proceedings is both inefficient and regressive); Eyal Zamir, 'The Inverted Hierarchy of Contract Interpretation and Supplementation', 97 *Colum L Rev* (1997) 1710, pp. 1782–4, 1788–1801 (arguing that the inverted hierarchy model of contract interpretation is both efficient and progressive); Hanoch Dagan, 'Takings and Distributive Justice', 85 *Va L Rev* (1999) 741, pp. 748–56 (a takings compensatory regime that is insensitive to the relative economic and political power of the parties involved is both regressive and inefficient).

106 K&S I, *supra* note 63, p. 668.

107 Ibid., p. 674 n.7.

engagement in redistribution is susceptible to the efficiency-loss critique, *and more generally to the excessive cost critique* (such as loss of liberty, predictability and so on). The following three observations should not be forgotten: (1) 'Legislatures never, ever pass statutes that adjust tax and transfer programs to make up for the impact of modifications of private law rules (though of course they could if they wanted to).'[108] (2) An attempt to have a tax response to the regressive redistributive results of legal rules will involve formidable administrative costs. (3) Tax-based redistribution is not fully commensurable with legal rule redistribution, given the symbolic aspects of the law and the fact that legal rules distribute broader goods than the tax system does.

The considerable weight the analysis accords to the likelihood that an optimal alternative mechanism would be used lies at the core of the critique of Logue & Avraham's independence assumption. According to their approach, which they contrast with both K&S and Sanchirico, a redistributive rule should correct the narrow inequality which is otherwise created by the regulated activity (assuming institutional capacity to do so) without heed to the direction of the distribution – whether the rule benefits the 'haves' or the disadvantaged. For example, they would support taking accident proneness into account by tort rules, even if it were proved that the accident prone have higher income than their victims, and would leave the redress of income inequality to the tax system.[109] Similarly, they support prohibiting sex-based insurance premiums even if such prohibition works to the detriment of women (and provided the difference between men and women is the result of brute rather than option luck).[110]

Such an approach might be defended in an ideal world. Indeed, one of the authors' significant contribution is to clarify that even in a world in which tax and transfer work ideally to effect progressive redistribution there is still room left for redistributive-oriented private law. However, when we take into account reality and its imperfections, the independence assumption is rendered unpersuasive. Given the weak political influence of the disadvantaged, adopting the independence assumption without heed to the direction of the redistribution and its results, might end up worsening the lot of the disadvantaged. Private law rules that worked (or might have worked) to their benefit will be cancelled, while the background discriminatory infrastructure will remain. If, for example, courts have reason to believe that the gender gap in earnings is not likely to disappear soon, allowing a progressive cross-subsidy in insurance is desirable, even though men will be subsidizing women through no fault of their own.[111]

---

108 Duncan Kennedy, 'Law-and-Economics from the Perspective of Critical Legal Studies', in Peter Newman (ed.), *The New Palgrave Dictionary of Economics and the Law* (vol. 2, London, 1998) 465, p. 469.

109 Logue & Avraham, *supra* note 59, pp. 243–8.

110 Ibid., pp. 221–6.

111 For applications of the approach that the direction of the redistribution matters see below Ch 4.IV, Ch 5, Examples 1, 2, Ch 6.IV.C, Ch 7 notes 45–7 and accompanying text. Cf Part II.B above.

IV. Ineffectiveness

Perhaps the strongest claim against an attempt to promote distributive goals by private law rules is that such an attempt is ineffective. Scepticism regarding the effectiveness of such an attempt is based both on comparative institutional analysis and on the way legal rules function and affect people's behaviour. Section A examines whether courts aiming to promote desirable distributive goals are likely to promote equality more than courts that shy away from dealing with distributive considerations. Section B inquires whether egalitarian legal rules can achieve the intended distributive results given problems of over- and under-inclusiveness, passing-on, pricing and backlash.

A. Comparative Institutional Inquiry: Will Judicial Egalitarian Commitment Bring About More Egalitarian Results?

In Part I.E. above it was argued that even if courts' involvement in egalitarian redistribution is problematic from a procedural justice perspective, it can still be defended if it brings about better results from a substantive justice perspective. It remains to be examined whether a system that expects courts to develop egalitarian rules will achieve better results than a system that expects courts to avoid such a task and entrusts the accountable branches alone with the duty to narrow gaps in society. The extent to which courts' involvement in an egalitarian agenda is likely to bring about desirable results seems to depend on two variables. One is the relative progressiveness of the two institutions – courts and legislatures. The other is the extent to which the 'haves' can exert their influence in the rule-making process.

Note that the two variables are not affected by the answer given to the question whether in a certain legal system judicial engagement in redistribution is deemed legitimate. If judges have regressive inclinations compared to legislators, these inclinations will remain (and will bring about negative results) even if we adhere to an approach that denies the legitimacy of judicial involvement in redistribution. Similarly, the advantages of the 'haves' in the legal process remain even if courts do not attempt to narrow gaps in society. With these insights in mind the discussion first deals with the question of relative progressiveness and then with the relative advantage of the 'haves' in the two processes.

1. The Relative Progressiveness of the Institutions The relative inclination of the courts to egalitarianism compared to that of legislatures depends on political and sociological variables that differ over jurisdictions and time. In the similar area of judicial review, left-wing scholars – Michael Mandel, to name one example – often argue that courts are more likely to be conservative and that they impede rather than further an egalitarian agenda.[112] Mandel, however, concedes that this

112 Mandel, *supra* note 19; Democracy in Israel, *supra* note 37, pp. 259–60. See also Frederick Schauer, 'The Calculus of Distrust', 77 *Va L Rev* (1991) 653, pp. 659–61; John H. Ely, *Democracy and Distrust* (Cambridge, 1980), pp. 58–9.

tendency is not universal and that at least in one country, the court consistently produces better results, egalitarian-wise, than the legislature.[113]

In any event, even judges with regressive inclinations will achieve more egalitarian results in a culture requiring them to take into account the distributive effects of the private law rules they develop. This is so, since the rhetoric of discrimination is politically costly for its announcer.[114] While it is especially true for elected politicians, it is also true for judges. Indeed, not only competing political theories purport to promote equality,[115] but also opposite judicial results are supported by conflicting perceptions of equality.[116]

One advantage of the approach insisting that judges take into account distributive considerations in crafting private law rules is that it requires an open discussion by judges of the distributive effects of their decisions. While it might be true that judges, due to their socio-economic background, might have a conservative inclination, the worst thing we can do, as progressivists, is to allow them to hide behind a formal approach which rejects the relevance of distributive considerations. Such a formal approach enables judges, consciously or not, to create rules which are inegalitarian. No matter what the judges' real inclinations are, once considering distributive goals is mandated, and given the egalitarian ethos on one hand and the costs of endorsing explicit inegalitarian views on the other, judges are more likely to produce progressive results than regressive ones. At least that would be the case in comparison to the results they produce when they are not supposed to address distributive considerations.[117] True, egalitarian rhetoric can be used manipulatively, and an egalitarian ethos does not ensure progressive results. Still, raising judges' consciousness to the distributive effects of court-made rules and the normative relevance of the principle of equality should improve the progressiveness of the results achieved by courts compared with the results currently being achieved. Sunshine is the best disinfectant of the judicial distributive workings.

---

113 Democracy in Israel, ibid., pp. 295–301 (noting that the Israeli experience shows that the Israeli Supreme Court almost did not produce undemocratic interventions against government and that, uniquely, its interventions have done more democratic good than harm).

114 See note 49 above and accompanying text.

115 See Dworkin, *supra* note 38, pp. 297–301.

116 See e.g., *Adarand Constructors v Pena*, 115 S Ct 2097 (1995) (disagreement among the judges whether affirmative action is supported or opposed by the concept of equality); CFH 2401/95 *Nahmani v Nahmani*, 50(4) PD 661 (Israel) (several judges supporting either the husband or the wife in a dispute over frozen ova based on different conceptions of equality).

117 The ideal of transparency clearly demands that judges reveal the values that lie behind their decisions. In terms of the ability to promote a given agenda, Omri Yadlin has argued that a policy-based (as opposed to formalist) reasoning exposes courts to a greater degree to intervention in their decisions: Yadlin, *supra* note 33, pp. 705–8. If this thesis is true, the extent to which the shift to a policy discourse is desirable depends on the relative progressiveness of the judiciary compared to the legislature. If the court is more progressive, it follows that it should hide its progressive results behind a formalist reasoning, which is more immune from intervention.

Furthermore, the suggested model does not ascribe to judges the exclusive (or even the central) role in the battle to decrease gaps in society. Therefore, the correct question is not whether the judiciary alone will bring about better distributive results, given the legitimacy of judicial engagement in such a task. Rather, the correct question is whether the interaction between the judiciary and legislature according to the suggested model will bring about better results, compared with an approach according to which judicial attempt to narrow gaps in society does not enjoy legitimacy. A distributively-oriented rule made by the court might lead to a regressive result either directly or by triggering a legislative response that ultimately will make things worse. Recall that, according to the complement thesis, a judicial initiative to promote distributive goals through private law rules is likely to – or at least might – bring about a more comprehensive progressive result. If this is the case then not only is the randomness concern adequately answered, but so are the concerns of illegitimacy and ineffectiveness.

In order to show why this is so, the discussion of the complement thesis and the relative progressiveness of the institutions should be linked with the public choice literature, and, more broadly, with courts' legitimacy in engaging in redistribution. Recall that interest groups are more likely to succeed in blocking legislation undesirable to them than they are to succeed in passing legislation which serves their particular interests. This prediction provides us with a further justification for the use of courts in order to change the status quo progressively. Given the greater ability of the 'haves' to block unwanted legislation and their more limited ability to advance desired legislation, it follows that when and only when courts opt for a progressive rule and the legislature does not overrule it, it can be inferred that the legislature is really satisfied with the new result, as it has not amended it. The legislature's failure to initiate legislation that will bring about the same result achieved by the court should be attributed to the constraints rooted in the power that interest groups wield over legislatures. But if this is the case, there is a basis for the claim that the court's intervention is commendable, rather than problematic, from the perspective of procedural justice, since the result is supported by the majoritarian concern. Combining the responses given to the charges of illegitimacy and randomness suggests that not only might judicial engagement in redistribution not be problematic, but that it might in fact be desirable. This is so since the result of such involvement is both effective (it brings about more egalitarian results overall), comprehensive (given the complement thesis) and procedurally fair (since it is supported by an unconstrained majoritarianism).

2. The Relative Advantage of the 'Haves' in both Processes If the relative advantage of the 'haves' is more significant in litigation than in the legislative process, the attempt to partially shift the battle for equality from the accountable branches to the courts is a bad strategy. For reasons explained above, the relative advantage of the 'haves' is more significant in the legislative process. Recall that private law litigation does not give the 'haves' another bite at the apple.[118] Still, it is left to see whether the single bite given to the 'haves' in litigation is not likely

118 See Note 26 above and accompanying text.

to bring about a regressive result. Given the undisputed advantage that the 'haves' enjoy over the disadvantaged, the right comparison is relative – in which process (legislative or judicial) is their advantage likely to be more significant. Schlozman and Tierney's observation regarding the 'easier to block' phenomenon is not equally valid in the context of litigation. A major explanation for this asymmetry is the different extent to which manipulation is possible in the two proceedings, and the techniques for exercising influence. While some of the advantages of the 'haves' apply equally to both arenas,[119] other advantages, are much more available and significant in the legislative and executive process than in litigation.[120]

In any event, even if, contrary to the conclusion of the above analysis, the relative advantage of the 'haves' over the disadvantaged is more significant in litigation than in the legislative process, it is still left to be examined under which regime the 'haves' can exercise a greater degree of influence: a regime recognizing or denying the legitimacy of judicial redistribution. The discussion with respect to the political costs of endorsing inequality, the egalitarian ethos and the complement thesis[121] suggests that the advantage of the 'haves' in litigation will decrease once awareness of the inevitable distributive results of private law rules is increased. The same analysis suggests that the desired interaction between the two branches might bring about a progressive result (compared to the status quo).

To conclude: the question whether judicial intervention will bring about a desirable result is contingent and contextual and should be empirically examined. While the relative progressiveness of the two institutions and the relative advantage of the 'haves' in both processes are likely to influence the answer, there is reason to believe that more progressive results would be achieved under a regime holding courts accountable to the distributive results of their rule-making. The argument presented attempted to demonstrate that a sweeping scepticism of the courts' ability to bring about progressive results is unfounded, and to identify several structural characteristics that make the opposite conclusion to be at least plausible, if not likely.

B. Limited Ability to Achieve Distributive Results by Legal Rules

An attempt to achieve distributive results by legal rules faces at least three difficulties: (1) inability to identify and to assess the distributive effects of legal rules; (2) over- and under-inclusiveness; (3) failure to achieve the desired result due to the way the addressees of the legal norm respond to it. The first, and some aspects of the third problem are discussed in Chapter 4 Part III below. The remainder of this chapter deals with the other two problems.

---

119 Among these are included the ability to bear the cost of litigation and lobbying and the solidarity between the 'haves' and the governmental and judicial elite which is partially based on homogeneous background.

120 These include the ability to offer contributions and perks, making threats and exerting pressures, and lobbying secretly.

121 Part II.A3 above.

1. Over- and Under-Inclusiveness A distributive-oriented rule is likely to be both over- and under-inclusive. The egalitarian agenda is concerned with the socio-economic and demographic characteristics of individuals, with the group membership of these individuals and with their immutable characteristics (categories such as women, minorities, gays, low-class). By contrast, private law rules regulate interactions that focus on the functional capacity of individuals (categories such as consumers, landlords, trespassers). The problem of over-inclusiveness occurs, since even when we can identify high positive correlation between status and function, for example, assuming that land-owners, on average, are stronger than trespassers, still a pro-trespasser rule which is motivated by an egalitarian agenda, will also benefit the occasional strong trespasser and harm the weak land-owner. Similarly, if our aim is to help the weak, an adjustment of trespass law is under-inclusive, since most of the disadvantaged are not trespassers and the wealth of most 'haves' is likely to be marginally affected by changes to trespass law.[122] Any egalitarian rule which is not *ad hoc* is likely to suffer from the problems of over- and under-inclusiveness, and *ad hoc* solutions are problematic in terms of predictability, reliance and equality before the law. In addition to this being problematic in itself, the law's ambiguity might be problematic on egalitarian grounds as well, since the disadvantaged can be worn out by a lengthy litigation and since they are likely to be more risk-averse.[123] However, the problems of *ad hoc* redistributive rules should not be exaggerated,[124] and the assumption that vague rules have regressive distributive results is contested.[125]

Both manifestations of the inclusiveness problem relate to two other problems discussed earlier in this chapter, the problem of randomness and the problem of excessive cost. Of the two problems of under- and over-inclusiveness, the former is less problematic to those who believe (as was explained above) that a partial result in the right direction is better than the status quo. Moreover, if an egalitarian commitment is instilled in private law theory and doctrine, it will be manifested in many legal rules regulating a host of interactions, so that over time most individuals will be involved in the desired redistribution so that the problem of under-inclusiveness is not acute.

The extent of over-inclusiveness of a given suggested rule should be evaluated as one factor in the decision whether to adopt it. As the discussion in Chapter 4 Part

---

122 This problem can be rephrased as reflecting the tension between distributive and corrective justice. While the former deals with status, the latter deals with (inter)action and therefore, arguably, distributive considerations are irrelevant to private law. See Weinrib, *supra* note 3. However, one's status can affect the normative evaluation of one's conduct. See Ch. 5.II below.

123 Bernstein, *supra* note 105, pp. 2215–39; Uri Weiss, 'The Regressive Effect of Legal Uncertainty', *Tel Aviv University Legal Working Paper Series. Tel Aviv University Law Faculty Papers;* Working Paper 30 (December 2005) <law.bepress.com/taulwps/fp/art30>. See also note 105 above and accompanying text.

124 For the Scandinavian adjustment rule of damages see Ch. 5 below, note 53 and accompanying text.

125 See e.g., Charles T. McCormick, *Handbook of the Law of Evidence* (1st edn, St Paul, 1954), pp. 427–8 (arguing that formalities work to the detriment of the 'have-nots' and are relied upon by the 'haves'); Ch. 7.II.A5, B3 below.

V demonstrates, the more significant the distributive result of a given egalitarian rule and the less costly the rule in terms of not achieving other goals, the stronger the case for its adoption. Rules suffer from the problem of over-inclusiveness to a different degree. The more significant the problem, the weaker the case for adopting the rule. For example, being a parent is a poor proxy for being wealthy. Therefore, a rule purporting to curtail parental liability to third parties for damage caused by their children cannot be supported by egalitarian considerations, since it is highly over-inclusive. By contrast, a rule imputing liability to one parent for the negligent supervision of the other parent is desirable from an egalitarian perspective. Since by and large women are the primary care-givers of children, the rule's overall result is likely to be progressive, despite the fact that at times mothers will be found liable for the negligent supervision of fathers. Such a rule is also not under-inclusive. Since most women are mothers, rules targeting the functional capacity of individuals as parents are likely to respond well to the underlying gender-equality concerns. This point is demonstrated in the following chapters.[126]

2. Circumventing the Desired Result This section deals with the concern that once an egalitarian rule is adopted it will trigger responses from those subject to it that will reduce and might even annul its intended distributive effect, and it might even bring about a result inferior to the status quo. Such results might occur for several reasons and in different ways. First, those who are burdened by the rule ('the targets') might pass on the costs to third parties. Second, the targets might contract around the rule in a way that prices its costs *ex ante*, so that the rule's beneficiaries bear its costs. Third, the rule might cause a backlash, so that the rule's targets would change their behaviour in a way detrimental to the interests of some or all the rule's beneficiaries. A major manifestation of such a backlash is avoiding interaction with the beneficiaries, since under the egalitarian rule such interaction becomes more burdensome to the targets.

Assessing this aspect of the ineffectiveness charge cannot be done in isolation from the excessive cost and randomness arguments. If indeed a small change in the right direction is better than nothing, the fact that part of the desired effect of the rule is circumvented, is not a convincing reason against adopting an egalitarian rule with limited effectiveness, as long as the rule's egalitarian tilt does not cost us too much in terms of achieving other goals. Moreover, the extent to which a rule can achieve its distributive goal varies with the context. At times that ability will be very limited. At other times it might be quite significant.

(a) Passing-on. The ability of the rule's addressees to pass on its results on to others makes both the ability to predict and to achieve that rule's distributive effect harder.[127] The problem of pricing, discussed below, is a subset of the passing-on problem. In the general case, the cost of the egalitarian rule's effect is borne by third parties. In the case of pricing it is borne by the rule's beneficiaries. This leads to a conclusion that *usually* the problem of pricing should concern egalitarians more.

126 Ch. 6 (maternal prenatal duty); Ch. 5, Example 7 (disputes over frozen ova), Ch. 8 (parental liability), Ch. 4.III.B1 (same) below.

127 See Schwartz, *supra* note 4, p. 570.

To the extent that the purpose of the rule is to improve the well-being of the rule's beneficiaries, pricing undermines this goal while passing on does not. To the extent that the purpose of the rule is to improve the well-being of the rule's beneficiaries at the expense of the other party to the interaction regulated by the rule, both passing-on to third parties and pricing undermine that purpose. Moreover, if narrowing gaps in society is our concern, in evaluating the rule's distributive result the identity of the third parties to whom the costs are passed becomes crucial. If third parties are stronger than the rule's beneficiaries, the result is progressive. The opposite is true if they are weaker. The answer becomes more difficult when those to whom the cost is passed on are heterogeneous and when the ability to pass on the costs is limited. A contextual examination is always required. At any rate, the existence of the passing-on should always be taken into account, and its existence can justify the creation and modification of legal rules. For example, the problem of regressive cross-subsidy generates a cautious approach towards expansion of liability,[128] while the possibility of progressive cross-subsidy might support its imposition.[129] Passing-on relates to the problem of assessing the distributive results of a legal rule and the problems of intra-group justice and effects on third parties.[130] Most of the responses offered below to the claim that pricing prevents the ability to achieve distributive results apply to passing-on as well.

(b) Pricing and backlash. Arguably, redistributive-oriented rules cannot achieve their goals since targets will adjust their behaviour in anticipation of the rule in a manner that will harm the interests of the beneficiaries. Such adjustment can take two main forms. One is pricing – when the redistributive rule occurs in a market setting, prices will be raised to reflect the cost of the redistributive rules on those burdened by them.[131] A classic example is the increase in the price of product when a warranty is given. The other form of adjustment is backlash – avoiding contact or interaction with the protected group, since interacting with its members becomes more burdensome, given the effect of the redistributive rule. Classic examples include a reduction in employment caused, arguably, by minimum wage laws, and the reduction of available apartments as a result of the introduction of rent control.[132] Other examples include the fears that an egalitarian standard of care will isolate

128 See Ch. 4.II.B below; Cf. idem. Part IV.B below.

129 See note 59 above.

130 See Ch. 4.III below. Cf. Ch. 6 below, note 9 and accompanying text

131 See e.g., A. Mitchell Polinsky, *An Introduction to Law and Economics* (2nd edn, Boston, 1989), p. 123; Cf. Richard Craswell, 'Passing on the Costs of Legal Rules: Efficiency and Distribution in Buyer-Seller Relationships', 43 *Stan L Rev* (1991) 361; Duncan Kennedy, 'Distributive and Paternalist Motives in Contract and Tort Law, with Special Reference to Compulsory Terms and Unequal Bargaining Power', 41 *Md L Rev* (1982) 563, p. 619; Ian Ayers & Robert Gertner, 'Filling Gaps in Incomplete Contracts: An Economic Theory of Default Rules', 99 *Yale LJ* (1989) 87, p. 100.

132 See George J. Stigler, 'The Economics of Minimum Wage Legislation', 36 *Am Econ Rev* (1946) 358, pp. 362–3; Milton Friedman & George J. Stigler, 'Roofs or Ceilings? The Current Housing Problem', in Walter Block & Edgar Olsen (eds), *Rent Control: Myth and Realities* (Canada, 1981), p. 87. For empirical research disproving these trade-offs see David Card & Alan B. Krueger, *Myth and Measurement: The New Economics of the Minimum*

the poor,[133] and that a rule allowing women to continue with implanting frozen ova without their partner's consent will reduce men's willingness to start the process.[134]

Pricing and backlash share the following similarities: in both cases the advancement of equality creates costs which are borne by the protected group, and these costs are borne due to the *ex ante* effect of the rule – the way the rule changes the behaviour of those burdened by it for the sake of the protected group. In analysing the two difficulties one should distinguish between questions of inter- and intra-group justice. The extent to which the rule succeeds in redistributing wealth or other entitlements from the 'haves' burdened by the rule to the disadvantaged who are the rule's beneficiaries, is a question of inter-group justice. The greater the extent of pricing, the less progressive the result as a matter of justice between these groups. In addition, pricing might bring about problematic results as a matter of intra-group justice. The latter difficulty is paramount with respect to the problem of backlash. As the discussion will show, the effect of the redistributive rule is typically to improve the lot of some members of the disadvantaged group while hurting others.

Accordingly, in what follows two claims are made. First, the ability of the 'haves' to price in full the benefit given to the disadvantaged by the rule is in many instances limited. Therefore, redistributive rules can have progressive redistributive results as a matter of inter-group justice more often than is widely believed to be the case. Second, even when pricing can be done effectively, and notwithstanding the problem of backlash, which in turn implicates issues of intra-group justice, an overall desirable distributive result can be achieved. Such examination should be contextual and no *a priori* inability to achieve the desired result should be assumed.

(b1) Limited ability to price and avoid. Three preliminary points are in order. First, claims that adopting a redistributive rule will harm the disadvantaged should be taken with a grain of salt. Besides being speculative and a recipe for stagnation and perpetuation of the status quo, they might also be a tactical manoeuvre by the 'haves' who oppose progressive change. A good starting point would be to refuse to grant the 'haves' a guardian role over the interests of the disadvantaged. Nonetheless, the pricing and backlash concerns cannot be ignored and they deserve a response on the merits. Second, pricing is limited to contractual and market settings. Therefore, it has a very limited scope with respect to non-voluntary interactions, including tort settings, on which this study concentrates.[135] Thus, for example, a wealth-sensitive examination of standard of care which results in denying the liability of the poor

---

Wage (Princeton NJ, 1995); Robert G. Lee, 'Rent Control – The Economic Impact of Social Legislation', 12 *Oxford J Leg Stud* (1992) 543.

133 See Tsachi Keren-Paz, 'Egalitarianism as Justification: Why and How Should Egalitarian Considerations Reshape the Standard of Care in Negligence Law', 4 *Theor Inq L* (2003) 275, pp. 336–7.

134 Ch. 5 below, note 78.

135 In several contexts, pricing and passing-on are relevant in tort settings as well, such as employers' liability, malpractice and products liability. Moreover, regressive cross-subsidy caused by liability insurance (for the phenomenon see Ch. 4.I.A below) is a very common phenomenon in torts. Nonetheless, the ability of the 'haves' to price in the burden they incur by a tort redistributive rule is less significant than their comparable ability in a contractual interaction.

will not enable the rich plaintiff to price the cost of this egalitarian rule on the poor. Third, pricing can thwart rules which aim to redistribute *wealth*. Egalitarian rules targeting the redistribution of other entitlements such as dignity and freedom, are less susceptible to pricing.[136]

Even in the contractual setting, the ability of the 'haves' to price in full the costs of the distributive rule they incur is limited for several reasons: (1) The ability to price depends on the structure of the market, and more specifically on the elasticity of demand and supply.[137] (2) The ability to price assumes that targets are fully aware of the rule and its redistributive effects and are free from cognitive biases. To the extent that these assumptions are false or overstated, pricing will not occur or will be partial.[138] The same is true with respect to backlash. More generally, the more one is sceptical, in a given context, of the behaviour-guiding potential of legal rules, the more significant becomes the *ex post* distributive effect of the rule, since the desirable result achieved *ex post* by the rule's redistributive result is thwarted to a lesser extent by the rule's *ex ante* regressive results caused by pricing and backlash.[139]

(b2) Pricing and backlash do not necessarily render the progressive redistribution ineffective. Even when pricing occurs, attaining an overall desired distributive result is possible. Richard Craswell distinguishes between the goal of improving the well-being of a party to an interaction and the redistributive goal of improving that party's well-being at the expense of the other party. The first goal can be achieved even if the benefit the beneficiaries receive is priced over the cost to the targets of providing that benefit, as long as the benefit is worth more to the beneficiaries than the price they pay. In such a case the rule's result, which is Pareto superior to the status quo, does not necessarily reduces the gap between the parties but it improves the well-being of the rule's beneficiaries.[140] If indeed egalitarian rules should be pro-disadvantaged rather than anti-'haves' oriented, such a result might be satisfactory. The rule's result would be satisfactory especially when the disadvantaged are likely to benefit from the rule while the targets' status is not high enough to justify stripping them of their wealth out of an independent egalitarian motivation, or in situations where the targets' identity is either unknown or heterogeneous.

The understanding that pricing does not prevent a desirable distributive result is also supported by the endowment effect.[141] In the default rules literature it has been argued that redistributive rules can have a redistributive result even if they are contracted around, since the weaker party will demand (and receive) compensation for giving away the entailment given to her by the default rule. But the (re)distributive effect will be reached even if the rule is mandatory. Since the value of the entitlement increases to those endowed with it, an initial allocation of

136 Compare Part III.B3(a) above. See also Logue & Avraham, *supra* note 59, p. 182.

137 Bruce A. Ackerman, 'Regulating Slum Housing Markets on Behalf of the Poor: Of Housing Codes, Housing Subsidies and Income Redistribution Policy', 80 *Yale LJ* (1971) 1093; Craswell, *supra* note 131; Kennedy, *supra* note 131, pp. 611–13.

138 Cf. Jolls, *supra* note 65 (redistribution through legal rules might be more effective due to cognitive biases).

139 See Part III.B1, 4 above.

140 Craswell, *supra* note 131, p. 372.

141 For the endowment effect see note 94 above and accompanying text.

entitlement to the disadvantaged increases the likelihood that the entitlement's value to the disadvantaged will exceed the target's cost of being subject to this entitlement, so that when this cost is priced the well-being of the disadvantaged will be increased. The analysis teaches us that the initial allocation of entitlements has redistributive significance. Not only can it increase the well-being of the disadvantaged, but it also affects the extent of the gap between the parties participating in the interaction that is regulated by the rule.

Another distinction made by Craswell is between homogenous and heterogeneous beneficiaries of rules. This distinction relates to the issue of intra-group justice. At times the rule will benefit some members of the protected group and harm others. In the context of pricing, those valuing the benefit received by the rule more than the increase in price benefit from the rule; the opposite is true for those valuing the benefit less than the increase in price.[142]

At times, the pricing takes a form of insurance in which many consumers will pay a small increase in price for the warranty protecting a few from a grave loss.[143] The extent to which such a result is desirable depends on the likelihood and significance of such a rise, on the existence of a regressive cross-subsidy, and on whether those benefiting from the warranty are likely to be stronger, weaker, or as strong as the average consumer.[144]

With respect to backlash, the crucial point to understand is that some of the members of the protected group will benefit from the rule (non-marginal consumers in Craswell's terminology) and others will lose from it (marginal consumers).[145] Therefore, evaluating the rule's overall distributive effects as a matter of intra-group justice becomes difficult. Such an evaluation depends on the following factors: (1) the relative size of the marginal and non-marginal members of protected group; (2) the significance of the benefit conferred and the cost incurred by each group; (3) the likelihood that the negative result will occur (which relates to the tension between the *ex post* and *ex ante* results of the rule); (4) the relative strength of marginal and non-marginal members; (5) the strength of interests involved (both those advanced and those hampered by the rule); and (6) the transformative potential of the rule to protect in the long run the interests of those losing from the rule in the short run.[146]

When the redistributive rule causes an increase in price, it has been justly mentioned that the marginal consumers who lose from the rule are likely to be the most vulnerable.[147] However, the losers from protective rules will not always be the worst-off.[148] But even when they are, this fact alone should not serve as a clinching

142 Craswell, *supra* note 131, pp. 376–7.

143 See Polinsky, *supra* note 131, p.123.

144 For an application in the context of informed consent see the example listed at no. (6) in Ch. 4.IV.A, below.

145 Craswell, *supra* note 131, p. 370.

146 An example of an application of such an analysis can be found in Ch. 5, Example 7 below, n.78.

147 Kennedy, *supra* note 131, p. 619; Craswell, *supra* note 131, pp. 374–380.

148 See Ch. 5 below, Example 7 note 78; in the context discussed there we have no reasons to believe that the women losing from the rule are weaker (or stronger) from the women benefiting from the rule. Cf. Ch. 6.IV.D below.

argument against adopting the rule. In this sense, this approach rejects Rawls' difference principle.[149] We should not strive to improve at all costs the lot of the least advantaged. Rather, we should evaluate the overall distributive picture, including the interests of those who despite not being the least advantaged, are nevertheless disadvantaged.

* * *

While the concerns regarding the effectiveness of legal rules to achieve distributive result are weighty, they fail to show that legal rules cannot achieve distributive goals. The discussion has shown that the answer is contextual; in some circumstances a desired distributive result can be achieved, in others it cannot.

Conclusion

This chapter has demonstrated that none of the main four arguments against promoting equality through tort law is convincing. The *illegitimacy* concern fails to convince for four reasons: sanctifying the status quo is as political as modifying it; courts are not necessarily at disadvantage, from a procedural justice perspective, to affect changes; the legislature's ability to amend the judicial rule is an adequate response to the majoritarian concern; any remaining deficiency from a procedural justice perspective of courts engaging in progressive redistribution, might be outweighed by the better attainment of substantive justice.

The *randomness* concern fails to convince for two reasons. First, redistribution by tort law is not particularly random in comparison to other forms of redistribution. The prevalence of liability insurance further decreases the random nature of tort-based redistribution as does the likelihood that partial judicially-crafted redistribution will be complemented by the legislature. Second, random progressive redistribution is fairer than the status quo, at least when the redistributive rule is 'pro-Ds' rather than 'anti-Hs'.

The *excessive cost* concern is unconvincing under a pluralist framework since trade-offs between better attainment of some goals and lesser attainment of others are inevitable and there is no *a priori* reason to believe that the equality gain is outweighed by the lesser attainment of other goals. With respect to the efficiency-equality trade-off, such trade-off does not always exist. Furthermore, even if a redistributive legal rule is less efficient than a tax-based redistribution, the former method might be more effective in promoting equality. Moreover, in comparing the two methods of redistribution, not only the theoretical superiority of the tax method matters, but also the likelihood that it will be used.

The *ineffectiveness* concern is unconvincing as a blanket response to an attempt to promote equality by tort law. From an institutional perspective, courts which are guided to take egalitarian considerations into account are likely to achieve more progressive results than courts which are guided to ignore these considerations,

149 For Rawls' approach see Rawls, *supra* note 12, pp. 65–73. For Dworkin's critique along the lines presented in the text see Ronald M. Dworkin, *Sovereign Virtue: The Theory and Practice of Equality* (Cambridge, 2000), pp. 330–31.

notwithstanding the relative advantage of the 'haves' in litigation and the relative progressiveness of courts and legislatures. Structural limitations of private law rules, such as rules' over- and under-inclusiveness and the possibility that the rules' addressees will circumvent the desired result, merely limit, rather than prevent, the ability to achieve the desired distributive result. The degree to which these constraints hinder the achievement of the desired distributive result depends on varying factors. Accordingly, the case studies in the rest of this book – egalitarian standard of care, the scope of maternal prenatal duty, combating discrimination with the tort of negligence and reformulating damages rules – show how tort rules and doctrines can be reformulated in order to be more egalitarian and can bring about a desired progressive redistribution. Before getting to these case studies, Chapter 4 continues the inquiry conducted in Parts III and IV of this chapter, by examining the ways in which the equality effects of tort rules can be assessed, and by suggesting a framework for balancing egalitarian commitment with other policy considerations.

Chapter 4

Applicatory Framework

Introduction

This chapter lays the ground for the application of an egalitarian approach to tort theory. First, it explains the reasons for the inherent regressive bias of existing tort law. Second, it explores the ways in which an egalitarian commitment can reshape tort law. Third, it presents the difficulties involved in an attempt to assess a rule's equality effect, given the multiplicity of participants and entitlements affected by a given rule. It discusses and explains issues of intra-group justice, the rule's equality effects on third parties, and the occasionally conflicting dimensions of distribution that occur when a given rule distributes material and symbolic goods in opposite directions. Fourth, it explains the two possible egalitarian recommendations: to expand liability in favour of the disadvantaged (plaintiffs) or to limit the liability of the disadvantaged (defendants). Fifth, it sketches a framework for balancing the dictates of egalitarianism with other competing goals of tort law.

I. The Regressive Nature of Existing Tort Law

Existing tort law is regressive by nature. One reason for this is the basic compensation principle: full compensation or *restitutio ad integrum*. Another reason lies with the principles that govern the scope of liability and the objective standard for liability.

A. The Principle of Restitutio Ad Integrum

The principle of *restitutio ad integrum* (RAI) is the cornerstone of tort compensation rules,[1] and is by nature inimical to redistributive considerations because its purpose is to perpetuate the status quo. By perpetuating the existing distribution of wealth in society, RAI assumes at the ideological level the justness of such distribution[2] and is instrumental in legitimizing such distribution, viewing it as natural, neutral and unproblematic.[3] RAI is also inimical to the idea of social responsibility, and

---

1 Much of the critique suggested here can be generalized to all areas of private law whose remedial goal is to achieve RAI. However, in contract law, for example, the ability of the parties to price the risk reduces the regressive nature of contractual RAI.

2 See Jules L. Coleman, *Risks and Wrongs* (Cambridge, 1992), pp. 350–54.

3 Richard L. Abel, 'A Critique of Torts', 37 *UCLA L Rev* (1990) 785, p. 803.

it promotes an atomistic, individualistic and libertarian approach that denies the existence of non-consensual obligations to improve the lot of others.[4]

Ideologically, different rates of compensation for identical injuries sends the message that the rich, the young and the healthy are worth more than the poor, the old and the sick.[5] This ostensible neutrality of the principle conceals both the ideologically motivated decision to respect and perpetuate the existing order and the disparity, discussed below, between this pretence and the principle's effect – a hidden, albeit consistent, regressive redistribution from the poor to the rich.

In practical terms, RAI involves regressive distribution of risk and wealth for four reasons:

Incentive to risk the poor. First, RAI makes it cheaper (and therefore more advantageous) to risk the poor.[6] Since the poor have less to lose, it is cheaper to compensate them. While tortfeasors cannot always channel the risk they create and choose their victims, in many circumstances they can. The concentration of NIMBYs and LULUs (locally undesirable land uses) in low income neighbourhoods is an obvious example of this fact.[7] Therefore, even if the ideal of RAI were attainable, it would nevertheless result in regressive distribution of risk in society, with the disadvantaged disproportionally subject to risks.[8]

In practice, compensation is not full. Second, because the ideal of RAI is not attainable in practice, regressive distribution of risk is translated into regressive distribution of wealth. To begin with, conceptually, no amount of money can compensate for loss of life or limb. When one adds to this the prevailing lack of information, limited legal consciousness, compensation rules regarding foreseeability and remoteness, liquidity problems, collective action problems and power disparities between disenfranchised victims and powerful institutional tortfeasors, the result is that tort law generally undercompensates, especially those who have been seriously injured.[9] Such effects are more significant when the victims are poor.[10] Since the disadvantaged are subject to risks disproportionally and since

---

4 Cf. Hanoch Dagan, *Unjust Enrichment: A Study of Private Law and Public Values* (Cambridge, 1997), pp. 35–40.

5 Abel, *supra* note 3, p. 803.

6 For conceding this point see Richard A. Posner, 'Wealth Maximization and Tort Law: A Philosophical Inquiry', in David G. Owen (ed.), *Philosophical Foundations of Tort Law* (Oxford, 1995) 99, p. 110.

7 See Denis. J. Brion, 'An Essay on LULU, NIMBY, and The Problem of Distributive Justice', 15 *BC Envtl Aff L Rev* (1988) 437.

8 Abel, *supra* note 3, pp. 813–14, 829; Cf. idem, p. 825.

9 Marc Galanter, 'Why the "Haves" Come Out Ahead: Speculations on the Limits of Legal Change', 9 *L & Soc'y Rev* (1974) 95; Michael J. Saks, 'Do We Really Know Anything About the Behavior of the Tort Litigation System – and Why Not?', 140 *U Pa L Rev* (1992) 1147, pp. 1271–80, 1286–9; David Duff, Donald N. Dewees & M. J. Trebilcock, *Exploring the Domain of Accident Law: Taking the Facts Seriously* (New York, 1996); Mancur Olson, *The Logic of Collective Action: Public Goods and Theory of Groups* (Cambridge, 1965).

10 See Gregory T. Miller, 'Behind the Battle Lines: A Comparative Analysis of the Necessity to Enact Comprehensive Federal Products Liability Reforms', 45 *Buffalo L Rev* (1997) 241, p. 273.

compensation is not full, it follows that tort law, while masquerading as neutral and non-distributive, brings about in fact a regressive redistribution of wealth. Moreover, the fact that the poor are both less likely to sue and less likely to succeed in their suits,[11] creates an additional incentive to risk-creators to channel risks towards the poor.

Regressive cross-subsidy. Third, the regressive redistribution of wealth is exacerbated by the prevalence of liability insurance. In liability insurance, neither the insurer nor the insured knows in advance the identity of the victims of the insured's activity. Therefore the insurer cannot calculate the expected liability of the individual insured. The insurer will collect a premium that is based on the expected loss of the *average* victim – rich and poor alike. It follows that the insured group (the potential tortfeasors) pay roughly equal premiums, while victims, because of RAI, receive different amounts that are a function of their pre-accident wealth.[12] The regressive distribution that results from tort law is based on two insights: (1) that tort law is but one possible compensation system among others, and (2) that there is a partial correlation between the identities of potential victims and of potential tortfeasors (that is, that the same person may be either a victim or a tortfeasor).[13] Liability insurance is much more susceptible to the problem of regressive cross-subsidy than is first-party insurance, since it is easier for an insurer to calculate the expected loss of the individual insured than it is to calculate the expected loss of the insured's victims.[14]

Ignoring the diminishing marginal utility of money (DMU). Finally, RAI ignores the importance of DMU. Since the first dollar received has greater utility than the last dollar, a compensation system which spreads compensation among a larger number of people has greater utility than the classic tort system which concentrates the same amount of compensation among fewer people.[15]

B. Scope of Responsibility

Tort liability is based on an objective standard. This means, on the one hand, that no leeway is given to those who find it harder to meet the required standard – whether for lack of funds or lack of skill – and, on the other hand, that the duty imposed on potential tortfeasors does not take sufficiently into account the interests of the

11 Ibid. Cf. Ch. 3.IV.A2 above and note 119 ibid. But see Ch. 5.VI.A3 below and note116 ibid. and accompanying text.

12 The situation is analogous to an agreement between two friends, A and B, that requires each one to put $500 in a common pot. A will receive $800 on his birthday, while B will receive $200 on hers. B will thus have subsidized A in the amount of $300.

13 Even if one disputes the significance of this phenomenon, regressive cross-subsidies are still problematic as a matter of intra-group justice.

14 For a classic treatment of this problem, mainly from an efficiency perspective (also termed 'adverse selection'), see George L. Priest, 'The Current Insurance Crisis and Modern Tort Law', 96 *Yale LJ* (1987) 1521, pp. 1546, 1559–60, 1565–6.

15 Cf. Patrick S. Atiyah, *The Damages Lottery* (Oxford, 1997), pp. 143–50. For a brief discussion of possible reforms with respect to damages, remoteness and causation, see Ch. 8 below.

disadvantaged. Here too, the fact that tort law ignores the marginal utility of money is highly problematic. Two examples which are discussed at length in the chapters below serve to clarify this point. (1) A standard of care analysis that compares precaution costs to accident costs in terms of their absolute value is likely to lead to a conclusion that the same activity may be considered negligent if it risks the rich but not negligent if it risks the poor.[16] Since a person who takes a reasonable risk does not have to compensate those harmed by the negative result of such risky behaviour, tort law provides potential tortfeasors with yet another incentive to risk the poor. The result is regressive distribution of wealth, because the poor bear the loss without having a right to compensation. (2) Any consequential loss to the victim that is the result of his lack of funds is considered too remote to be compensated for, even if it is foreseeable.[17] By contrast, when there is substantial loss to high-value property or to earning capacity, such loss is compensable in full. While in both cases the victim's wealth (or lack thereof) is a relevant factor that contributes to the harm and its consequent disutility, tort law favours the rich.

II. Levels of Operation

Egalitarianism can play a role on three different levels of tort law.[18] One level is the desirability of the existence of tort law as institution, a second is the choice of liability regime, and the third is the desirability of specific torts and doctrines.[19]

A. Tort Law and Alternative Compensation Schemes

Tort law is just one of several possible systems of compensation. Some are complementary to each other, while others are mutually exclusive. In evaluating the desirability of tort law as an institution, egalitarian analysis is one relevant factor that should be taken into account. Many commentators on the left (or even centre-left) who are committed to the goal of progressive distribution of income have criticized tort law for the haphazard, lottery-like compensation mechanism it provides victims (as well as the collateral burden it imposes on injurers), and for its selectivity of compensation for certain misfortunes but not for others, and in particular for its exclusion of misfortunes that are poverty-related. Some have placed their critique within the framework of a wider attack on the liberal individualistic philosophy of

---

16 See Ch. 5.IV.B1(d), Example 3 below.

17 See example listed as no. (7) in Part IV.A below and Ch. 8 below (but see Ch. 8 below for a discussion of *Lagden v O'Connor*).

18 In principle, the analysis applies also to other non-egalitarian distributive considerations.

19 A possible distinction here may be made between, on the one hand, doctrines with an overt distributive or egalitarian result – a husband's common law right to consortium (nowadays largely abolished or amended to be gender-neutral) is an obvious example – and, on the other, doctrines in which the distributive effects are less clear and are the result of the disparate impact of the legal rule on different potential groups in society.

tort law (and of common law in general).[20] Since the fundamental problem with tort law, according to such views, is in its inherent nature of selective and partial compensation, some scholars have a fierce disbelief in, and scepticism of, tort law in general, calling for its abolition in its current form and its replacement with alternative compensation schemes.[21] Some scholars have expressed a more limited scepticism concerning the efficacy of the use of tort law to respond to specific predicaments of the disadvantaged. Catharine MacKinnon, to take one example, has argued that tort law cannot play a significant role in combating the social problem of the sexual harassment of women.[22]

B. *Choice of Regime*

Tort law, unlike most compensation mechanisms, is based on a particular notion of the individual responsibility of the injurer for the act that is causally related to the victim's loss. Tort liability can be established based on one of two basic theories: fault-based liability and strict liability.[23] The former limits liability to circumstances in which the injurer's behaviour deviated from an objective threshold standard of behaviour. The latter imposes liability without the need for demonstrating a deviation from such standard. The following analysis suggests that the two regimes can be compared in terms of their equality effect according to three dimensions. According to one dimension, strict liability is superior, according to a second, it is inferior, and according to the third, the desirability of either regime depends on the context. To complicate matters further, it is hard to know the effect of which dimension is controlling.

First, one may regard strict liability as superior to a negligence regime on the grounds that that latter (but not the former) creates an incentive to risk the poor in the hope that such risk will be considered reasonable. Under a strict liability regime the defendant pays for the harm it caused. However, and this is the second consideration, since under a strict liability regime defendants pay greater damages, the incentive to channel risks towards the poor increases in order to reduce the total amount of damages paid. The cross-subsidy effect pertains to intra-group effects among potential plaintiffs. As long as the principle of RAI governs torts damages, poor victims will continue to subsidize (by way of premiums) affluent victims. The greater the amount transferred by tort damages, the greater the subsidy. Viewed in this light, expanding liability is problematic from an egalitarian perspective.[24]

---

20 Abel, *supra* note 3, p. 831; Allan C. Hutchinson, 'Beyond Non-Fault', 73 *Cal L Rev* (1985) 755, p. 756.

21 See Abel, *supra* note 3, pp. 822–31; Joanne Conaghan & Wade Mansell, *The Wrongs of Tort* (London, 1993), p. 155.

22 Catharine A. MacKinnon, *Sexual Harassment of Working Women: A Case of Sex Discrimination* (New Haven, 1979), pp. 164–74.

23 A more nuanced quintuple classification distinguishes between intentional torts, negligence, presumed negligence, strict liability and absolute liability.

24 In this respect, there is a tension between, on the one hand, the dictates of fairness and loss-spreading and, on the other hand, the dictates of egalitarianism. See generally, Ch. 5.II.B1 below, note 20 and accompanying text.

Moreover, even if we disregard the effects of the cross-subsidy, to the extent that increasing liability results in the increased cost of a commodity or a service, it is the poor who are more likely to be burdened by such increase. No *a priori* conclusion can be reached as to which effect – cross-subsidy or the likelihood that risking the poor would be deemed reasonable – is more controlling, although I suspect that it is the former.[25] Third, since strict liability tends to be pro-plaintiff, a strict liability regime is more desirable than a negligence standard, whenever the typical plaintiff is more disadvantaged than the typical defendant. Conversely, if it is the typical defendant who is more disadvantaged, a negligence standard is preferable. To take one example, Morton Horowitz has argued that the adoption of the negligence rule with regard to enterprise liability has resulted in a regressive redistributive effect, by which workers and consumers subsidize entrepreneurs.[26] When potential plaintiffs are more disadvantaged than potential defendants, a tension arises between inter-group analysis favouring strict liability and intra-group justice favouring negligence. The greater the extent to which potential defendants are able to pass the cost of increased liability on to potential plaintiffs, or the greater the overlap between the groups of potential plaintiffs and potential defendants, the more likely the intra-group (cross-subsidy) effect controls the inter-group effect, so that a negligence regime is to be preferred. By contrast, the greater the homogeneousness of potential plaintiffs as a group and the more significantly disadvantaged they are compared to potential defendants, the more preferable a strict liability regime becomes.[27]

Finally, negligence-based liability is related to notions of fault and desert. And these notions in turn tend to be endorsed by the right, which emphasizes choice and personal responsibility, and downplays social construction and misfortune as explanations for behaviour and status. As such, the right, or at least those who believe in desert-based compensation, oppose projects of universal compensation supported by the left.[28] Strict liability is philosophically closer to universal compensation for misfortunes than negligent liability. It is therefore more often favoured by those on the left. However, sensitivity to intra-group analysis urges caution before adopting a strict liability regime unless such regime also contains a deviation from the principle of RAI.

---

25 If this is the case, it follows that, at least in the absence of a deviation from RAI, egalitarianism dictates a negligence regime coupled with the development of an egalitarian jurisprudence of standard and duty of care. Such an approach is developed in Chs 5–7 below.

26 Morton Horwitz, *The Transformation of American Law, 1780–1860* (Cambridge, 1977), pp. 99–101; This point is disputed; see e.g. Gary T. Schwartz, 'Tort Law and the Economy in Nineteenth-Century America: A Reinterpretation', 90 *Yale LJ* (1981) 1717; for general scepticism regarding the significance of the distributive results of opting for either negligence or strict liability see Richard A. Epstein, 'The Social Consequences of Common Law Rules', 95 *Harv L Rev* (1982) 1717, pp. 1724–40; Moreover, entrepreneurs' ability to pass the costs of liability on consumers complicates the ability to determine whether the result discussed by Horwitz is in fact regressive.

27 Cf. Part IV.A below, the discussion of the example at no. (6) for a situation in which the inter-group effect controls the intra-group effect.

28 Cf. Hutchinson, *supra* note 20, p. 756; Abel, *supra* note 3.

C. Desirability of Specific Torts and Doctrines

At times, tort rules have discernible equality effects. When they do, the burden created by these rules is borne disproportionately by individuals who are identifiable by immutable characteristics such as sex, race, ethnicity, class and sexual orientation. As explained below, these effects can be financial or not, symbolic or practical, and may be borne by typical litigants or third parties. They can be desirable from an egalitarian perspective if the burden is progressive or, alternatively, undesirable if it is regressive. It is often difficult to establish the existence of an equality effect.[29] Nevertheless, the existence of some cases in which such disparate impact exists cannot be disputed.

III. Multiplicity of Participants and Entitlements

Egalitarian analysis of tort rules is seldom easy. This is because of the multiplicity of participants and entitlements affected by any given rule. As mentioned above, the distributive result of the legal rule in question should generally be evaluated in terms of potential litigants.[30] It would seem that the relevant axis for distribution is plaintiffs–defendants. The relative strength of the two groups should therefore be compared, and the effects of the rule in question on them evaluated. The following discussion refines this crude starting point to include the rule's effects on different members within each group of potential plaintiffs and defendants, as well as on third parties. In addition, given the multiplicity of entitlements distributed by tort rules, the rule's potentially conflicting distributive effects on the same person should be assessed.

A. Factual and Conceptual Problems

Once the parties that are typically affected by the rule are identified, the court should attempt to evaluate the relative strength of the potential defendants and plaintiffs. At times, no conclusion can be drawn regarding the relative strength of the potential parties, either because their identities are unknown or because we have reason to believe that the affected parties are heterogenic. For example, it is doubtful whether there is a significant discernible equality effect to a rule that governs the right to, and extent of contributions among, a group of defendants who are all vicariously liable for another person's tort.[31] At other times there are problems of multiplicity of disadvantage, that is, the difficulty in determining which of several disadvantaged groups is at the greatest disadvantage. For

29 Some of the concerns regarding the feasibility of such a task (and, as a corollary, the wisdom of pursuing the achievement of distributive goals through tort law) were discussed in Chapter 3 above, and will be discussed in Parts III and IV below.

30 For one exception, see Ch. 5.IV.B2(c) below (standard of care should take into account the economic means of actual defendants).

31 See *Viasystems (Tyneside) Ltd v Thermal Transfer (Northern)* [2005] 4 All ER 1181 (CA).

example, views might differ as to whether black men or white women are more disadvantaged in contemporary United States. However, the fact that questions of relative disadvantage are ideologically-driven and are disputed should not prevent courts from attempting to take the equality effects of the rules into account. When no conclusion regarding the relative strength of the affected parties is possible, the egalitarian consideration is irrelevant.

B. Identifying those Affected by the Rule

1. Intra-Group Justice: Three Axes of Distribution At times, the problem with a given rule is not necessarily or directly due to the way it affects the status of plaintiffs vis-à-vis defendants, but rather with its distributive effects *within* one or both groups. The need to expand or limit liability in such cases derives from concern for the well-being of some potential plaintiffs compared to others, or for the well-being of some potential defendants compared to others. It follows, then, that there are at least three axes of distribution. Plaintiffs–defendants, plaintiffs–plaintiffs, and defendants–defendants. Horizontal redistribution (within each group) occurs both because of the (limited) ability of those burdened by a given rule, be it plaintiffs or defendants, to pass on the costs of these rules to those benefiting from them, and because the membership of each group is heterogeneous, as are the members' preferences. These points, which have been explained above, are invaluable to a complete, accurate and nuanced distributive analysis, since it is the *overall* effects of any legal rule that should be taken into account. The discussion in the following chapters provides examples of intra-group sensitivity.[32]

Inter-relatedness. The analytical distinction between inter-group justice and intra-group justice is blurred by life's complexity, as demonstrated by the issue of the scope of parental liability for negligent supervision of their children.[33] One way to analyse the issue is through the prism of defendants' intra-group justice. Individual liability (which is not imputed to the other parent) is seemingly non-problematic as between parents (potential defendants) and potential plaintiffs. Rather, it is the fact that the effect of the rule is more burdensome on mothers than on fathers (given gendered division of labour and patterns of custody) that renders the individualistic common law approach problematic. However, the rule may also be problematic in terms of inter-group justice. Since, on the side of potential defendants, the rule burdens women disproportionally while its benefits are distributed roughly equally among female and male potential plaintiffs,[34] it results in a regressive distribution among plaintiffs and defendants, due to the different proportion of men and women in these groups.[35]

---

32 See Ch. 6.IV.B–D below (intra-group justice among potential defendants); Ch. 5.V.B Examples 9 & 10 below (intra-group justice among potential plaintiffs).

33 Ch. 5.V.B below, Example 8.

34 While one might assume that women, given their greater proximity to and interaction with children, are somewhat more likely than men to be victims of children's acts leading to parents' liability for negligent supervision, such disparity can hardly equal the disparity in care for children in contemporary societies.

35 While these effects are attenuated by some social structures, such as the pervasive existence of joint finances of married couples and cohabitants, they do not disappear even in

2. Effects on Third Parties While potential plaintiffs and defendants are those mainly affected by a given rule, at times the rule may also affect third parties who are typically unlikely to be directly implicated in the litigation. A comprehensive egalitarian approach mandated by a commitment to instrumentalism is bound to take these effects into account. An example of such an effect is the impact on the status of gays in society of a decision to recognize as defamatory a false statement that characterized the plaintiff as gay.[36] The typical litigants in such a scenario are the defaming defendant (who is not likely to be gay), and the defamed plaintiff who in fact is not gay. However, the decision to find the defendant liable for defamation is ideologically charged, given the legal requirement that the statement is likely to bring the plaintiff into hatred, contempt or ridicule.[37] The court, by finding the defendant liable, gives its imprimatur to the claim that being gay could be considered shameful. This approbation may have (or at least might have) a negative ideological effect on gay people and their status in society. At other times, the legal rule might *benefit* third parties. For example, the imposition of maternal prenatal duty is likely to increase the relative power of men who typically are not litigants in maternal prenatal negligence cases. Consequently, imposing such a duty benefits this class of men by restricting women's autonomy and reinforcing ideologies that hurt women's status in society.[38] In this manner, regressive redistribution occurs by virtue of the fact that it increases the disparity between defendants and third parties who are already better off.[39] Effects on third parties can also be financial and mundane, such as the effect on workers of injunctions in nuisance cases.[40] Such an effect is caused mainly by the passing-on phenomenon.[41]

3. Balancing the Effects on Different Groups As outlined in the previous two sections, a given rule can affect one or more of the axes of plaintiffs–defendants, plaintiffs–plaintiffs and defendants–defendants, or even third parties. Since a rule will often benefit some and hurt others, it is difficult to evaluate the overall equality effect of the rule. Such evaluations depend on three main factors: (1) the relative strength or weakness of affected parties, (2) the size of the group affected and (3) the magnitude of the rule's negative or positive equality effect on each group.[42] There

---

practice, let alone symbolically.

36 See e.g., Patrice S. Arend, 'Defamation in an Age of Political Correctness: Should a False Public Statement That a Person is Gay be Defamatory?', 18 *N Ill UL Rev* (1997) 99, p. 111 (citing arguments that if courts recognize that calling an individual a homosexual damages an individual's reputation, it is the same thing as saying that homosexuality is offensive or somehow shameful); Cf. *Donovan v Fiumara*, 442 SE 2d 572, 580 (NC Ct App 1994).

37 *Parmiter v Coupland* (1840), 6 M & W 105, 108.

38 See Ch. 6.III.B, C1 below.

39 It also might hurt the newborn (plaintiffs) by entrenching patriarchy. See Ch. 6.III. C1 below.

40 *Boomer v Atlantic Cement Co. Inc.*, 257 NE 2d 870, 873 (NY Ct App 1970).

41 See Richard Craswell, 'Passing on the Costs of Legal Rules: Efficiency and Distribution in Buyer–Seller Relationships', 43 *Stan L Rev* (1991) 361.

42 Compare Craswell, ibid., pp. 372–7; Duncan Kennedy, 'Distributive and Paternalist Motives in Contract and Tort Law, with Special Reference to Compulsory Terms and Unequal

is no one-size-fits-all formula. The following chapters analyse several interactions in a more nuanced way, and demonstrate the promise of an egalitarian analysis, as well as its limits. All that can be said at this level of generality is that no single factor should *a priori* be given precedence over the others; it is the combined weight of all the factors that should lead to the overall evaluation of the rule from an egalitarian perspective. Similarly, no lexical priority should be given to promoting the lot of the worst-off.

C. Conflicting Dimensions of Distribution: Material and Symbolic Goods

Egalitarian analysis is further complicated by the fact that tort law redistributes not only wealth but also freedom, security, status, power, dignity, and notoriety. At times, even the equality effect of a given rule on one homogeneous group of people will be hard to evaluate, as the rule that benefits them on one distributive level burdens them on another. This problem of conflicting distributive results is endemic to egalitarianism, given the inherent trade-off that protectionist rules entail: the benefit conferred to the protected person by the protectionist rule (which is often material and concrete) often comes at the cost of symbolic and long-lasting effects.[43] For example, not to recognize a duty of care of pregnant women (out of concerns for the status and freedom of women) leaves one exposed to a charge that one is diminishing women's agency. To recognize a duty that hinges on the existence of insurance creates a trade-off between women's economic and freedom interests and certain negative symbolic effects. Furthermore, the multiplicity both of affected groups and of dimensions in which those groups are affected by a given rule require a very nuanced, contextual and careful analysis. The discussion in Chapter 5 below elucidates the symbolic meaning attached to negligence liability and its distributive effects, and draws from it doctrinal conclusions regarding the role that egalitarianism should play in the tort of negligence. Through the examination of maternal prenatal duty, the discussion in Chapter 6 demonstrates the complexity of egalitarian analysis, which takes into account intra-group justice and the trade-offs between material and symbolic goods. The analysis in Chapter 7 further demonstrates these themes by analysing the structure of the tort of negligence.

IV. Direction of Distributive Result

Taking into consideration all the dimensions of distribution, a rule's overall equality effect on all groups can be either regressive, progressive, or unclear. Egalitarian considerations call for expanding liability when the likely net effect of such liability is to benefit the disadvantaged, and for limiting liability when the likely net effect of such liability is to burden them. But sometimes it is unclear whether

---

Bargaining Power', 41 *Md L Rev* (1982) 563, pp. 609–13.

43 See e.g., Richard Delgado, 'Affirmative Action as a Majoritarian Device: Or, Do You Really Want to Be a Role Model?', 89 *Mich L Rev* (1997) 1222, p. 1226 ('A white-dominated institution hires you not because you are entitled to or deserve the job').

an egalitarian approach should lead to a rule resulting in an overall expansion or limitation of liability. A few non-exhaustive examples follow.

A. Expanding Liability

Egalitarian principles call for expanding liability with respect to (1) the scope of duty of lender's lawyer towards an unrepresented borrower;[44] (2) allowing a woman to continue with implantation in disputes over frozen ova;[45] (3) the duty not to discriminate;[46] and (4) a physician's duty towards women who become pregnant as a result of the botched vasectomy of their partners.[47] Albeit less clearly, egalitarian principles may also support an expansion of liability in the following situations: (5) compensation of minor female plaintiffs on the basis of a unisex average earning index (because using a female average earning index to calculate girls' lost earning capacity puts girls at a disadvantage compared to boys);[48] (6) cases involving the loss of autonomy by patients who did not give informed consent but who would have, had it not been for the violation of their autonomy;[49] (7) indigent incapacitated patients who, according to RAI, were supposed to live at home rather than in an institution, and who, prior to the final judicial decision in their favour and damages being paid to them, were unable to finance the cost of living at home. An egalitarian approach calls for awarding them an amount reflecting the cost of living at home from the time they were physically able to do so, rather than merely from the date of the judgment.[50] Similarly, egalitarianism might support expanding liability (8) by relaxing the strict factual causality requirement in cases of mass torts.[51] As will be explained below, egalitarianism occasionally calls for expanding liability out of a desire not to leave plaintiffs at a disadvantage compared to other potential plaintiffs (examples 5, 6 and 7).[52] It should be recalled that as long as RAI dominates tort law, any expansion of liability is potentially problematic from an egalitarian perspective. However, when potential plaintiffs are overwhelmingly disadvantaged, expansion of liability is likely to be desirable from an egalitarian perspective. Example 6 clarifies this point. Since violations of the duty to receive a patient's informed consent are more likely to occur in the case of disadvantaged patients, and assuming damages awards that are not income-based, an increased liability rule – that is, making moderate compensation awards even to patients

44 See Ch. 5.V.A, Example 6 below.

45 Ibid., Example 7.

46 See Ch. 7 below.

47 See *Goodwill v British Pregnancy Advisory Service* [1996] 2 All ER 161 (CA); Ch. 6 below notes 5–8 and accompanying text.

48 See Ch. 8 below.

49 See *Snider v Henniger* (1992) 96 DLR (4th) 367, 374–5 (Can); CA 2781/93 *Daaka v Carmel Hospital*, PD 53(4) 526 (Israel) ; Cf. *Chester v Afshar* [2004] 4 All ER 587 (HL).

50 See Ch. 8 below.

51 Principles of intra-group justice and the possibility of passing on costs to consumers complicate the analysis. See Ch. 8 below.

52 See Part III.B1 and Ch. 3.II.B3(c) above.

who would have granted their consent had they been provided all the relevant information – is desirable from an egalitarian perspective.[53]

B. Limiting Liability

Egalitarian principles require limiting liability with respect to (1) maternal prenatal duty of care;[54] (2) scope of investment in precaution by the poor when damage is wealth-dependent;[55] (3) awarding compensation for wealth-dependent components, such as damages for lost years;[56] and (4) when imposing liability harms the status of the disadvantaged, such as recognizing as defamatory the false depiction of a straight person as gay.[57] Similarly, it might be desirable not to impose liability on (5) a defendant who shifts a risk progressively by channelling it to stronger potential victims, even though an alternative channelling of the risk would have minimized it.[58] Limiting liability may also be desired with respect to (6) negligent parental supervision of children for reasons of intra-group justice among parents.[59]

C. Unclear Recommendation

In some of the examples discussed above, as well as in others, there is uncertainty either as to whether egalitarianism supports expanding or limiting liability, or as to whether adopting the more egalitarian rule would lead to the expansion or the limitation of liability. For example, (1) the scope of public authorities' liability involves significant difficulties from egalitarian perspectives, given their ability to pass costs on to others, and the difficulty in measuring the relative strength of the affected parties.[60] (2) A standardization of awards, which is desirable from an egalitarian perspective, might lead either to the expansion or to the limitation of liability in comparison to awards paid today, depending on the levels of compensation that are established. This point is demonstrated by the example of compensation for the lost earnings of minors. If a unisex index is applied to claims of boys as well as of girls (as it should), it is not clear that the egalitarian approach would lead to an overall expansion of liability.[61] An egalitarian approach can also lead to contradictory recommendations (3) regarding the scope of liability for negligent parental supervision,[62] and, as we have seen, (4) regarding the shift from negligence

53 See Tsachi Keren-Paz, 'Compensating Injury to Autonomy: Normative Evaluation, Recent Developments and Future Tendencies', 11 *Colman LR* (forthcoming 2007).

54 For a discussion of this issue and an important qualification see Ch. 6 below.

55 See Ch. 5 below.

56 See e.g., *Pickett v British Rail Engineering Ltd* [1979] 1 All ER 774 (HL).

57 See Part III.B2 above, note 36 and accompanying text.

58 See Ch. 5.V, Examples 5, 9 & 10 below.

59 Ibid., Example 8.

60 See Ch. 5.V.B below.

61 See Ch. 8 below.

62 See Ch. 5, Example 8 below and note 93 and accompanying text; Ch. 3 above, notes 101–102 and accompanying text.

to strict liability regime.[63] Finally, (5) it is unclear whether or not an egalitarian approach should entail support for relaxed requirements of factual causation.[64]

V. Balancing Egalitarianism with Other Policy Considerations

A commitment to pluralism entails that the demands of egalitarianism should be balanced against other goals that also need to be promoted through tort law. This leads to the following conclusions: first, the distributive-egalitarian concern will almost always be a relevant criterion for the evaluation of the legal rule. Second, the distributive concern is an independent consideration that either favours liability or militates against it; it is not derived from other considerations. Third, egalitarianism does not take precedence *a priori* over other considerations. Accordingly, the equality effect of the rule should seldom be determinant in deciding whether to adopt or reject the rule. Fourth, egalitarianism is not subordinated to other policy considerations. Finally, the weight that should be accorded the distributive-egalitarian concern when balancing it against other policy considerations will change with the context.

A. Relevance

The first point is quite straightforward. If indeed tort rules should be evaluated in terms of their social consequences, and if society is under a duty to improve the lot of the disadvantaged, it follows that one of the consequences of the rule – its potentially regressive distributive effect – should be taken into account. According to the progressive commitment, such an effect should weigh against the imposition of such a rule. Under rare circumstances it might be inappropriate to consider egalitarian principles. Such situations arise when the disadvantage is deemed to be irrelevant to the proper allocation of the burden.[65]

B. Autonomous Nature: Egalitarianism is Broader than Anti-Discrimination

To the extent that a rule distributes its burdens and benefits regressively, the distributive-egalitarian concern weighs against adoption of that rule. It is important to notice that the regressive distributive effect is in itself a reason to oppose the legal rule that creates it even if: (1) the rule is desirable from other policy perspectives; and (2) the increased burden on the disadvantaged is rational. 'Rational' means that the disparate effect of the rule on the disadvantaged is justified on the basis of their characteristics, which call for the imposition of a unique burden upon them or, in the alternative, provide an explanation for the fact that they bear the burden disproportionately. The distributive-egalitarian concern therefore is different from a charge of discrimination, which is based on the claim that the different treatment is not grounded in a relevant distinction. Even if the different treatment is required in

---

63 See Part II.B above.

64 See the example in Part IV.A at no. (8) above; Ch. 8 below.

65 Ch. 5, Example 10 below discusses one such example, the distribution of the risk of being a victim of sexual assault. For an alternative analysis, see note 73 below.

order to achieve a legitimate tort law goal, the mere fact that the tort rule increases disparities of wealth and other entitlements to the detriment of the disadvantaged is sufficient for the distributive-egalitarian concern to weigh against the adoption of the rule. Thus, for instance, even though the burden imposed on pregnant women is justified by the unique woman-foetus dyad, egalitarianism still views imposition of such a duty as problematic due to the disparate impact such a rule imposes on an already disadvantaged group in society.

C. Lack of Conclusiveness

Tort law should promote other goals in addition to equality, and the egalitarian concern does not enjoy philosophical precedence over the other goals of tort law. Therefore the fact that a given rule does not best serve equality does not necessarily disqualify it. Sometimes the result of the balancing will be a rejection of a certain kind of liability, at other times it may lead to the modification of the rules, and in other situations still, rules may be adopted despite their regressive distributive effect. A possible (ostensible) exception to this principle might be when the suggested rule is discriminatory. When it is, the rule should be opposed without the need to balance the considerations supporting it against its regressive distributive results. For example, it is possible to justify the Canadian Supreme Court's refusal to issue an injunction to confine a pregnant woman who was sniffing glue during pregnancy[66] by pointing out that in cases of domestic violence against women there is no equal preventive confinement accompanied by treatment.

D. Egalitarian Consideration Should Not Serve Merely as a Veto

Contrary to some suggestions raised in the literature,[67] the view taken in this book is that distributive considerations in general, and egalitarian considerations in particular, should not serve merely as a veto. A veto approach is binary; it proposes that the distributive deficiency should not be taken into account at all, as long as the deficiency of the distributive result does not exceed a certain limit. However, the egalitarian concern should almost always be relevant, but should seldom, if ever, by itself be conclusive. In essence, the question is one of balance, not of relevance.

E. Weight

Because the distributive-egalitarian concern is not *a priori* conclusive, this consideration needs to be balanced against others. According to the model of

66 *Winnipeg Child and Family Services (Northwest Area) v DFG* [1997] 3 SCR 925 (Can).

67 Guido Calabresi, *The Costs of Accidents* (New Haven, 1970), pp. 32–3. In subsequent writings, Calabresi leaves more room for distributive considerations; see Guido Calabresi & Jon T. Hirschoff, 'Toward a Test for Strict Liability in Tort', 81 *Yale LJ* (1972) 1055, pp. 1083–4; Guido Calabresi & Alvin K. Klevorick, 'Four Tests for Liability in Torts', 14 *J Leg Stud* (1985) 585.

pluralism endorsed here, the distributive-egalitarian interest should be accorded a different weight in different situations. The question of weight is especially context-dependent. Therefore only some general remarks can be made at this stage about the ways courts should approach the question of relative weight. Three factors should be mentioned here: (1) the significance of the equality effect entailed by the rule (that is, to what extent equality is promoted or forgone); (2) the importance of promoting equality in a given context; and (3) the cost in terms of the reduced furtherance of other goals due to the adoption of the egalitarian-motivated rule. Since the dilemma arises when there is a trade-off between egalitarianism and other goals, the less costly the promotion of the desired distribution in terms of forgoing other goals, the more weight should be given to the egalitarian concern. Similarly, the more effective a rule is in bringing about the desired distributive result, and the greater the urgency to promote equality in a given situation, the greater the weight that should be given to the egalitarian concern.

1. The Magnitude of the Distributive Result Entailed by the Rule Parts III and IV above demonstrated that the overall equality effect of a given rule may vary considerably. The groups affected may not be identified, or, if identified, the equality effects of the rule may not be observable or significant. Even when significant equality effects can be observed, their classification as regressive or progressive may be disputed. And even when not disputed, regressive and progressive effects might cancel each other out in whole or in part, due to the multiplicity of participants and entitlements. As mentioned above, it is the net equality effect of the rule that should be taken into account. The more blurred or insignificant this net equality effect is, the less the weight that should be accorded to the egalitarian concern.

2. Relative Contextual Importance of the Need to Promote Equality Different contexts call for different degrees of egalitarian zeal. The main relevant factors in deciding the relative importance of promoting equality are: (1) the initial status of the affected parties; (2) the extent to which the equality effect of the rule is either under-inclusive or over-inclusive; and (3) the extent to which egalitarian concerns are appropriate.

(a) Status of parties. The more disadvantaged one of the parties is, or the more substantial the disparity between the parties, the greater the importance of promoting equality. While the goal of promoting the lot of those who are worst off should not be given lexical priority, all things being equal, greater weight should be given to the need to improve the lot of those at the bottom of the ladder. Therefore, even a relatively small redistributive gain may be desirable when those whose lot is improved are very needy. Similarly, it would seem that when both litigants are artificial persons, the relative weight of promoting equality is less significant than when both litigants are individuals.[68] This is not to say that equality has no place in the case of the former, particularly given that a comprehensive distributive inquiry will look at the way the corporation spreads the benefit or burden allocated to it.

---

68 Cf. Allan C. Hutchinson, *Waiting For Coraf: A Critique of Law and Rights* (1995), pp. 31–4 (criticizing the conferring of constitutional rights upon corporations).

However, in such situations the relative weight of equality compared to other values seems to be less significant.

(b) Over- and under-inclusiveness. When the relevant rule suffers from significant over- or under-inclusiveness, the weight of the egalitarian concern diminishes. The more under-inclusive the rule is, the less appropriate it is to adopt the rule as a response to the need to solve the underlying unjust redistribution. Moreover, the more under-inclusive the rule is, the more its adoption creates problems of intra-group justice that stem from the disparity between those who benefit from the rule and those who do not (and whom we would like to see participate in the redistribution). While, as explained above, such under-inclusiveness is not in itself a reason to avoid adopting a redistributive rule, it does make such adoption appear less warranted. The extent to which over-inclusiveness diminishes the weight of egalitarianism depends on the rule's cost in terms of the reduced promotion of other goals and the extent to which the receipt of the unwarranted benefit by intended recipients deviates from the ideal distributive scheme.

(c) Relevance and appropriateness of egalitarianism. The extent to which egalitarian concerns are appropriate and central to solving the parties' conflicting interests in tort cases changes with the context. Some of the relevant considerations are: (1) the parties' expectations regarding the relevance of egalitarian considerations as formed from the context of the interaction, the relationship between them, and their identities; (2) the extent to which equality and needs are relevant criteria for distributing the burden and resolving the conflict; and (3) the manner in which the regressive result is created by the rule, and the justification for such result.

(c1) Parties' expectations. In any given context, the greater the expectation of potential actors that an efficient (rather than egalitarian) rule will be applied, the less the relative weight that should be accorded to egalitarianism. Such expectations may be formed when the actors are risk-neutral, either because they are repeat players or because they can spread the loss.[69] The more commercial the context, the more likely it is that the relative weight of non-egalitarian considerations (such as efficiency, loss spreading and fairness) will increase. It follows that when the potential plaintiff is a one-shot player (for example, a person who is discriminated against in his search for a rental apartment) and when the context of the interaction is more personal, the relative weight of egalitarian considerations increases.[70] Parties derive expectations

69 Cf. Gregory C. Keating's argument with respect to the choice between strict liability and negligence from a fairness perspective, 'Distributive and Corrective Justice in the Tort Law of Accidents', 74 *S Cal L Rev* (2000) 193, pp. 213–14.

70 The idea that parties' expectations with respect to the way they will be treated are relevant for the allocation of burdens is well known in contract theory, and Macneil's distinction between relational and discrete contracts comes to mind. See Ian R. Macneil, 'Contracts: Adjustment of Long-term Economic Relations Under Classical, Neoclassical and Relational Contract Law', 72 *Nw UL Rev* (1978) 854. While, admittedly, there is a stronger reason to take into account expectations in the contractual arena in which both parties act voluntarily, the distinction should not be overemphasized. First, from the contractual aspect, freedom of contract is limited by market constraints and social structures. Second, both potential tortfeasors and victims take calculated and uncalculated risks in the knowledge that there exists the possibility of a tortious interaction.

from the type of interaction they have with the other party, as well as from the latter's identity. For example, when public authorities are implicated in a tort interaction, one might expect the relative weight of egalitarian considerations to increase, given the public law duty of public authorities to respect equality.

(c2) Equality as an appropriate criterion for distribution. In several situations egalitarian considerations seem less appropriate, since the initial inequality is deemed irrelevant or out of place for resolving the conflict at hand. Such a view might be based on the idea that any conscious redistribution of some devastating burdens seems inappropriate even if it is progressive. In such cases, it is better that the burden stay where it falls, rather than it be intentionally shifted, especially if the allocation is based on substantive criteria such as desert or need.[71] The discussion in Chapter 5 below of the risk of being the victim of sexual assault exemplifies this claim.[72] Arguably, egalitarian considerations are irrelevant, or at least peripheral, to the proper solution of some conflicting interests. Perhaps the incommensurability of the type of loss in such cases with the parties' wealth or social status accounts for the marginalization of egalitarianism in such a context.[73]

(c3) Justification of regressive result. Finally, the way the rule creates the regressive result and the extent to which this result can be adequately justified affect the extent to which ignoring egalitarianism is offensive or understandable. The more overt and less rational the burdensome treatment of the disadvantaged, the greater the weight that should be given to egalitarianism. When the interests of the disadvantaged are ignored, the insult of devaluing the worth of the disadvantaged is thus added to the injury of the regressive distributive effect. This might suggest that placing a unique burden on the dissimilarly-situated disadvantaged (as does, for example, the maternal prenatal duty) is symbolically more harmful to their status than a seemingly neutral rule resulting in an adverse effect on them (as does, for example, the rule regarding parental negligent supervision of their children).[74] Accordingly, the weight of the egalitarian concern in the former type of rules should be increased.

3. The Strength of Other Policy Considerations The more costly the adoption of a given rule in terms of attaining other policy considerations, the less the relative weight of the egalitarian concern. Since we are dealing with a trade-off, society

---

71 Cf. Michael Otsuka, 'Killing the Innocent in Self-Defense', 23 *Phil & Pub Aff* (1994) 74, pp. 76–90.

72 See Ch. 5.V.B, Example 10 below.

73 However, an alternative account is possible, according to which egalitarian considerations are relevant even in the context of sexual assault. The prohibition on increasing the aggregate risk of becoming a victim of sexual assault for its more progressive redistribution can be explained on the grounds of the precedence of inter-group justice over intra-group justice. According to such an approach, the egalitarian gain from decreasing the aggregate risk to women of being sexually assaulted by men takes precedence over the egalitarian loss of the regressive distribution of risk among women of different classes and races. It is submitted that to decide intentionally to channel the risk of being sexually assaulted, even in a progressive manner ('we prefer more white women and less black women get raped') is highly problematic.

74 See Ch. 5.V.B, Example 8 below.

might be willing to pay in the currency of distributive justice in order to achieve a very good result in terms of other goals, but might not be willing to pay in the same manner for a less certain promotion of those goals. For example, when comparing two alternative rules, one rule's small deficiency in egalitarian terms might be outweighed by its superior results in terms of efficiency. A rule that results in a distribution of $15 to 'A' and $50 to 'B' might be inferior overall to a rule that results in an alternative distribution of $14 and $100 respectively. As the discussion above demonstrates, the extent and significance of such a trade-off change with the context. At times, the more egalitarian rule is also the more efficient one, or else the egalitarian rule may be supported by other goals of tort law.

F. Conclusion

According to the suggested model, the policy maker should do the following: (1) identify the typical litigants; (2) determine who is more disadvantaged; (3) decide whether the rule in question results in progressive or regressive distribution; (4) evaluate whether such rule is desirable from the perspective of other considerations; and (5) balance the postulations of the different policy considerations, including distributive-egalitarian concerns, and only then reach the decision. In essence, these five stages may be reduced to two main steps: First, identify what the postulation of the distributive-egalitarian concern is, and second, balance this postulation against the postulations of other policy considerations.

Chapter 5

Standard of Care

Introduction

This chapter presents an egalitarian reformulation of the standard of care. First, it explains why it is important from a normative perspective to incorporate egalitarian sensitivity into the concept of negligence. Second, it suggests that an egalitarian reformulation of the concept of negligence should be based on needs, equality, and desert, as criteria for distribution. Moreover, it argues that, quite surprisingly, egalitarianism fits well with the basic understanding of negligence law as reflecting *corrective* justice and notions of *fault*, provided that fault is reformulated to accommodate egalitarianism. Third, it maintains that for egalitarianism to fit well with notions of corrective justice, the egalitarian concern should be incorporated not only into the analysis of the duty of care but also into the analysis of the standard of care. At the level of the standard of care, the egalitarian concern functions as a justification for legitimizing otherwise wrongful activity. As will be explained, morally, we should usually hold the better-off individual to a higher standard of care than we do the disadvantaged. Fourth, it shows how the egalitarian concern can be used to reformulate the standard of care analysis. Fifth, the practical usefulness of sensitivity to egalitarianism in standard of care analysis is examined, by discussing a few examples dealing with active risk creation and failure to prevent risk by third parties. Finally, it is argued that the approach advocated for in this chapter is not incongruent with existing tort law.

I. Insights from Other Approaches

When introducing egalitarianism into the tort of negligence, there are lessons to be learned from other theoretical approaches to tort law. A theoretical account of tort law usually revolves around one or more of the following three themes: corrective justice, whose goal is remedying the plaintiff's loss caused by a wrongful act by the defendant;[1] economic analysis of law, whose goal is the prevention of all – and only those – accidents worth preventing, and the achievement of allocational efficiency;[2]

---

1 See, e.g., Ernest J. Weinrib, *The Idea of Private Law* (Cambridge, 1995); Richard W. Wright, 'Right, Justice and Tort Law', in David G. Owen (ed.), *Philosophical Foundations of Tort Law* (Oxford, 1995), p. 159. For corrective justice approaches which are based on strict liability see George P. Fletcher, 'Fairness and Utility in Tort Theory', 85 *Harv L Rev* (1972) 537; Richard A. Epstein, 'A Theory of Strict Liability', 2 *J Legal Stud* (1973) 151.

2 See e.g., Richard A. Posner, 'A Theory of Negligence', 1 *J Legal Stud* (1972) 29; William M. Landes & Richard A. Posner, *The Economic Structure of Tort Law* (Cambridge,

and distributive justice, whose goal is the fair distribution of burdens and benefits in society.[3] Distributive considerations in tort law are usually of two kinds. The first, which, following Keating, is referred to as 'fairness', is based on the idea that those who benefit from a given activity should bear its costs.[4] The second, which is referred to as 'loss-spreading', is based on the idea that it is better to spread losses across many individuals and across time.[5]

Egalitarians should learn important lessons from these four other theoretical approaches. Corrective justice teaches us that establishing that an act was wrongful is a precondition for a finding of negligence. Economic analysis teaches us that in the context of negligence law, in order to evaluate the wrongfulness of the activity and the desirability of the legal rule, it is necessary to examine the consequences of both. Loss-spreading approach teaches us that the needs of the parties (namely, the effects of the loss resulting from the accident on the parties' well-being) are both relevant and important. Fairness perspective teaches us that the distributive effects of the legal rule are important and that individuals have a fairness-based claim for equal treatment. These insights help defending in Part II the incorporation of egalitarianism into the tort of negligence.

A. Corrective Justice

Upon first glance, corrective justice approaches are most inimical to the inclusion of distributive considerations into the tort of negligence. Corrective justice theoreticians as diverse as Fletcher, Epstein, Weinrib, and Coleman assert that a tort regime that is based on corrective justice should ignore distributive consequences and motives, including egalitarianism.[6] Indeed, corrective justice operates, according

---

1987); Steven Shavell, *Economic Analysis of Accident Law* (Cambridge, 1987).

3 See e.g., Gregory C. Keating, 'Distributive and Corrective Justice in the Tort Law of Accidents', 74 *S Cal L Rev* (2000) 193; Alan L. Calnan, 'Distributive and Corrective Justice Issues in Contemporary Tobacco Litigation', 27 *Sw UL Rev* (1998) 577; Guido Calabresi, *The Costs of Accidents* (New Haven, 1970), pp. 27–8, 39–67. For pluralist approaches, see Gary T. Schwartz, 'Mixed Theories of Tort Law: Affirming Both Deterrence and Corrective Justice', 75 *Tex L Rev* (1997) 1801; Izhak Englard, *The Philosophy of Tort Law* (Aldershot, 1993); Guido Calabresi & Jon T. Hirschoff, 'Toward a Test for Strict Liability in Tort', 81 *Yale LJ* (1972) 1055; Guido Calabresi & Alvin K. Klevorick, 'Four Tests for Liability in Torts', 14 *J Legal Stud* (1985) 585; Ariel Porat & Alex Stein, *Tort Liability Under Uncertainty* (Oxford, 2001).

4 See Keating, ibid.

5 See Calabresi, *supra* note 3, pp. 39–45. Calabresi views this consideration as constituting part of efficiency. Indeed, it is supported by reasons of efficiency as well, namely, the fear of over-deterrence. Nonetheless, it has a justice component to it.

6 Fletcher, *supra* note 1, p. 547 n.40; Richard Epstein, 'Intentional Harms', 4 *J Legal Stud* (1975) 391, p. 441; Weinrib, *supra* note 1, pp. 36–7, 74–5; Jules L. Coleman, *Risks and Wrongs* (Cambridge, 1992), pp. 350–54. However, in a later co-authored article, Coleman has shown the similarity between the questions tort law deals with and those dealt with by distributive justice. Jules L. Coleman & Arthur Ripstein, 'Mischief and Misfortune', 41 *McGill LJ* (1995) 91.

to conventional wisdom, against the background of, and based on the assumed desirability of, initial distribution.[7]

According to conventional wisdom, corrective justice approaches are all based on the correlation between the doer's duty and the sufferer's right; they are all agency-dependent; and they all impose liability based on the activity that caused the interaction between the parties, rather than on the respective status of the parties prior to the tortious action.[8] For our purposes, the last two features are of the most importance. First, liability should be dependent on the tortfeasor's action. Second, the gist of corrective justice is that this action should be classified as morally wrong. The wrongfulness of the tortfeasor's action singles out some (but not other) actions as creating a duty to compensate the victim. Now, one might dispute the justification of these requirements as general preconditions to tort liability, and one might dispute (as is suggested in this chapter) the principle of disregarding of the parties' prior status for purposes of determining whether to impose liability or not. However, in the context of the tort of negligence, *the identification of a given action by the tortfeasor-agent as morally wrong is a necessary condition for the imposition of liability under the tort of negligence.* The tort of negligence includes an important moral and evaluative component. Negligent activities are wrong and should not occur. Some activities are appropriate, and some are not. Imposing liability in negligence should target only activities we deem wrongful. As will be explained below, the tort of negligence should not impose liability on all wrongful activities. However, it should impose liability only for wrongful activities. To the extent that society would like to impose liability on non-wrongful activities, the basis for such liability should differ from the basis for a finding of negligence. It follows then, that normatively a finding of negligence has a symbolic as well as practical outcome: it does not extract a price for legitimate activity; rather, it imposes a sanction for illegitimate activity.[9] It says that the negligent activity is wrongful and should not be carried out.

B. Efficiency

A law and economics approach has an important lesson for us in the context of negligence: the moral relevance of consequences. As the leading instrumentalist theory in legal academia, law and economics teaches us a lesson that is forgotten by many other theories: that in evaluating whether an activity is negligent or not, the costs of precaution (that is, the benefits of the activity that harmed the victim) should be compared with the costs of accidents (the costs of bearing the accidents). The basic law and economics formula for the standard of care in negligence – the Hand formula – engages in cost-benefit analysis: it measures the benefits of the activity against its costs and imposes liability if, and only if, the costs of the activity outweigh its benefits.[10] It does so by comparing accident costs with precaution costs. Note that on its face, the activity's benefits do not

7 Coleman, ibid.

8 Cf. Porat & Stein, *supra* note 3, p. 12; Keating, *supra* note 3, p. 197.

9 See Robert Cooter, 'Prices and Sanctions', 84 *Colum L Rev* (1984) 1523.

10 *United States v Carrol Towing Co.*, 159 F 2d 169, 173 (2d Cir 1947).

seem to be calculated at all. However, they are included in the calculation of the precaution costs. True, it is well known that courts do not take into account activity levels when determining negligence (and, hence, they seemingly disregard the opportunity costs of foregoing an activity that is alternative to the risk-creating one).[11] However, variations of the Hand formula that were adopted in England and Israel, as well as by the Restatement (Second) of Torts, do consider the social value of the risk-creating activity.[12] The social value calculus inserts into the cost-benefit analysis the opportunity cost of not foregoing the risk-creating activity as part of the precaution costs of the accident. At times, the only way to prevent an accident will be to cease from engaging in the risk-creating activity. If the benefits from the activity outweigh its accident costs, refraining from the activity becomes the cost of precaution. When the activity is cost-justified (that is, when its benefits outweigh its costs), engaging in that activity is not considered negligent. While economic analysis is inadequate, in that it ignores distributive results and attempts to aggregate wealth, its basic consequentialist insight is valid, namely, that in order to evaluate the desirability of an activity, both its costs and benefits should be given weight and compared.

Corrective justice, despite its appeal as a non-cost-justified definition of negligence, misses a very important (and intuitive) point. It is unreasonable to evaluate the reasonableness of a given activity without comparing the actor's purpose and the cost at which this purpose was achieved. Looking only at one side of the equation – the risk imposed on others – is insufficient; one needs to assess why the risk was imposed. Shooting a gun in the middle of the street creates a huge hazard to passers by and therefore would usually constitute negligence. However, if the shooting is by a police officer attempting to stop a person on a shooting rampage, it will not, and should not, be considered a negligent action.[13] In such cases, corrective justice approaches run into trouble. Under corrective justice, the injured innocent bystander should not be subject to such a risk, regardless of the fact that the police officer's shooting advanced a legitimate (cost-justified) action. Under corrective justice approaches, or at least some versions thereof, such a shooting is wrong.

Note, however, that a duty to compensate the innocent bystander is desirable based on notions of distributive – and not corrective – justice. It is fairer to spread the loss from an activity that benefits the general public across the public by imposing

11 See, e.g., Shavell, *supra* note 2, p. 25.

12 See, e.g., *Watt v Hertfordshire County Council* [1954] 2 All ER 368, 371 (CA); *Dabron v Bath Tramways Ltd* [1946] 2 All ER 333, 336 (CA); CA 343/74 *Groobner v Municipality of Haifa*, PD 30(1) 141, 158 (Israel); Restatement (Second) of Torts, s. 292(a) (1965) (US). See also ibid. s. 293(a) (social value of the interests under risk from the actor's activity as a factor in determining the magnitude of risk from such activity); *Meyers v Robb*, 267 NW 2d 450, 452 (Mich Ct App 1978); W.V.H. Rogers, *Winfield and Jolowicz on Tort* (16th edn, London, 2002), pp. 199–202; Simon F. Deakin, Angus Johnston & Basil Markesinis, *Markesinis and Deakin's Tort Law* (5th edn, Oxford, 2003), pp. 177–82; R.F.V. Heuston & R.A.B. Buckley, *Salmond & Heuston on the Law of Torts* (21st edn, London, 1996), pp. 225–31.

13 Cf. *Hatfield v Gracen,* 567 P 2d 546 (Or 1977); see also Watt, ibid.; Restatement (Second) of Torts, s. 296 (1965).

liability on the police, rather than placing the burden on the shoulders of the innocent victim. However, if proponents of corrective justice insist that liability in negligence necessarily implies that the actor has acted wrongfully (towards the plaintiff), such a conclusion is problematic on the facts of the example. What the officer did was desirable and commendable, not negligent and wrongful. We would like any officer to act in the same manner under similar circumstances. Economic analysis, unlike corrective justice, captures the intuition that the officer's action was not wrongful. However, due to its insensitivity to distributive considerations, economic analysis fails to see the case for compensating the innocent bystander. Under the Hand formula, as long as the officer's action produced more aggregate benefit than cost, the officer should not have to compensate those harmed from his activity.

Thus far the discussion has shown that both the law and economics approach and corrective justice yield unsatisfactory results due to their disregard for the distributive results of legal rules. The following two approaches, loss-spreading and fairness, do reveal sensitivity to particular distributive considerations. In examining these approaches the following insight derived from law and economics should be employed: *in evaluating the wrongfulness (or reasonableness) of an activity, the costs and benefits of alternative courses of action should be considered as well.*

C. Loss-Spreading

Guido Calabresi has argued that one of the goals of tort law should be to reduce the negative effects of accident losses on those who bear them (secondary accident costs, in his terminology), rather than reducing merely the overall size of these losses (primary accident costs, in his terminology).[14] Indeed, if society is concerned not merely with deterrence but also with compensation, with meeting the needs of individuals, the questions of who bears the loss and what are the effects of bearing the loss upon those who bear it become crucial. One of the critiques of law and economics is relevant in this context. Measuring efficiency in absolute figures ignores the diminishing marginal utility of money, and hence is unsuitable if what we are concerned about is individual (or even aggregated individual) well-being. The morality concern underlying loss-spreading is that, all other things being equal, the disutility from bearing a small and predictable loss over time is much smaller than the disutility from bearing a considerable abrupt loss. Therefore, all things being equal, accident losses should be spread across many bearers. The idea of spreading *accident* losses (as distinguished from precaution costs) is quite openly accepted by many courts and serves as a hidden persuader in other jurisdictions in which its legitimacy is formally disputed. Of course, from an egalitarian perspective the underlying initial distribution of wealth is crucial if our goal is to reduce disutility. Therefore a deep-pockets policy might be preferable to a loss-spreading mechanism. The lesson taken from a loss-spreading morality is this: *meeting the needs of individuals and reducing the negative effects of losses they bear are worthy goals.*

---

14 Calabresi, *supra* note 3, pp. 26–7.

D. Fairness

A fairness approach maintains that those who benefit from a given activity should bear its costs and risks. As such, the fairness approach is hostile to the notion of subsidy and therefore seems at odds with an egalitarian approach favouring progressive subsidizing. Fairness and egalitarianism seem to be merely two competing criteria for the distribution of costs and risks in society. In fact, however, the relationship between fairness and egalitarianism is more complex than that. First, egalitarianism shares with the fairness approach the idea that *the distributive effects of a legal rule, including its effects on third parties, are relevant for the assessment of the rule's desirability*. Thus, both approaches take issue with both corrective justice and economic analysis of law. Second, it is worth noting that these two criteria for distribution will not always conflict with one another. At times, liability will be justified on grounds of both prevention of subsidization (the fairness approach) and of regressive distributive effect (egalitarianism). This will happen when the subsidy given by uncompensated victims to the tortfeasors' activities that harmed them is regressive.

More importantly, *one should take from the fairness approach a commitment to equality*. Fairness and egalitarianism differ, however, with respect to the definition of the desired equality. For example, Gregory Keating's justification of the fairness approach is Rawlsian and, as such, committed to a particular type of equality. To Keating, the meaning of a fairness approach in tort law is to equalize burdens (including risks and their materialization) and benefits across society.[15] In essence, his claim is that individuals have a fairness-based claim for equal treatment. Imposing the risks of a given activity that benefits all members of a given group only on specific members of this group amounts to unequal treatment of those members.

The difference between fairness and egalitarianism is that the former is interested in equalizing the absolute value of the risks and losses, whereas egalitarianism is interested in equalizing the negative effects created by such losses, an examination that mandates consideration of the parties' prior holdings. Fairness could be equated with formal equality, and egalitarianism with substantive equality. By failing to take into account the parties' prior holdings for purposes of equating the burdens imposed by tort law, a fairness approach reflects formal equality.

As for the conflict between the two approaches with respect to the worthiness of progressive subsidization, there is a great deal of appeal in the anti-subsidy sentiment. We often feel it is fair to demand that those who benefit from a given activity pay its costs. Nonetheless, this anti-subsidy sentiment does have its limits. In many circumstances we feel that subsidy is warranted. The predominant tax-and-transfer system in modern society is progressive and, as such, is founded upon a subsidy regime. Patrons of public transportation on central lines subsidize those in the periphery. Indeed, the most fundamental social structure, the parent–children relationship, is all about subsidization.[16] Since subsidization

15 Keating, *supra* note 3, pp. 202–7.

16 For a similar critique of the labour-desert justification for copyright, see Wendy J. Gordon, 'On Owning Information: Intellectual Property and the Restitutionary Impulse', 78

is not necessarily bad in general, it is not necessarily bad specifically in the field of tort law. Therefore, to the extent that distributive considerations should play a part in tort law (a theme underlying the fairness approach itself), egalitarianism is yet another legitimate and relevant distributive consideration that should be taken into account.

II. Normative Defence

A. The Intuition

Consider the following example:

Example 1. George is Elaine's neighbour. To heat his house, George uses a cheap kind of coal, which costs him $200 per month. George is very poor, and his monthly income is $1,000, from which he has to feed his sick and hungry daughter. The cheap coal causes pollution that costs Elaine $900 per month. Elaine's monthly income is $18,000. Had George used a more expensive coal, which costs $800, the pollution would have been prevented.

Under the Hand formula, George is negligent. He could have prevented a loss of $900 by spending another $600. Not doing so is negligent. George, as a rational actor, would have to spend 60 per cent of his monthly income in order to prevent a loss of 5 per cent of Elaine's monthly income. As a result, his daughter might not get adequate nutrition, proper clothing, adequate school supplies, or simply a treat. In contrast, if Elaine is not compensated for her loss, no major negative effect on her well-being or future plans will result. Under these circumstances, can we really say that if George decides not to buy the more expensive coal, he is acting negligently?

Example 2. Elaine and George have the same income as in the previous example. Elaine uses the cheap coal, which causes George a loss of $600 per month. Elaine can prevent this loss by using a more expensive coal, which would cost her an extra $900 per month.

Under the Hand formula Elaine is not negligent for not using the more expensive coal. She is not required to spend $900 in order to prevent a $600 loss to George. The fact that the burden that she would be required to shoulder would amount to only 5 per cent of her monthly income whereas the loss to George amounts to 60 per cent of his monthly income is irrelevant.

In both examples, the moral intuition of many will lead to the opposite conclusion to that reached using the Hand formula. The intuition is especially strong in the first example. George should not be considered negligent for opting not to spend $600 in order to prevent a $900 loss to Elaine. Our moral evaluation is (and should be) that George has not acted improperly by reaching this decision. Furthermore, we do not think that George should be absolved from liability, despite the fact that he acted wrongfully;[17] rather, we think that he is not liable since he acted reasonably and his decision was justified.

Va L Rev (1992) 149, p. 170.

17 Such an approach can be based on compassion towards George or derive from a need-based argument that overrides the instinct to hold George liable due to his faulty decision.

Similarly (although it is conceded that the moral intuition in less obvious) in Example 2, Elaine should be considered negligent for not preventing the loss to George. True, Elaine's decision is cost-justified. Yet the combination of fairness and egalitarianism leads us to believe that the fact that George is forced to provide regressive subsidization for Elaine's heating activity (by not being compensated for his loss, which is created by Elaine's activity) makes Elaine's decision not to use the more expensive heating method negligent. The next section defends this intuition based on notions of needs, equality, and desert as criteria for distribution.

B. *Justifications*

Tort law can be viewed as one mechanism for distributing burdens and benefits across members of society. There are at least three relevant criteria for the distribution of the burdens allocated by tort law: needs, equality, and negative desert. The criterion of needs requires that losses should be distributed in a way that minimizes the negative effects of the loss on its bearers. The criterion of equality requires that the burdens that society imposes on the liberty of its members for the sake of the security of others should be substantively equal, so that the less advantaged will not be burdened disproportionately. Finally, the criterion of negative desert requires that those who act unacceptably should bear the losses created by their unacceptable behaviour. All three criteria support the incorporation of egalitarianism into tort doctrine. They all support the conclusion that the distributive effects of liability under negligence should affect the decision of whether liability should be imposed. Moreover, at least the equality and negative desert criteria support the conclusion that the distributive effects of liability under negligence are relevant in the moral assessment of the defendant's activity as blameworthy (negligent) or not.

1. Needs One criterion for the distribution of burdens (both risks and losses) by tort law should be the allocation of burdens to those who can bear them with the least disutility. The rationale behind such a criterion is that losses are a bad thing and we would like to minimize their bad effects for those who have to bear them.[18] More fundamentally, such an approach is based on a commitment to fulfil the basic needs of individuals. Under this view, individuals should be assured a minimum set of material conditions in order to be able to fulfil those needs.[19] Losses, including losses caused by human agency, can jeopardize the agent's ability to fulfil her basic needs. Therefore, a relevant criterion for distributing tortious losses is the identification of the individual who can bear the loss with the least disutility. The phenomenon of diminishing marginal utility clearly suggests that the parties' prior holdings are relevant for purposes of determining

18 Cf. Christopher T. Wonnell, 'Replacing the Unitary Principle of Unjust Enrichment', 45 *Emory LJ* (1996) 153, p. 177 ('harms are bad things which the system should seek to discourage [...] benefits are good things which the system should seek to encourage').

19 David Wiggins, 'Claims of Need', in Ted Honderich (ed.), *Morality and Objectivity: A Tribute to J.L. Mackie* (London, 1985), p. 149.

loss-bearing capacity. Note that there may be a tension between the policies of loss-spreading and egalitarianism,[20] and in many cases, in order to stay true to the rationale of fulfilling the individual's needs, priority should be given to egalitarianism.

To be sure, needs are not the only, or even the controlling, criterion for distribution. A competing criterion is negative desert, which requires that those who wrongfully created losses should be the ones who bear them. For current purposes, however, there is no need to decide how to balance the needs criterion with other criteria. All that is required is the acknowledgement of the following three propositions: one, that needs are a legitimate criterion for deciding where tortious losses should lie; two, that existing tort doctrine recognizes the validity of this concern; and three, that a proper application of this concern requires that courts also take into account the parties' relative ability to bear precaution costs and that they compare the parties' relative ability – based, amongst other things, on their prior holdings – to bear *either* accident or precaution costs.

Loss-spreading and deep-pockets considerations should and do play a role in tort law. These considerations convey the significance of fulfilling the individual's needs as a morally relevant criterion for distribution. They mandate that in deciding whether liability should be imposed or not, the effects of the relevant legal rule on the well-being of its addressees (or subjects) should be taken into account.[21] Some view needs-based considerations (in some circumstances, at least) as subordinate to negative-desert-based considerations,[22] but this can be disputed.[23] Indeed, as tort doctrine teaches us, needs-based considerations can serve as the basis for allocating the accident loss to the innocent victim rather than to the faulty tortfeasor. This is done by refusing to recognize a duty of care and by curtailing liability by means of the doctrines of proximate cause and remoteness of damage. Doctrinally, needs-based considerations influence tort law in at least three ways. First, they support imposing liability if the defendant is likely to be a good loss-spreader (by purchasing insurance or through other loss-spreading mechanisms).[24] Second, they support imposing liability on the basis of the defendant's deep pocket.[25] Third, they support an exemption from liability for negligent defendants on the ground that potential liability is too burdensome for potential defendants. This is done by not

20 A loss-spreading approach advocates spreading the loss across as many loss-bearers as possible. An egalitarian approach advocates allocating losses to deep-pockets loss-bearers who would suffer little disutility from bearing the loss.

21 See Calabresi, *supra* note 3, pp. 27–8; Menachem Mautner, '"The Eternal Triangles of the Law": Toward a Theory of Priorities in Conflicts Involving Remote Parties', 90 *Mich L Rev* (1991) 95, pp. 105–6, 139–41, 149, 151–2; John G. Fleming, *The Law of Torts* (9th edn, Sydney, 1998), pp. 11–13; Cf. Peter Cane, *Atiyah's Accidents, Compensation and the Law* (London, 1993), pp. 354–7.

22 See Mautner, ibid., pp. 100, 107, 116, 118.

23 See e.g., Hanoch Dagan, 'The Craft of Property', 91 *Cal L Rev* (2003) 1517, pp. 1544–7.

24 See e.g., *Escola v Coca Cola Bottling Co*, 150 P 2d 436, 440–41 (Cal 1944).

25 See e.g., Patrick S. Atiyah, *Vicarious Liability in the Law of Torts* (London, 1967), p. 22.

recognizing a duty of care.[26] This denial can be regarded as a manifestation of the loss-spreading idea: it is preferable that potential victims remain uncompensated for the losses they suffered from certain negligent activities than that potential negligent tortfeasors are made to bear in full the losses created by their negligent behaviour.

All three paradigms mentioned above draw on the moral imperative of fulfilling the individual's needs as a basis for allocating *accident* losses to either of the parties. The paradigms are based on the idea that the ability to bear the burden of the accident loss is morally relevant to the decision regarding who should bear the loss. The extent of the burden created by the requirement to incur precaution costs is equally morally relevant. From the point of view of the potential bearer of those costs, there is no distinction between accident costs and precaution costs. The loss is the same, and the burden is the same.[27] Needs-based considerations call our attention to the actor's ability to bear losses as a relevant factor in deciding how to allocate the losses. Since the accident loss and precaution costs should be treated as one and the same, courts should allocate that loss to the party who has the greater ability to bear it. Therefore, if the victim has the greater ability to bear the loss, liability should be denied; but if the victim has less ability to bear the loss, liability should be imposed on the tortfeasor.

Given the diminishing marginal utility of money, it is better that those with higher loss-bearing capability ('the rich') bear losses of higher absolute value than that the poor bear losses of lower absolute value. For that matter, it is immaterial whether the loss is an accident loss or a precaution cost. This is justified from a needs-based perspective, since the disutility caused to the poor from bearing the loss (in either form) would be more significant than the disutility caused to the rich from bearing the loss (in either form), even if the loss suffered by the rich is higher in absolute value than that suffered by the poor.

The discussion so far has not suggested that the decision not to impose liability on the less able loss-bearer implies that the latter's activity (assuming she is the defendant) was not negligent. Rather, it suggests that for reasons of policy or justice, we would like to exempt her from liability, even if she were negligent. The next section defends the proposition that the agent's means are relevant for purposes of deciding whether her activity is negligent or not.

2. Equality A fairness approach is based on the idea that burdens and benefits should be distributed in an equal way among members of society. There are, of course, competing conceptions of equality. Those who endorse a substantive concept of equality, one that takes into account some measure of equality of results rather than

26 See e.g., *Hercules Managements Ltd v Ernst & Young* [1997] 2 SCR 165 (Can) (policy concerns surrounding indeterminate liability negate imposing a duty); *Caparo Industries Plc v Dickman* [1990] 2 AC 605 (HL); *Ultramares Corp v Touche*, 174 NE 441 (NY Ct App 1931).

27 It should also be recalled that according to conventional economic wisdom, in some situations the potential victim can 'bribe' the tortfeasor and thereby achieve the efficient result by bearing the cost-effective precaution costs himself, instead of the tortfeasor.

equality of opportunity, should agree that the relevant burden should be measured against the prior holdings of parties.

The question essentially is how should burdens and benefits be measured. Presumably, all those who support the basic fairness intuition agree that benefits and burdens should be borne equally by all members of society, so the question boils down to what the guideline for measuring burdens and benefits should be. The prevalent view, based on economic analysis, compares burdens according to their absolute monetary value. However, absolute value is a poor guideline for the real-life effect of bearing the burden (or enjoying the benefit). Put simply, we should include the concept of diminishing marginal utility into the evaluation of the magnitude of the burden borne by different members of society.

Applied to negligence, the argument goes as follows. Negligence law balances the competing claims for liberty by potential tortfeasors and for security by potential victims. The moral rationale behind such a balancing is that the actor is required to refrain from creating risk for another only to a certain degree: there comes a point when the requirement to protect the interests of others comes at a cost deemed too high to the actor's liberty. When this line is crossed, the actor is not required to prevent the risk to another simply because the burden of doing so is deemed excessive. Equality dictates that all actors be subject to the same burden when required to consider the interests of others. The Hand formula systematically subjects the poor to a higher burden than the rich bear, since they are required to spend the same amount of money as precaution costs, which imposes a greater burden on the poor than on the rich. Similarly, when unavoidable accidents occur, the burden the poor have to bear as potential victims is greater than the burden borne by the rich when the absolute value of the loss is the same.

This view finds support in another approach emphasizing positive liberty. Obviously, tort law affects potential defendants' negative liberty by proscribing certain kinds of behaviour. However, the distributive effects caused by the duty (or lack thereof) to compensate others for certain activities affects both parties' positive liberty. The individual's positive liberty – her ability to pursue her own goals and to have effective choice regarding her life plans – derives partially, yet significantly, from her financial resources.[28] If we strive to ensure an adequate and equal degree of positive liberty for all individuals, we must take into account the distributive consequences of the relevant legal rule.

Below, it is explained that the Hand formula has the result of a regressive distribution of wealth in society due to the systematic incentive it gives tortfeasors to harm the poor. The analysis here adds the insight that even if we put aside this effect, the Hand formula brings about regressive results by ignoring the fact that equal losses (be it accident losses or prevention losses) have greater adverse effects on the poor than on the rich, and result in greater disutility to the poor. Viewed this way, the problem seems one of horizontal equality and as more reflective of notions of distributive justice than corrective justice. The problem appears to be that as among

28 See Note, 'Distributive Liberty: A Relational Model of Freedom, Coercion, and Property Law', 107 *Harv L Rev* (1994) 859, p. 859 ('changes in property rules redistribute liberty, as well as material well-being').

potential victims or tortfeasors, respectively, the poor are required to forego a greater amount of security or liberty in order to achieve the same degree of protection of the liberty or security of others. Unlike the needs-based argument, however, the equality criterion reveals the unfairness of morally assessing as equally wrong the failure of poor and the rich to take the same degree of precaution. This suggests that exempting the poor from liability in situations like Example 1 above is based on the idea that the poor individual's behaviour was not negligent, not on the idea that despite his negligent behaviour, it is unjust to hold him liable. While a needs-based rationale is derived from mercy and excuse, an equality-based rationale is derived from notions of rights and justification. If individuals do have a right to equal treatment and to expect to be subject to equal burdens in order to achieve the same goals, they are seemingly justified in not taking precautions that overly burden them.

A fairness approach that demands placing equal burdens on actors might require that inequality in initial holdings of resources other than wealth (including personality traits) also be taken into account in determining the expected standard of care for each individual. This amounts to a shift toward a subjective standard of care. The question whether such a proposition is true or whether for purposes of a standard of care analysis there are grounds for distinguishing wealth and social power from other resources is not explored here.

3. Desert Notwithstanding the dictates of substantive equality, an approach advocating that the parties' respective status be taken into account for purposes of evaluating the reasonableness of the activity in question arguably misses an important feature of negligence law which is related to corrective justice: namely, that in order to support liability in negligence, the agent's activity should be considered as blameworthy vis-à-vis the victim. It might seem that if, as a matter of negative desert, the agent's activity wrongfully risked or harmed the victim, the former should compensate the latter, irrespective of the equality criteria. Put differently, the advocate of corrective justice might argue that the apparent unequal burden is justified and in fact equal since it subjects all agents to an equal criterion of negative desert: those who harmed others wrongfully should compensate them. As should be clear from the discussion thus far, the crucial question is the following: what should be the standard for measuring 'wrongful' or 'negligent' activity? The concept of negative desert should be reformulated in an egalitarian-sensitive way, so that the magnitude of the burden created by the duty to take precautions or by the freedom of the other side not to take precautions will affect the moral assessment of the defendant's activity as negligent. To substantiate this point, two notions will be discussed: desert as a criterion for distribution and the idea that negligent behaviour is conduct that fails to balance properly between self-interest and other-regarding. The ensuing discussion will establish the claim that, even as a matter of corrective justice, it is unjust to disregard the actual burden involved in bearing accident or precaution costs for purposes of evaluating in moral terms a given activity as negligent or not.

Negative desert as a criterion for distribution is based on the idea that those who wrongfully harm others should bear the resulting loss. As it is well accepted that mere causation is not a sufficient ground for liability, corrective justice theorists, as well as others who support negative desert as a criterion for distribution, have to define what will be considered as wrongful or negligent. As explained in Part I, the moral evaluation of a given activity as negligent is based on an improper balancing of costs and benefits (broadly defined) of the activity. For this reason, we should reject definitions of negligence that ignore the purpose for which the activity was engaged in, the benefits it produces, and the way in which its benefits and burdens are distributed. Similarly, we should reject the Hand formula for its inherent regressive effects and its disregard for distributive considerations and effects on the well-being and welfare of the affected individuals.

In defending this view, three insights are combined: an understanding of negligence law as balancing the competing claims of individuals for liberty and security; an understanding of negligence law as balancing the underlying tension between self-regard and altruism; and a progressive and somewhat materialistic understanding of desert and moral agency as influenced by the agent's means and practical ability to choose.

(a) Balancing security against liberty, and self-interest against altruism. Egalitarianism can justify a different moral evaluation of the same act committed by two different individuals based on their prior holdings. Such a conclusion can be supported by the understanding of negligence law as the arena in which the law balances competing claims for security and liberty and prescribes the desired balance between altruism and self-interest. The core of negligence law is the balancing of the interest of potential victims to be secure from harm and the interest of potential tortfeasors' in their freedom of action.[29] Built into this analysis is the idea that a restriction on liberty which may be justified in order to further certain worthy goals (such as preventing a significant decrease in the security of potential victims), may be unjustified to further other goals (such as preventing an insignificant decrease in the security of potential victims). Similarly, a certain reduction of the security of potential victims can be justified if it serves some goal deemed worthy enough (primarily ensuring a certain minimal degree of liberty to potential injurers), but not if it serves less worthy goals (such as the prevention of an insignificant decrease in the liberty of potential injurers).

But if liberty and security are what we should be concerned about, surely the extent to which the applicable legal rule will in fact affect security and liberty is relevant, if not crucial. The intuition in Example 1 and Example 2 (that George is not negligent for not spending $600 in order to prevent the loss to Elaine, whereas Elaine would be deemed negligent in the opposite case) is formed precisely because we think that the burden that should be imposed on the two should be substantively equal. The law of negligence calls for a compromise between one's natural inclination toward self-regarding behaviour and the requirement to take the interests of others into account. The moral judgment of a given course of action as negligent is due when the agent fails to take appropriate account of the interests of others.[30] The morality of negligence law is this: individuals live in society and interact with each

29 This proposition is often presented more broadly as reflecting the law of torts in general. See e.g., Keating, *supra* note 3, pp. 196–7, 202–3; Calnan, *supra* note 3, p. 588.

30 See e.g., Stephen G. Gilles, 'On Determining Negligence: Hand Formula Balancing, the Reasonable Person Standard, and the Jury', 54 *Vand L Rev* (2001) 813, p. 834; Richard

other. Some of these interactions result in harm to some people from the activities of moral agents. A balance must be struck between the agent's liberty and the security of others. The reality of coexistence entails that not all harms that individuals incur from moral agents should be compensated for. It also entails that moral agents have to take into account the interests of others while acting. Negligence law is the forum in which individuals are required to balance their self-interests and altruism. The moral evaluation of deviation from the acceptable standard of care is a determination that the agent failed to consider the interests of others adequately. Since individuals should enjoy equal rights and equal treatment, they can expect that the assessment of their acts as negligent (or not) will respect their interests to the same extent that it respects the interests of others.

The previous section explained this expectation as a matter of horizontal equality; here, vertical equality is at the centre. The determination of whether the agent's activity was negligent should be based on a balance of equities. A conclusion of negligence means that the agent has failed to accord enough weight to the interests of others. In order to reach such a conclusion, it is vital to see what burdens and benefits are created by the activity and what burdens and benefits are created by an alternative course of action. Imposing risks on others is justified if an alternative course of action (that prevents the risk) will burden the agent excessively. True, an agent is required to take into account the interests of others. Yet, he is also morally entitled to take into account his own interests. Since we seek equal treatment, the burdens and benefits of the activity should be compared. There is no dispute that individuals must bear a small loss from the activity of moral agents, if requiring the agent to prevent the harm to others that would result from his activity would excessively impair his freedom. For this reason, those who choose to fly without taking their small children and even those who choose not to bring children into the world cannot prevent parents from flying with their children or get compensation for their loss of convenience. Parents who fly with their children are not considered negligent, since they did not fail in a balancing of the competing interests by according greater weight to their interest to fly with their children than to the interests of the other passengers to fly undisturbed.

The common-sense understanding of the reasonable person standard is that a reasonable person will take precautions when those precautions will prevent a significant loss to others and do not constrain the person's liberty excessively. Negligence law can be viewed as one manifestation of the golden rule 'Do unto others as you would have them do unto you'. A common justification of the Hand formula is that it treats individuals equally: individuals will prevent accidents to their own property only if it is cost-effective; therefore, they should be required to prevent losses to others also only if it is cost-effective.[31] This will be referred to as 'the single-owner test'. But the fallacy in the argument is obvious. A person who does not prevent a loss of 600 to herself that she can prevent by spending 900

W. Wright, 'The Standards of Care in Negligence Law', in *Philosophical Foundations of Tort Law*, *supra* note 1, pp. 249, 256.

31 See Stephen G. Gilles, 'The Invisible Hand Formula', 80 *Va L Rev* (1994)1015, pp. 1034–5.

in precautions is left with that loss of 600. A person who does not prevent a loss of 600 to her neighbour by not spending 900 is externalizing that loss to another rather than bearing it as she would under the single-owner test. It follows that if only the absolute monetary value is considered, a regime of strict liability rather than negligence better serves the logic of the single-owner test.[32] More importantly, the disregard shown by standard economic analysis for the diminishing marginal utility of money further undermines the persuasiveness of the single-owner test. When the parties' extents of disutility from bearing the loss are compared, the result will often differ from the dictates of cost-effective analysis. Let us consider a single-owner test of the respective disutility of the two parties in Example 1. Let us assume that George will suffer the same degree of disutility Elaine suffers from the use of the cheap coal. This disutility is that created by the loss of 5 per cent of one individual's high income (Elaine's in Example 1), and it is incurred in order to prevent the disutility resulting from a loss of 60 per cent of one individual's low income (George's in Example 1). A single-owner test of utilities would lead George *not* to shift to the more expensive coal.

Again, a single-owner test suggests that on grounds of fairness, George should bear a disutility created by the loss of 5 per cent of *his* income.[33] Were this approach adopted, George would have to compensate Elaine with a damages award of 50. Note the following two points: First, in these circumstances, egalitarianism and fairness prescribe different results. The former opposes even this kind of modified compensation, whereas the latter supports it. Second, and more importantly, if compensation is due, it is due based on grounds of distributive, rather than corrective, justice. George would have to compensate Elaine not because he was wrong to prefer his interests over hers, but because fairness (arguably) mandates that despite the fact that George acted in a justified manner, he still has to bear the costs of his justified decision. Grounds of responsibility, and not only the monetary result, are important here. Liability in negligence is based on the moral evaluation that the actor acted wrongfully. By contrast, other grounds of liability, mainly strict liability, are based on an idea that the agent has acted properly but should bear the costs of her justified activity.[34] Not only the fairer distribution of wealth but also the symbolic aspects of negligence liability strongly support including egalitarianism in the standard of care analysis.

(b) Moral agency, means, and needs. The call to reformulate the concept of reasonableness to be egalitarian-sensitive is inspired by the view that the satisfaction of basic needs is a necessary condition for the individual's ability to develop and exercise agency. Accordingly, there is no room for any desert-based moral assessment

---

32 For a critique of the single-owner test, see John Rawls, *A Theory of Justice* (rev. edn, Cambridge, 1999), pp. 23–4; Ronald M. Dworkin, 'Is Wealth a Value?', 9 *J Legal Stud* (1980) 191, p. 200.

33 The analysis in the text should be refined. What matters for purposes of utility is wealth and not merely income. A loss of 5 per cent from a high income creates less disutility than a loss of 5 per cent from a low income. This, however, can be partially overcome by some reduction of the amount George would have to pay Elaine.

34 Cooter, *supra* note 9, p. 1524; Keating, *supra* note 3, pp. 200–202.

of the agent's behaviour if her basic needs have not been fulfilled, something that impairs her free will. As Wojciech Sadurski has stated, meeting basic needs should be a precondition to the operation of desert as a criterion for distribution, since the failure to satisfy those needs prevents the needy from becoming the subjects of other principles of justice: '[Q]uestions of desert do not even arise where basic needs are not satisfied.'[35] A similar line of thought might call for giving priority to social rights over political rights[36] or to recognizing a criminal law defence based on underprivileged social background.[37] The logic behind such an approach is clear: agency is about the ability to choose, and in order to be able to choose, the agent's basic needs must be fulfilled.

The argument defended here, however, seems to go beyond the approach represented by Sadurski. Presumably, once Sadurski's threshold for the desert criterion of fulfilling basic needs is met, the criterion operates without regard for egalitarian considerations. The argument takes the logic of that approach one (significant) step further. Whenever we evaluate in moral terms the worthiness of an agent's activity, the effects of that activity on the fulfilment of the basic needs of all relevant parties should be taken into account. For the purposes of deciding whether the activity is negligent or not, the disutility it causes to all affected parties is an important (although not a conclusive) factor.

It follows that even a corrective justice approach that is based on notions of negative desert should, when properly understood, take into account the distributive effects of the relevant negligence rule and the parties' prior holdings in the moral evaluation of the worthiness of an agent's activity. At first glance, this conclusion is surprising, given the distinction corrective justice theory mandates between action and status. Yet the approach defended here conforms to the requirement that an agent's activity should dictate the moral evaluation of her duty to compensate the victim. Egalitarianism uses the parties' prior status not as an independent reason for redistributing wealth, but rather as a vital component in the moral evaluation of the activity itself. It paints the activity as negligent or not based on the extent to which the agent has properly balanced her self-interest against the interests of others. It does so by calling to our attention the consequences for the well-being of the parties of burdening one side with precaution costs or the other side with accident costs. It teaches us that we are entitled to expect a greater degree of altruism from the better-off than from the worse-off.[38] One is required to protect another's interests only up to a certain point, and in deciding where this point is, it is essential to take into account the consequences of alternative courses of action for both parties. These consequences hinge on the parties' prior holdings.

---

35 Wojciech Sadurski, *Giving Desert Its Due: Social Justice and Legal Theory* (Dordrecht, 1985), p. 169.

36 See, e.g., Rhoda Howard, 'The Full-Belly Thesis: Should Economic Rights Take Priority Over Civil and Political Rights? Evidence from Sub-Saharan Africa', 5 *Hum Rts Q* (1983) 467, p. 469.

37 Richard Delgado, '"Rotten Social Background": Should the Criminal Law Recognize a Defense of Severe Environmental Deprivation?', 3 *Law & Ineq J* (1985) 9.

38 Eyal Zamir, 'The Inverted Hierarchy of Contract Interpretation and Supplementation', 97 *Colum L Rev* (1997) 1710, pp. 1783–4.

Arguably, the interests of all involved could be better served by requiring the potential tortfeasor to incur precaution costs when the expense is cost-justified, and to reimburse him for his expense if he is needy. However, such a solution is not practical. Reimbursement from potential victims is impossible due to transaction costs. A more progressive tax and transfer system would fail to reimburse accurately due to administrative costs, and is in any event, not likely to arise due to public choice pressure. The claim made by Louis Kaplow and Steven Shavell that progressive redistribution would be achieved more efficiently by taxation than by changing the legal rules is disputed on many grounds, including on the basis of insights taken from behavioural law and economics and a real-politics approach. From a moral perspective, we are left with the truism that as long as society does not create an effective and just procedure to reimburse the needy who expend cost-effective precaution costs to prevent losses to others, society cannot hold those who fail to incur this cost as negligent, given the financial and symbolic consequences of holding such defendants negligent.

III. Standard or Duty?

It is yet to be determined at which stage egalitarianism should come into the picture: at the stage of determining the existence of a duty of care or at the stage of examining the standard of care. The desert-based and equality-based justifications of egalitarianism show a strong preference toward incorporating egalitarianism into the standard of care analysis. In order to give full weight to both equality and notions of fault, the standard of care analysis should be reformulated to reflect egalitarian concerns, and this should be based on the distinction between excuses (operating at the duty stage) and justification (operating at the standard stage) as grounds for not imposing liability.

A common understanding of the duty of care element of the tort of negligence views it as a mechanism for restricting the potential liability of negligent actors. According to this understanding, the duty stage responds to the question of whether we should impose liability on a defendant, assuming she was negligent. The existence of a duty is rejected when policy considerations weigh against imposing liability, *even though* the defendant was negligent.[39] These policy considerations do not render the defendant's activity non-negligent. Thus, the duty of care serves as a reason to *excuse* the defendant from liability.

Philosophers distinguish between excuses and justifications as different types of reasons for absolving individuals from liability.[40] While this dichotomy works usually at the level of defences (which negate liability that is otherwise established), it is not limited to that realm alone. More broadly, the dichotomy implies a distinction between wrongful actions and legitimate actions. Quite simply a justified action is one that is not wrongful and therefore is legitimate. Society (or whoever is making the relevant moral judgment about the activity in question) would not seek to prohibit

39 See Ch. 6 below.

40 See, e.g., John L. Austin, *A Plea for Excuses*, in James O. Urmson & Geoffrey J. Warnock (eds), *Philosophical Papers* (2nd edn, Oxford, 1970), p. 175.

such an action and would even sometimes seek to encourage it. The agent's course of action is therefore justified. A classic example of justification in tort is the defence of necessity. The starving mountain-climber is encouraged to break into the cabin and take refuge from the storm, despite his activity's violation of the sanctity of private property. Criminal law likewise recognizes situations of necessity and self-defence as justified and legitimate activities. By contrast, excuses are based on the idea that the defendant's action was wrongful. Society would rather the action not occur. Nonetheless, liability is not imposed because we think that it would be unfair to hold the agent liable for his wrongful action. The classic example in criminal law of excuse is the defence of duress.[41] In tort, the 'defence' of *novus actus interveniens* works similarly as an excuse: the intervention of a third party does not make the defendant's activity legitimate, rather it provides an excuse for not being held accountable for what she did.

Seen through this prism, there are two different grounds for not imposing liability on a defendant in negligence litigation. The defendant might be released from liability simply because she was not negligent. In such a case, her activity is legitimate and therefore justified. As noted in Part I, the purpose of the standard of care is to distinguish between activities deemed wrongful and those deemed legitimate by society. By contrast, negligent behaviour, which is wrongful, might not trigger liability if the activity is excused, through non-recognition of the existence of a duty of care based on policy considerations.

It is no doubt possible to adhere to a standard of care that is indifferent to egalitarianism and yet still release the defendant from liability based on egalitarian considerations at the duty stage. However, such a strategy misses the moral intuition presented and defended in Part II. If indeed the standard of care strikes a balance between the interest of potential defendants in liberty and the interest of potential plaintiffs in security, and if indeed the burdens of taking precautions and of bearing the accident costs are influenced by the prior holdings of the parties, it follows that the same failure to take precautions might be viewed as wrongful in certain circumstances but legitimate in others. As explained in Part II, we should not really expect from a defendant to expend all of her meagre wealth to prevent a small loss to the well-off. For the reasons explained above, such a failure simply is not faulty or wrongful. If one accepts this view, one should support, both analytically and morally, the incorporation of egalitarianism into the stage of standard of care analysis: analytically, because the standard stage is the correct one for dealing with activities we deem legitimate, and morally, because it is unfair to tarnish the defendant with the label of negligent activity, even though we release her from liability. Symbolically, there is a difference between the proposition 'You acted rightly and hence bear no liability' and the proposition 'Despite your wrongful action we do not hold you liable'. In addition to being more correct and just, the former proposition is more empowering: rejecting liability at the duty stage can be interpreted as an act of mercy or charity on the part of society toward the disadvantaged. In contrast, determining that there was no deviation from the expected standard of care interprets the denial of

41 See George P. Fletcher, *Rethinking Criminal Law* (1978), § 10.4.2.

liability as a matter of the right of the disadvantaged to equal treatment and respect and to share in society's basic goods.

IV. Reformulating the Standard of Care

A. The Role of Egalitarianism in Standard of Care Analysis

1. The Analysis in General A finding of negligence is based on a cost-benefit analysis that is both approximate and broad. The analysis is approximate in the sense that neither the actor nor the court conducts the cost-benefit analysis rigorously, and instead do it intuitively most of the time. This means that technical rules, a rigorous model, and exact valuation and interpersonal quantification of utility or welfare levels are neither required not assumed to be feasible. Rather, the courts should take into account rough evaluations of disutility that are based in part on the affected parties' holdings and status in society, in so far as these can be assessed by the courts.

The analysis is broad in that it takes into account many factors, both welfare- and non-welfare-based. It is also consequential, in that the normative evaluation is based, to a large extent (but not solely), on the consequences of the activity. The test respects *moral agency* in that the evaluation of the actor's behaviour derives from the actor's choice regarding how to act based on knowledge available to her prior to taking action. In evaluating whether the imposition of risk by the defendant was negligent or not, the court must weigh the reasons for expecting the defendant to bear the burden of taking precautions, against the reasons for expecting potential victims to bear the burden of not being compensated for their losses.

2. The General Role of the Egalitarian Concern in Standard of Care Analysis One relevant (yet not conclusive) consideration in this assessment is the parties' relative ability to bear these losses. There should be a lesser expectation from a poor than from a rich defendant to incur big expenses to prevent harms to others if those expected to be harmed are less likely to suffer greater negative consequences from the losses. Similarly, there should be a greater expectation from a rich than from a poor defendant to take precautions to protect others from harm, since the disutility to the former from the burden would be small and the loss to others would create significant disutility if no compensation is awarded to the victim. In estimating disutility, the absolute magnitude of the losses and their proportion to the respective holdings of the parties (both before and after the loss is borne) should be taken into account. By considering the proportion of the loss to the parties' situation prior to bearing the loss, weight is given to disutility due to the endowment effect.[42] Greater weight should be accorded to disutility caused by diminishing marginal utility, which is determined by the parties' remaining holdings. When the identities of potential victims is known in advance, their expected disutility should be taken into account by the defendant and by the courts. When the victim's identity is unknown

42 See Section B1(a) below.

in advance, the average disutility from bearing the loss should be compared with the actual defendant's disutility.[43]

3. Balancing Egalitarianism Against Other Considerations In deciding whether to adopt a certain rule, courts should not rely solely on the egalitarian consideration. First, courts should also consider efficiency. Second, courts should evaluate the legitimacy of the competing claims of the parties according to other considerations, some distributive and some not. For example, the fairness consideration – who stood to benefit from the risk-creating activity – is an important factor in the evaluation of reasonableness of the risk that was created. The social value of the activity and the actor's motives should also be taken into account. No rule of thumb can be given to resolve the question of the relative weight that the egalitarian consideration should be given in relation to other considerations.

4. The Multifaceted and Contradictory Nature of the Egalitarian Concern Identifying the dictates of egalitarianism raises factual conceptual and normative questions. The more egalitarianism is concerned with issues of power and status that defy monetary valuation, the thornier the determination becomes. These difficulties influence the egalitarian standard of care analysis as follows: First, with respect to standard of care analysis, due to the inherently relative, narrow, and contextual nature of litigation, these difficulties are easier to deal with than, for example, duty of care issues. Second, the more courts stick to narrow conceptions of welfare (which are more wealth-oriented) in standard of care analysis, the less acute these problems become. Third, although at times the egalitarian consideration will have no effect in the courts' determination of negligence, it does not follow that courts should not take egalitarian considerations into account when possible. Fourth, many determinations of relative disadvantage are value-laden and contested. However, this should not prevent courts from making such determinations.

5. The Roles of Egalitarian Considerations Outside Standard of Care Analysis When the risk imposition was deemed to be reasonable *ex ante* (based also on average disutility) but resulted, in fact, in a loss to the plaintiff whose disutility is greater than the defendant's disutility in bearing precaution costs, egalitarian considerations might justify imposing a duty to compensate the victim.[44] However, such a duty cannot be grounded in a finding of negligence, since when the risk-creating activity is examined *ex ante*, as it should be, the defendant did not impose an unreasonable risk. Similarly, non-egalitarian results that are produced by compensation rules may have to be repaired by changing the compensation rules. This question, however, exceeds the matter of the proper delineation of the standard of care analysis.

To conclude, egalitarian considerations should serve as one in a range of considerations in determinations of reasonableness. This consideration is almost always relevant but seldom conclusive. The weight that should be accorded to it

43 See Section B below.

44 Such a result might also be supported by non-egalitarian considerations such as fairness.

varies with the context, as does the extent to which it can guide courts. The parties' respective ability to bear the loss should be one consideration in deciding who should bear that loss, and an important one in evaluating the morality of the actor's behaviour.

B. Comparing Disutility: The Difficulties and Guidelines for Courts

Egalitarian reformulation of standard of care analysis advocates a comparison of the parties' disutility from bearing the loss as one consideration in deciding whether the defendant's activity was negligent. The disutility to the actual defendant of bearing the loss should be compared with the average disutility to the typical victim. This test raises two difficulties. First, measuring utility and disutility is impossible. Therefore, an egalitarian-oriented court should develop some guidelines, or proxies, for measuring disutility. Second, it is necessary to explain why the test takes into account the disutility to the *average* victim (as opposed to that to the actual victim or to the below-average victim), but the disutility to the *actual* (rather than the average) defendant. This is related to the distinction between liability rules and compensation rules as sources of non-egalitarian results.

1. Proxies for Disutility *(a) In general.* Loss causes disutility. The absolute magnitude of the loss can serve as a proxy for the resulting disutility. However, absolute magnitude cannot act as the sole proxy for that disutility. Diminishing marginal utility suggests that the individual's remaining wealth after bearing the loss is relevant as a proxy for disutility. The endowment effect, according to which individuals give added value to endowments they possess simply by virtue of possessing them, suggests that one's holdings prior to the loss affect one's disutility from the loss. This suggests that one's holdings prior to the loss and the proportion of the loss are relevant as proxies for the disutility. What is important to understand is that no single proxy is sufficient in itself.

(b) Proportion. Seemingly, a good proxy for disutility would be a comparison of the proportions of the losses of the parties (measured in dollars) to their respective wealth prior to the loss. The sum of the precaution costs should be divided by the total assets of the defendant. The plaintiff's expected loss should be divided by the total assets of the plaintiff. A finding of negligence should follow if the former figure is lower than the latter one. The appeal of this test is that in theory it is simple, it is easy to apply, and it enjoys a 'scientific' pedigree. It leads to clear results and is rigorous, and it seems to exclude judicial discretion and bias. It also seems to respond well, and in a comprehensive manner, to the underlying difficulty of the regressive nature of a cost-benefit analysis that compares losses of wealth. Such a rule, however, leads to undesirable results from an egalitarian perspective, since it does not reflect accurately enough the disutility caused by diminishing marginal utility. A proportional comparison does not solve the problem of unequal burdens caused by diminishing marginal utility of money; it merely alleviates it. The reason is that a larger proportional loss of one's wealth might still inflict a lesser burden on the bearer's well being, given the magnitude of her remaining wealth. For example, a billionaire who loses 90 per cent of her wealth would still fare better than a person

with an average income who loses 50 per cent of his wealth. The latter might fare better than the poor person who loses 10 per cent of her wealth. It seems, then, that if we are concerned with the magnitude of the burden that the loss causes to the bearer, what should interest us is not the percentage of the loss relative to one's prior holdings, but, rather, the effect of the loss on the remaining wealth of the parties.[45]

(c) Remaining wealth. Given the inability of the proportion test to solve the problem of the diminishing marginal utility of money, one might opt for a rule that allocates the loss to the more affluent party. Such a rule would disregard proportion and would instead compare the parties' absolute wealth after the tortious loss has been taken into account. The outcome would deny a victim compensation if, after the loss, his wealth were to exceed the defendant's wealth. Adopting remaining wealth as the only proxy for disutility, however, would not suffice, since it ignores the endowment effect as a source of disutility. What matters to people is not only how much they have presently, but also how much they have in comparison to what they had in the past, how much they lost, and how abrupt the loss was. Abrupt loss of wealth imposes two kinds of disutility. One resulting disutility is due to the *temporal aspect of the loss*. Abrupt losses negatively affect one's ability to plan one's life. They are harmful to stability and predictability. The other kind of disutility derives from the *magnitude of the loss*. Individuals have subjective and relative concepts of welfare. They get used to living at a certain level of welfare and compare what they have with what they had and lost. Therefore, *A*, who is left with more than what *B* has, might still suffer more disutility if her loss is much greater than *B*'s loss. For this reason, ignoring initial wealth altogether is problematic. It is too burdensome on the rich and is morally doubtful. Under a remaining-wealth test, a defendant with an average income would not be required to spend even one dollar, even if by spending this she could prevent a loss of millions of dollars to the plaintiff, provided the plaintiff would be left with more money than the defendant after bearing the loss.

(d) Pecuniary loss of the average victim. This test compares, as does the traditional application of the Hand formula, the marginal costs and benefits of the activity *measured in dollars*. The test differs from the Hand formula in that it calculates the expected loss of the activity according to the loss of the average victim, even if the typical potential victim is likely to be below average. Note that average figures are already calculated by both potential tortfeasors and courts[46] whenever the identity of typical victims cannot be assessed in advance. The difference is that even when the victim's identity can be established in advance, potential tortfeasors will have to take into account the expected loss to the average, rather than the actual below-average, victim. This will reduce (but not eliminate) the incentive to channel risks to the poor, and will at least reduce the regressive effect that compensation rules create.

---

45 Economists face similar problems when trying to determine the appropriate distributive weighting factor to account for different income levels. For a suggestion to consider the 'diminishing marginal utility of utility', see David W. Pearce & Christopher A. Nash, *The Social Appraisal of Projects: A Text in Cost-Benefit Analysis* (London, 1981), p. 33.

46 Assuming courts make any use at all in practice of the Hand formula, either rigorously or intuitively.

Consider the following example:

Example 3. J.R. has to decide where to build a refinery. The choices are Poortown and Richtown. A given safety device would cost $800,000 and would decrease the probability of an explosion by half (from 0.2 to 0.1). An explosion would cause damage of $7 million in Poortown, but $10 million in Richtown. (The difference in the expected loss is due to both the value of the property and future lost earnings.) The cost of prevention is $800,000; the savings in expected loss from installing the device are $700,000 in Poortown, but $1 million in Richtown.[47]

According to the average-loss test, the court would determine the expected loss of the accident to be $850,000 (the average of the expected losses in Richtown ($1 million) and Poortown ($0.7 million). Therefore, J.R. would be considered negligent if he did not spend $800,000 in precaution costs. Under the assumption that compensation law still adheres to the principle of *restitutio ad integrum*, J.R. would prefer to build the refinery in Poortown, bear the expected loss of $0.7 million, and not incur the $0.8 million precaution costs. However, if the risk materializes, J.R. will have to compensate the victims for their losses.[48] Note that under this outcome, the efficient result has been achieved. J.R. did not prevent a loss of $0.7 million by spending $0.8 million in precaution costs. The difference is distributive. J.R., rather than the victims, bears the costs of this unavoidable accident. In this respect, the effect of the rule is akin to that achieved under a strict liability regime.

However, the loss-of-the-average-victim test will not be always sufficient for protecting the interests of the poor. Let us change the numbers in the previous example, so that the expected loss in Poortown is $0.2 million rather than $0.7 million. In this case, the expected loss that courts would take into account would be $0.6 million (the average of the expected loss in Richtown ($1 million) and Poortown ($0.2 million)). Assuming precaution costs remain at $0.8 million, J.R. would not be negligent if he avoids incurring those costs. Assuming the principle of *restitutio ad integrum*, J.R. would build the refinery and would not have to pay for the loss caused if the risk were to materialize. While in theory, J.R. might decide to build the refinery in Richtown (and, in such a case, the result of not investing in precautions is also inefficient), we have a reason to believe that it would still be built in Poortown.[49] In this case, J.R. would not invest in precaution costs and the residents of Poortown would not be compensated for their losses. A rule awarding average loss (rather than actual loss) in the event that liability is established would not be relevant here, since compensation requires a finding of liability and J.R. is not negligent under these

47 The first three examples are analysed under a rule of negligence, despite the fact that they might give rise to a nuisance cause of action.

48 By contrast, under the traditional version of the Hand formula, J.R. would be considered negligent if he were to build the refinery in Richtown without investing in loss reduction, but not if he were to build the refinery in Poortown without such an investment. He would build the refinery in Poortown, and its residents would become even poorer, in the amount of their increased expected loss ($700,000), which would not be compensated for.

49 Among the reasons supporting such a conclusion are: the political power of Richtown residents to prevent the building of a refinery there; their ability to bribe J.R.; J.R.'s fear that courts might err and impose liability on him; and that it is better to build the refinery in Poortown, due to economic incentives external to tort law such as cheaper labour.

figures.[50] The discussion so far has demonstrated that the loss-of-the-average-victim test, although reducing the regressive effects entailed by the Hand formula, does not reduce them enough. It has also demonstrated a difficult result from a distributive perspective: the more disadvantaged the potential victim, the less she is protected by such a test.

(e) Pecuniary loss of a victim with the same status as the particular defendant. Under such a test – the 'same-status-victim test' – the precaution costs measured in dollars should be compared to the expected loss as measured in dollars of a same-status victim. To better understand the test and its limits, let us consider the following example.

Example 4. Installing a special device in the defendants' cars reduces by 1 per cent the incidence of skidding accidents that result in a total loss of the plaintiffs' cars. There are five types of drivers, all of whom are both potential plaintiffs and potential defendants:

Type of victim	Magnitude of loss if accident happens (car's value)	Adjusted accident cost per type of plaintiff (1% of car's value)	Proportion of all cars that are of this type	Expected loss per group (assuming there are 100 cars)	Overall expected accident cost per group
Very rich	300,000	3,000	0.1	30,000	300
Rich	100,000	1,000	0.2	20,000	200
Average	30,000	300	0.5	15,000	150
Poor	10,000	100	0.15	1,500	15
Very poor	4,000	40	0.05	200	2
TOTAL	–	–	1	66,700	667

Under the traditional application of the Hand formula, the accident cost would be calculated as 667. Bear in mind that the main part of this amount is to be attributed to the cars of the rich and very rich. Under the traditional application of the Hand formula, all potential tortfeasors would be treated alike. If, for example, precaution costs (the price of installing this device) are 500, all drivers will be considered negligent if they do not install it, both the owners of cars worth 4,000 and those with cars worth 300,000. Conversely, if the precaution costs are 800, no driver will be considered negligent if he or she did not install the device.

Under the adjusted-accident-cost rule, the expected cost of the accident is determined on the basis of the defendant's status. It would be calculated under the

50 This analysis implies that in order to prevent completely regressive results, tort law must move to a strict liability regime as well as provide, as accompaniment to such a regime, equalization of the awards given as compensation.

assumption that all drivers own cars with the same value as that of the defendant. Hence, each driver's accident cost is simply 1 per cent of the value of his or her car. Accordingly, if precaution costs are 500 or 800, only the rich and the very rich drivers will be considered negligent if they do not install the device.

There are two problems with this solution, however. First, it might not afford enough protection to the interests of the very poor. Assume that the defendant is the average-status driver, whose accident costs are 300. If precaution costs are 350, the shift from the traditional Hand formula to the adjusted one would result in a reduction of the driver's liability. It is true that he would not be liable toward the rich and very rich; however, he would also not be liable toward the poor and the very poor. The second problem is that the adjusted rule might seem too harsh toward the better-off. Recall that a finding of negligence entails not only a duty to compensate, but also a condemning moral evaluation of the actor's behaviour. The adjusted rule miscalculates the risk the actor created, making it more significant than it really is. The real risk he created is lower than that calculated: in reality, not all cars are worth 300,000; most of them are worth much less. On the other hand, the phenomenon of the diminishing marginal utility of money lends support to such a calculation for two reasons. First, the burden the better-off have to bear is not so heavy given their holdings. Second, the small financial loss that the better-off injurers impose on the poor victims might bring about greater disutility than would a great financial loss borne by better-off victims. For example, the very poor might not be able to insure their cars, and of course, the less money one has, the greater the relative disutility from small losses.

This test has several advantages. To begin with, it reflects well egalitarian morality: the rich are required to spend more in precaution costs than the poor. Note, however, that given the anonymity of the potential victims, the test does not reflect the flip-side of egalitarian morality, namely, that one should spend more in precaution in order to prevent a loss to the poor rather than to the rich (given the larger ensuing disutility from the loss to the poor). All potential victims, poor and rich, enjoy greater protection from a rich defendant and lesser protection from a poor defendant. The second advantage of the test is that it is easy to employ intuitively. One does not have to calculate the exact expected loss in order to understand that while a demand to spend 500 in precautions in a car worth 4,000 is excessive, such a demand is not excessive for a car worth 300,000.

(f) Conclusion. The discussion so far has revealed the well-known difficulty of computing disutility. None of the proxies suggested above is sufficient in itself to adequately advance egalitarianism. The disutility of a loss derives significantly from one's remaining holdings after bearing the loss. It is also influenced by the magnitude of the loss and its proportion of the actor's holdings prior to the loss. In evaluating reasonableness, we are influenced by three notions: efficiency (big losses should be prevented by expending small amounts); the diminishing marginal utility of money (the party who would be left with more wealth after bearing the loss should bear that loss since her disutility is smaller); and the endowment effect (the party who will be left with more wealth might still suffer more disutility if she loses a larger proportion of her wealth). Of these three notions, only the second reflects egalitarianism. The more one leans

toward egalitarianism, the more one will emphasize the weight of diminishing marginal utility in assessing disutility. There is no need to determine the priority and weight that should be given to the suggested tests, since courts make determinations about negligence intuitively. Courts should consider disutility (and not absolute magnitude of loss measured in dollars) as one relevant factor in evaluating a defendant's conduct, and in so doing, they should compare the burden to the defendant given her status and holdings and the burden to the average typical victim given his or her status. Since in many situations, the court (and the defendant) do not know the identities of the potential victims prior to the materialization of the risk, the egalitarian concern boils down to an examination of whether the actual defendant – the actual creator of the risk – is disadvantaged or well-off and, accordingly, take into account the magnitude of the disutility to her from incurring precaution costs. Whenever the identity or socio-economic status of potential victims can be identified in advance, their expected disutility from bearing the loss should be compared to that of the actual defendant. Whatever proxies are used, several theoretical difficulties about the identification of those whose disutility has to be compared should be addressed.

2. Average Victim versus Actual Defendant The model calls for comparing the disutility to the average typical victim with that to the actual defendant. In what follows, four issues are dealt with: First, why does the model choose for the disutility comparison the typical victim's disutility as opposed to that of the actual victim? Second, why does the model choose, for purposes of comparison, the disutility to the average victim rather than the disutility to potential victims who are below average (whose disutility is higher), which would afford better protection to the interests of the disadvantaged? Third, why does the model choose the disutility to the actual, rather than to the average, defendant? Fourth, should the defendant be liable to the victim when the defendant's disutility is higher than that of the average victim, but lower than that of the actual victim? Conversely, should the defendant be not liable to the victim when the defendant's disutility is lower than that of the average victim, but higher than that of the actual victim?

(a) Average victim versus actual victim. The model takes, for purposes of comparison, the *ex ante* average disutility to potential victims. In theory, the disutility to any potential victim who might bear the loss should be calculated, averaged, and then compared with the actual defendant's disutility from incurring precaution costs. The support for the *ex ante* average disutility test derives from the moral aspect of negligence liability and the requirement of foreseeability. The problem of the lottery-like effect of tort law and the lack of necessary connection between one's *ex ante* culpability or the magnitude of the risk that one imposes and the magnitude of resulting liability was largely commented upon and is indeed problematic.[51] This difficulty, however, is broader than the one dealt with

51 Christopher H. Schroeder, 'Corrective Justice and Liability for Increasing Risks', 37 *UCLA L Rev* (1990) 439; Patrick S. Atiyah, *The Damages Lottery* (Oxford, 1997); Jeremy Waldron, 'Moments of Carelessness and Massive Loss', in *Philosophical Foundations of Tort Law*, *supra* note 1, p. 387.

here. Within the negligence framework, the moral evaluation of whether the risk imposed was reasonable should always be based on an *ex ante* examination. If I drive 200 miles per hour and am lucky enough to cause only a scratch to someone's old car, I may not argue that I was not negligent since the resulting harm that I caused was in fact outweighed by the benefit I derived from driving quickly. The court would justly judge the *ex ante* risk I imposed, which included serious harm to life, limb, and property. The model suggested here maintains that in evaluating expected loss, the expected disutility should be taken into account. In the same example, the expected average disutility to victims from my reckless driving exceeds my disutility from driving at the normal speed, even if I am poor. Therefore, the moral evaluation of the risk I imposed is that it is unreasonable, and this conclusion should not change even if I happened to cause property loss to someone so rich that the actual disutility to her from that loss is less than the disutility to the poor driver of driving slowly (for example, driving quickly in order to get to a job interview that might take the driver out of the ranks of the unemployed and the poor).

(b) Average versus less than average victim. To what extent further allowance should be given to the interests of the disadvantaged under conditions of imperfect information? The question essentially is whether in comparing a defendant's disutility from incurring precaution costs with the unknown victim's disutility from incurring the expected loss, the interests of the average victim, or the below-average victim, should be taken into account. The problem with adopting average figures of victim disutility from bearing accident losses is that it produces actual results that are undesirable from an egalitarian perspective, even though the evaluation process is sensitive to that perspective. When the *average* victim's disutility is higher than the (actual) defendant's disutility, the defendant will be liable, even if the disutility to the *actual* victim is lower than that to the defendant, and vice versa. Such a gap is inevitable if we seek to preserve negligence liability as based on notions of fault. Below, it is suggested how this problem might be solved or alleviated by extending liability beyond the scope of fault and by changing compensation rules. However, modifying the test to include disutility to the below-average victim will not necessarily serve egalitarian concerns.

According to this test, actors would have to take into account a potential disutility that is higher than the average. This means that they would have to take into account the possibility that the victim is disadvantaged. Theoretically, such an approach can be supported by ideas of social responsibility toward the weak, Rawls' difference principle,[52] or ideas similar to the eggshell skull rule. The problem with such an approach is that it might bring about results that are just as undesirable from a distributive perspective as the average disutility test, and perhaps worse. Adopting a higher-than-average disutility test would bring about two contradictory distributive results. It would result in greater transfer of wealth from the average and poor to the very poor, but would also result in a transfer of wealth from the average and poor to the rich and the very rich. Determining what

52 Rawls, *supra* note 32, p. 220.

is the overall distributive effect from adopting a higher-than-average disutility test is not easy. On the one hand, it seems to protect the very poor (and in this sense, it seems to be in accord with Rawls' difference principle). On the other hand, this added protection to the very poor might be too costly in terms of the added burden to the poor. Bear in mind that under existing compensation rules liability results in regressive redistribution of wealth: the wealthier receive a bigger piece from the compensation pie. Therefore, extending the scope of liability, which is the result of adopting a higher-than-average disutility test, would probably result in overall regressive distribution of wealth. Taking further into account the reality that deserving poor victims file fewer suits only exacerbates this problem. Finally, let us remember that from a moral perspective, the average disutility test seems more adequate. After all, a finding of negligence tells us that the actor did not balance properly his interests and the interests of others. Adopting a higher-than-average disutility test would lead to findings of liability in circumstances in which the overall risk to society, given the uncertainty of the victim's identity, seems to be justified.

(c) Actual versus average defendant. The model treats the defendant and plaintiff differently, by comparing the disutility to the actual defendant with the disutility to the average victim. While prior to the accident, the identity of the victim is unknown, the identity of the potential tortfeasor is known. The potential tortfeasor knows her status prior to the activity in question and therefore can make the cost-benefit analysis based on her actual data. The test should take defendants' *actual* disutility, but victims' *average* disutility into account since: (1) the magnitude of precaution costs remains constant across defendants with different holdings; (2) the disutility caused by the burden of incurring precaution costs varies according to defendants' means; (3) the defendant knows, and courts can relatively easily assess, the defendant's means; (4) the moral evaluation of one's activity derives from a comparison of disutility; and (5) the identity of the typical victim is not typically known in advance and the identity of the actual victim is seldom known.

(d) Resolving remaining non-egalitarian results caused by imposing liability. Two sources of non-egalitarian results will remain even under an egalitarian-sensitive standard of care analysis. One is due to the fact that the test compares the defendant's actual disutility with the disutility to the average, rather than actual, victim. The second source of non-egalitarian results derives from the principle of *restitutio ad integrum*, and will be discussed in Chapter 8 below.

The first problem is composed of two problems, which are the mirror images of each other. In one type of case, a defendant who is found to be negligent (partially since his disutility from incurring precaution costs *was outweighed* by the average disutility that the expected loss causes) *in fact incurs greater disutility* from bearing the precaution costs (and the expected loss) than the disutility to the actual victim. This problem might be alleviated by giving courts discretion to reduce the amount to be paid as compensation. Such a solution has been adopted in certain civil law jurisdictions, such as Finland and Sweden. This adjustment rule qualifies the general duty to compensate the victim in full by affording courts the discretion to reduce the damages award based on the defendant's means and on a comparison to the victim's means.[53] In the second type of case, a defendant who is found to be not negligent (partially since his disutility from incurring precaution costs *outweighs* the average disutility that the expected loss causes) *in fact incurs less disutility* from bearing the precaution costs than the disutility to the actual victim from bearing the loss. This is part of the general deficiency of negligence-based liability on fairness grounds. The victim subsidizes the defendant's non-negligent activity. A general shift to strict liability might solve this problem, but with no corresponding change in compensation rules, such a shift will cause other problems from an egalitarian perspective. However, even if one is reluctant to move generally to a strict liability regime, one might think of a rule that would give courts discretion to require the defendant to compensate the victim for her loss, in full or in part. A factor in exercising this discretion should be the egalitarian concern, namely, that the actual victim damaged by the activity is poor or otherwise disadvantaged. What is important to note is that such a duty to compensate is not grounded in notions of negligence. The defendant has to compensate the victim based on notions of distributive justice (fairness and/or egalitarianism), but not on notions of corrective justice and fault. With respect to the symbolic aspects of liability, such liability does not imply culpability on the part of the actor.

V. How Does It Work?

This Part briefly shows how the approach defended and explained above can work in practice. It explores cases of active risk creation and failure to prevent risk by third parties.

A. Active Risk Creation

1. Few Examples *Examples 1 & 2: Using cheap coal.* These examples have been discussed above.[54] While the use of cheap coal by the poor is reasonable, its use by the rich is negligent.

Example 4: Not installing brakes. As explained above, the scope of the driver's duty to install the supplementary braking device would hinge on the ratio between the expense required and the value of car. Therefore, if Jane's car is worth $4,000, her decision not to install the device (which costs $500) would be deemed reasonable, while in the case of Louise, whose car is worth $100,000, the same decision would be deemed negligent. This solution is especially fair since it ameliorates the problem of regressive cross-subsidy, according to which the owners of cars that are low in value currently pay premiums that go disproportionately to cover risks to cars that are high in value.

---

53 See Act of Tort Ch. 2 § 1.2 (Finland) (general adjustment rule); Ch. 2 § 2 (adjusting liability of minors); Ch. 2 § 3 (adjusting liability of the mentally ill, mentally retarded and persons of unsound mind); Ch. 4 § 1 (adjusting employee's liability); Sv. Prop. 1975:12, at 177 (Sweden) (general adjustment rule in Sweden). For a review of these provisions, see Thomas Wilhelmsson, *Critical Studies in Private Law* (1992), pp. 113–24.

54 See Part II.A above.

Example 3: The refinery. As discussed above,[55] the conclusion was that J.R. should be found liable for negligence toward the residents of Poortown. A finding of negligence is important here, as it is contrary to the economist's intuition. The poorer the victim, the less cost-justified the precaution. Economic analysis bluntly suggests channelling risks to the poor, since the resulting loss measured in dollars is the lowest. Here the progressive potential of the egalitarian approach is realized in full. When examined in terms of welfare, the loss to the poorest entails the largest disutility. Hence, courts should adopt what is in practice a strict liability rule regarding risks that are channelled downwards to the disadvantaged, based on their lower expected loss. This would prevent at least the result of regressive subsidy given by the poor to enterprises, a subsidy that results in systematic regressive redistribution of wealth. Therefore, courts should find such risk placement negligent, which they can do by means of a disutility comparison.

Furthermore, as Example 5 will show, an egalitarian-sensitive standard of care analysis might result in progressive redistribution of risk.

Example 5: The refinery II. Assume that J.R.'s refinery has to be built and that the only two possible locations are Richtown and Poortown. Moderate protection to the disadvantaged would require a finding of negligence wherever the refinery is built. This would still result in the refinery being built in Poortown. However, a truly progressive court would, based on a comparison of disutility, find only the building of the refinery in Richtown as reasonable.[56] In such a case, negligence law gives J.R. a strong incentive to locate the refinery in Richtown, and one of two things would happen. If negotiations are impossible, the residents of Richtown will bear the loss. What is important here is that the residents of Poortown will not bear any loss, and given the assumption that tort law generally under-compensates for losses, this is a desirable result.[57] If negotiations are possible, the residents of Richtown might bribe both J.R. and the residents of Poortown to build (or move) the refinery to Poortown. In such a case, a progressive redistribution of wealth is possible.[58]

Example 6: A lawyer's liability toward an unrepresented party. Jane is a lawyer representing a lender. She drafts a given transaction as a conditional sale according to which the borrower sells his house with an option to buy it within

---

55 See Example 3, and text accompanying notes 47–50 above.

56 A similar question was debated between Professor Doug Kysar and Professors Henderson and Twerski in the context of design defect in product liability and the reasonable alternative design test. Kysar's approach would allow a finding of liability for a product which minimizes the overall risk but distributes it unequally on women. Henderson and Twerski reject such an approach, and would allow, at best, a finding that the producer of the alternative product – which distributes the somewhat bigger aggregated risk equally among men and women – is not liable. See Restatement (Third) of Torts: Products Liability, s. 2(b) (1998); Douglas A. Kysar, 'The Expectations of Consumers', 103 *Colum LR* (2003) 1700, pp. 1768–9; James A. Henderson, Jr. & Aaron D. Twerski, 'Consumer Expectations' Last Hope: A Response to Professor Kysar', 103 *Colum LR* (2003) 1791, pp. 1797–9.

57 In addition, some would think that the decrease in the gap in holdings between the residents of Richtown (who do not get compensated) and Poortown is in itself desirable.

58 The ability of the residents of Poortown to enjoy part of the 'bribe' depends on whether they are protected by a property rule (injunction) or a liability rule (compensation).

45 days if he repays the loan. The borrower loses his house.[59] This case raises questions regarding both the scope of duty of care and the required standard of care. The basis for the claim that the lawyer was negligent hinges on her failure to explain to the borrower that in this kind of transaction he might lose the safeguards afforded to mortgagors by the relevant provisions of the law of secured transactions.[60] If such transaction is subject to these provisions as a hidden mortgage, the lawyer was negligent in not explaining to the borrower that he has the right to these safeguards. If such transaction is *not* subject to these provisions, the lawyer was negligent in depriving the client of these safeguards. On the assumption that the transaction is not subject to the safeguards afforded to mortgagors, it is clear that a finding of negligence is both motivated and explained[61] by an egalitarian approach. The fact that the borrower is unrepresented[62] and the power gap between the borrower and the lender account for the lawyer's duty to explain the meaning of the transaction and its risks. Had the client been represented, or, arguably, had the power balance between the parties been less pronounced, it is clear that the same behaviour would not have been deemed negligent. The relative status and strength of the parties, then, determines whether a given behaviour is negligent or not.[63]

2. Disputes over Frozen Ova *Example 7: Disputes over frozen ova.* Xavier and Britney have commenced an IVF fertilization procedure in which several fertilized

---

59 The example is based on the Israeli case of CA 2625/02 *Nahum v Dorenbaum*, PD 58(3) 385 (Israel).

60 The question whether such a transaction is subject to the provisions of the law of secured transactions is currently unsettled in Israeli law. While Israeli law adopted in principle the functionalist approach of the UCC (the American Uniform Commercial Code), the scope of transactions subject to the law governing secured transactions is still in flux. The Supreme Court in the *Nahum* case decided that this issue does not require determination since the lawyer acted negligently under either assumption.

61 Is it justified? If the relevant transaction is not subject to the safeguards afforded by the law governing secured transactions, it is not easy to defend the conclusion that the lender's lawyer is negligent in structuring the transaction in a way that better serves the interests of her client. In such a case, the extent to which the other party trusted the lawyer to serve his interests as well becomes crucial for the evaluation of both duty and breach.

62 This factor has led to a greater tendency to impose liability on lawyers towards non-clients in several common law jurisdictions, although in a narrower scope in comparison to the approach in the *Nahum* case. Liability is limited to circumstances of negligent misrepresentation and reasonable reliance. See e.g., *Granville Savings & Mortgage Corp. v Slevin*, [1993] 4 SCR 279 (Can); *Nelson v Nationwide Mortgage Corp.*, 659 F Supp 611 (DDC 1987); *Dean v Allin & Watts* [2001] 2 Lloyd's Rep 249 (CA). Interestingly, in the *Dean* and *Granville* cases, the liability was imposed on the borrower's solicitor, towards the unrepresented lender. The extent to which the approach in *Nahum* is an outlier, depends on the extent to which the borrower relied in fact on the lender's lawyer. The Justices disagreed on that point.

63 For a comparable approach within contract law regarding the scope of disclosure towards unrepresented guarantors in the context of 'sexually transmitted debt' see *Barclays Bank plc v O'Brien* [1994] 1 AC 180 (HL).

eggs were frozen. The parties have separated and no agreement exists regarding the disposition of the ova in the event of separation. Despite the relationship between the couple having ended Britney still wishes for the ova to be implanted whilst Xavier wishes to destroy it.[64] The following discussion will: (1) establish the relevance of an egalitarian analysis of reasonableness in general, and standard of care in particular, to the dispute over frozen ova; (2) explain the ways in which an egalitarian approach influences standard of care analysis of the dispute; and (3) draw doctrinal conclusions from the analysis.

(a) Relevance of reasonableness and standard of care. While this kind of dispute is usually analysed within a contractual framework,[65] the relevance of an egalitarian standard of care to its proper solution should not be overlooked. First, as several commentators and a few courts have observed,[66] the woman's reliance is a relevant factor in solving the dispute, and the doctrinal manifestation of such reliance is promissory estoppel. Promissory estoppel is a hybrid doctrine that draws on contracts and torts alike.[67] Second, the dispute can just as easily be framed as one of negligent misrepresentation by the husband,[68] or, less obviously, as a matter of negligent behaviour by him. With respect to the former option (misrepresentation), it can be argued that by agreeing to enter the IVF process, the husband consented to the implantation and the wife relied on this representation

---

64 The example is a variation of the American *Davis* case: *Davis v Davis*, 842 SW 2d 588 (Tenn 1992). In *Davis*, the ex-wife ultimately wished to donate the fertilized ova to another (unspecified) woman and the ex-husband, who opposed any use of the ova, prevailed. The example is based also on the Israeli *Nahmani* case in which the 7–4 panel which reheard the case granted the wife the right to continue in the process: CFH2401/95 *Nahmani v Nahmani*, PD 50(4) 661 (Israel). In the UK, a woman's suit was defeated in circumstances where the statutory framework requires the continuous consent of both partners prior to implantation. The husband reassured the wife that he would not withdraw his consent, after the wife was explained about the legal framework and considered whether she should explore other means of having her remaining eggs fertilized. *Evans v Amicus Healthcare Ltd*, [2004] EWCA Civ 727 (CA), *aff'm* [2003] 4 All ER 903 (Fam); 6339/05 *Evans v UK* [2006] 1 FCR 585 (ECHR). The analysis in this section is not meant to critically analyse *Evans*, despite the fact that part of that analysis is applicable. *Evans* does not deal with the proper default rule, but rather with the constitutionality of a rule requiring continuous consent by both parties. *Evans* does, however, raise the issue of estoppel.

65 See e.g., Donna M. Sheinbach, 'Examining Disputes over Ownership Rights to Frozen Embryos: Will Prior Consent Documents Survive if Challenged by State Law and/or Constitutional Principles?', 48 *Cath UL Rev* (1999) 989.

66 See e.g., Paula Walter, 'His, Hers, or Theirs – Custody, Control, and Contracts: Allocating Decisional Authority Over Frozen Embryos', 29 *Seton Hall L Rev* (1999) 937, p. 963; Alise R. Panitch, 'The Davis Dilemma: How to Prevent Battles over Frozen Embryos', 41 *Case W Res L Rev* (1991) 543, pp. 573–6; Tanya Feliciano, 'Davis v. Davis: What About Future Disputes?', *26 Conn L Rev* (1993) 305, pp. 344–9; *Nahmani*, *supra* note 64.

67 E. Allan Farnsworth, *Contracts* (3rd edn, New York, 1999), pp. 100–101.

68 The doctrine of estoppel by representation might be also relevant. Several Justices in *Nahmani*, *supra* note 64, dealt also with the claim of misrepresentation, usually in conjecture of the claim of estoppel. See ibid., pp. 689–90, 697–8, 699, 703–6, 717, 721–2, 732, 771, 784–5.

to her detriment by undergoing the painful and intrusive fertilization procedure.[69] Negligent misrepresentation doctrine examines both the reasonableness of the husband's representation and the wife's reliance.[70] The examination with respect to the former is whether the scope of the husband's representation includes consent for continuing the process without his continued consent, and whether the gap between the representation and his current position render such representation negligent.

With respect to the second – and more contested – option (negligent withholding of consent to implantation), it can be argued that even if the representation at the moment of deciding to undergo the treatment was not negligent misrepresentation,[71] the husband's refusal to allow the wife to continue the process despite his change of heart is nonetheless unreasonable given the balance of equities and the detrimental reliance of his partner. This approach which arguably imposes on the husband a duty to rescue in circumstances which are definitely not easy rescue[72] (given the costs of unwanted fatherhood) can be defended by the doctrine that the creator of reasonable risk has a duty to act reasonably in order to remove it.[73] Third, in the absence of actual agreement over how to dispose of the ova in an event of separation, the implied contract theory boils down to reasonable allocation of the risk between the parties. Whether frustration or interpretation is involved, the reasonable allocation of the risk is part of the process.[74] Whatever the doctrinal compartmentalization is, the dispute calls for evaluating the conflicting interests of the husband in not becoming an unwilling parent and the wife in bringing the painful and intrusive fertilization process into fruition. Two insights accordingly bear mention: first, the limited observation that the reach of an egalitarian reformulation of the concept of reasonableness extends beyond the scope of tort law, since this concept is relevant

---

69 Whether such misrepresentation exists on the merits, is debatable and depends on construing the implied content of the representation.

70 For the elements of doctrine of negligent misrepresentation see *Caparo plc v Dickman*, *supra* note 26, p. 638; Restatement (Second) of Torts, s. 90(1) (1981). Similarly, the doctrine of promissory estoppel requires that 'the promisor should *reasonably* expect' that his promise would induce reliance. Restatement (Second) of Contracts, s. 90(1). For the relevance of the reasonableness of the promisee's reliance see ibid. Cmnt b. For the more restrictive English approach to promissory estoppel see Hugh G. Beale (ed.), *Chitty on Contracts* (29th edn, vol. 1, London, 2004), pp. 263–88.

71 Such claim is based on interpretation of the man's consent as being limited in scope to either only commencing the process or to implantation conditional on family harmony.

72 Even those supporting the recognition of general duty for negligent nonfeasance limit it only to circumstances of easy rescue. See e.g., Ernest J. Weinrib, 'The Case for a Duty to Rescue', 90 *Yale LJ* (1980) 247, p. 250.

73 *Montgomery v National Convoy & Trucking Co.,* 195 SE 247, 251–3 (SC 1938); *Wright v Lodge* [1993] 4 All ER 299 (CA); Rogers, *Supra* note 12, p. 137.

74 See e.g., Patrick S. Atiyah, *An Introduction to the Law of Contract* (5th edn, Oxford, 1995), p. 204; Beale, *supra* note 70, pp. 777–8, 1314–15; Farnsworth, *supra* note 67, pp. 466–7, 645.

in other areas of private law.[75] Second, an egalitarian approach is needed not only in tort law but in other areas of private law.[76]

(b) Implication of an egalitarian approach. A standard of care analysis will identify the conflicting preferences of the parties whether to continue with the process or not as an accident; accordingly, the party whose preferences are thwarted bears the loss. The ability to clarify the situation in advance in order to prevent such a clash of preferences could be considered as precaution costs.[77] It is difficult to identify one of the parties to the conflict as having, at the moment when the decision to commence IVF treatment is taken, the greater ability to prevent the future disagreement. It is assumed that the instance of strategic behaviour – a party considering the possibility of changing his or her mind but preferring not to raise the issue – is negligible, so the reason there is no prior agreement regarding disposition of the ova in case of a dispute between the parties is that neither side considered this possibility.[78]

Against this background five ways in which an egalitarian-distributive approach can influence standard of care analysis can be identified. The first way is by mandating that the costs of precaution – the burden to clarify the situation – should be imposed on men. This should be so due either to men's generally enhanced status in society compared to women in general[79] or to the fact that the common goal of the IVF enterprise is having a child together and that the man's change of heart imposes much greater costs on his partner than on himself.[80] At

75 For other examples see, e.g., *Robbins of Putney Ltd v Meek* [1971] RTR 345 (liquidity as factor in assessing reasonableness of buyer's failure to mitigate by buying substitute). In civil law systems, unlike common law, reasonableness is relevant also for purposes of unilateral use of co-owned property in cases of disagreement between the owners. See Hanoch Dagan & Michael Heller, 'The Liberal Commons', 110 *Yale LJ* (2001) 549, pp. 609–16 & n.250.

76 Indeed, the theoretical normative argument offered in Ch. 3 above calling for incorporating egalitarianism into tort law, applies almost equally to other areas of private law.

77 Alternatively, at the moment the dispute arises, the cost borne by the losing party can be viewed as precaution costs borne in order to prevent the losses that the other party would have borne had the decision been reversed.

78 Distributive analysis has to take into account the concern of backlash with its ensuing intra-group justice issue. In the IVF context, a rule allowing women to continue with the process without continuous consent by the husband might be regarded as harmful to women since men will be less willing to start an IVF process. This fear is unconvincing for two reasons. First, the significance of such an effect is doubtful mainly due to psychological biases of over-optimism. Second, even if such an effect occurs, it is a price worth paying for protecting both the reliance interests of women who began the process and the interests of men not to become fathers unwillingly. From an intra-group justice perspective, the loss to women whose expectation that their partners will agree to commence an IVF process is outweighed by the gain to the reliance interest of women who started the process.

79 This approach is based on the idea that when the absolute burden of prevention is similar it should be borne by the better off since relatively it would impose less disutility on him.

80 See note 73 above and accompanying text. For a similar rationale which is based on the idea of 'he who alters (or retracts from) a contract is at a disadvantage', see *Nahmani*,

least when neither party enjoys preference in terms of accident prevention capacity, an important criterion for allocating the loss is distributive. The rule should prefer the party who would suffer the greater loss if the other party prevails.

A second – and perhaps the major – influence of egalitarian sensitivity is by calling into attention an andocentric bias which might lead to under-evaluation of women's interests in the conflict, interests that should be balanced against men's interests. Egalitarian sensitivity adequately weighs women's considerable interests, and by this leads to an evaluation that their loss would be more significant, measured in absolute terms, than that of men under an unfavourable rule. Accordingly, it supports a solution allowing women to continue with the process despite their partners' change of heart.

Much feminist critique of law emphasizes law's andocentrism and hence the importance of taking into account women's experience, epistemology and morality while (re)constructing legal rules.[81] In this respect both the gendered social costs for women of not becoming a mother and, more importantly, the value of autonomy and bodily integrity, namely the interest in not being subject to a futile intrusive medical intervention are relevant. Biological asymmetry in the reproductive process renders women systematically vulnerable to a unilateral change of mind by their partner, under a veto rule. Once the considerable emotional and physical costs for women of undergoing fertilization treatments are adequately appreciated, a solution declining to protect the woman's reliance on the man's consent to undergo the process appears to be highly problematic. As some judges and commentators have observed,[82] to the same extent that in natural pregnancies men's interest in not becoming fathers is subordinated to women's autonomy interest, so should it be too in the IVF context. In both cases the conception process and its ending involve considerable physical changes, such that women's right to bodily integrity should outweigh men's interest in changing their mind. The fact that in the IVF case, part of the physical intervention precedes conception, does not render women's interest in bodily integrity less real or less worthy of consideration. A default rule allowing the man to veto the process renders the intrusive intervention in the woman undergoing the fertilization treatment futile in retrospect and by this encroaches upon her bodily integrity.

Any legal system has to choose a point of no return for the regretting would-be-parent, and the biological differences between the sexes call for an earlier point for the potential father: the point at which women's physical integrity would be violated if the regret is to be acted upon, should be adopted across the board as this point

---

supra note 64, p 699 (Tal J.).

81 For the andocentric bias in defining reasonable person see Robyn Martin, 'A Feminist View of the Reasonable Man: An Alternative Approach to Liability in Negligence for Personal Injury', 23 *Anglo-Am L Rev* (1994) 334. For a call to incorporate women's values into tort law see Leslie Bender, 'A Lawyer's Primer on Feminist Theory and Tort', 38 *J Legal Educ* (1988) 3.

82 See, e.g., *Nahmani*, *supra* note 64, p. 694 (Tal J.); OM (Haifa) 599/92 *Nahmani v Nahmani*, PM 1994(1) 142, 157,158, 164 (Israel) (Ariel J.); Feliciano, *supra* note 66, pp. 347–8.

of no return.[83] Moreover, if in natural pregnancies men's interest is subordinated to women's, all the more so this should be the result in the IVF context. Men cannot prevent the pregnancy even if it was not planned and, indeed, even if they were defrauded. In the IVF context there is informed consent for a process whose goal is to bring a child into the world. Moreover, in natural pregnancies there is no equivalent reliance by the woman on the man in order to get pregnant; the process is typically much less lengthy, onerous and painful.[84]

A third influence of the egalitarian approach is by defending a distributive preference that men would bear the loss in this conflict given their better position in society, even if in absolute terms men's loss is more significant than that of women's, given men's better ability to bear this loss.

A fourth possible, and more contested influence of the egalitarian approach on standard of care analysis is by characterizing men's refusal to allow implantation as unreasonable and negligent. This conclusion can be grounded in women's vulnerability (given the biological asymmetry) and the fact that such vulnerability was enhanced by men's behaviour (the consent to commence the IVF process). Note that such vulnerability is not natural, despite the biological asymmetry. Rather, it is the result of a legal rule conditioning implantation (a process which in itself is not natural) on the continued consent of the man.[85] According to such an approach the law should not adopt a rule that systematically puts a group of people in a vulnerable position. *A fortiori*, such a rule should be opposed when those put in such a position are members of a historically disadvantaged group.

Finally, (and related to the fourth influence), even if an approach condemning men for attempting to veto implantation could be equated with a duty to rescue, it can be supported by an approach calling for greater incorporation of women's morality and epistemology.[86] Such morality entails, according to relational feminists, a greater commitment to imposing positive duties on others and belittling the relative weight that should be accorded to the values of negative liberty and the atomistic epistemology upon which it rests. Such an approach helps overcoming the bias towards (typically men's) negative freedom claim not to become an unwilling parent and against the (typically women's) seemingly positive claim for assistance in

83 This means that in cases in which the man gives his consent to undergo the fertilization process but no treatment has begun, the case for enforcing this obligation is weaker. Few European countries, such as Italy and Austria, set fertilization as the point of no return. See *Evans v UK*, *supra* note 64, para 32. This approach, which presumably was motivated by religious rather than egalitarian concerns, might theoretically differ from the solution suggested in the text where the change of heart occurs after harvesting and before fertilization.

84 For similar reasons, the child's best-interest argument in favour of demanding continuous consent by both parents prior to implantation is unpersuasive. The future child's interest to be born to a willing father is ineffective after conception has occurred in unassisted pregnancies. In any event, for reasons similar to those presented in Ch 6.III.C below, egalitarian commitment supports the analysis offered in the text even when the interests of the future children are taken into account.

85 See *Nahmani*, *supra* note 82, p. 164.

86 See, e.g., Bender, *supra* note 81.

becoming mother. According to such a view, resolving the conflict in a no-veto rule is justified not because (or at least not only because) women would typically benefit from such a rule, but rather because it incorporates women's values.

(c) Doctrinal ramifications. The main doctrinal ramifications of such an approach are these: first, balancing the parties' interests in coming up with a default rule should not hinge on the existence of reasonable alternatives to the claimant woman becoming a mother.[87] Even if such alternative exists, the woman is entitled not to have the intrusive treatment she was undergoing rendered futile. Second, prior agreements regarding the disposition of the frozen ova in case of future disagreement between the parties should be enforced. An agreement according to which implantation depends on the man's continued consent does not thwart the woman's autonomy since she was aware of the risk in advance and chose to bear it. Similarly, it goes without saying that men's explicit obligation to allow implantation without continued consent should be enforced. Invalidating such an obligation based on constitutional grounds is nothing less than outrageous: it prevents women from having any kind of protection of their autonomy interests, and subjects them to the painful dilemma of either not having a biological child or being subject to an intrusive treatment that can be rendered futile at any moment at their partners' sole discretion without any legal possibility of protecting their significant interests.

B. Failure to Prevent Risk Created by Third Parties

Generally, in this category there is a triangle of third parties (the immediate creators of the risk), potential victims, and potential defendants. Egalitarian considerations play a part at several stages here, including the duty of care stage. As for standard of care analysis, egalitarian considerations are relevant at two levels. First, as always, the question is whether the disutility caused by the burden to act (to prevent the risk to the third party) is outweighed by the victim's disutility from bearing the uncompensated loss. In this respect, to the extent that the defendant is a corporation or a public authority (as often is the case), the disutility of incurring the precaution costs (or the cost of liability) should be measured by the disutility to those to whom the loss is passed on. For example, if a public authority is under a duty to supervise a third party, the disutility should be determined according to the ways in which the costs of complying with the duty or paying for its breach are funded. (By a tax raise? If so, for whom? By reducing welfare benefits? By reducing financial support to the opera?) This disutility should be compared with the disutility to the victims. (Who are the victims? Investors in the stock market? Molested children?)

Second, determinations regarding the defendant's decision not to act should take into account the possibility that intervention would only channel the risk created by the third party to another victim, rather than reduce (or eliminate) the risk. As the discussion of the refinery example demonstrated, the reasonableness of putting the residents of Richtown at risk should (or at least could) be partially assessed by

---

87 The reasonable alternative test was set in *Davis*, *supra* note 64, p. 604.

the likelihood that a determination of unreasonableness would channel the risk to the residents of Poortown. Under instrumental approaches to tort law, the disutility to third parties is definitely a relevant factor in determinations of reasonableness.[88] Not only the utility or disutility to third parties from undertaking the risk-creating activity should be taken into account, but also the disutility to them from being the substitute victims of accidents, whether avoidable or not.[89]

With regard to substitute victims of accidents, it should further be observed that the egalitarian consideration (as well as other distributive considerations) might and usually should be relevant for purposes of evaluating the reasonableness of the defendant's failure to protect his victim. While under the economic analysis of law, an omission to act can be deemed negligent (and entail liability if a duty of care exists) only if that omission failed to reduce the overall risk (as opposed to merely channelling it to a substitute victim), the egalitarian approach would explore also the distribution of the risk entailed by the decision to act or to refrain from acting. It is possible that a failure to act that increased the overall risk would be deemed reasonable, since it would bring about a more equitable distribution of the risk.[90]

Example 8: Parental liability. At common law, parental liability for damage caused by their minor children to third parties is limited to circumstances of negligent supervision.[91] Courts (at least in the United States) usually place strict limits on the scope of liability, requiring a showing of the proclivity of the child to engage in the same (or, according to some versions, a similar) endangering activity that led to the plaintiff's loss.[92] The narrow boundaries delineated by the courts for the standard of care in cases of parental supervision (a narrowness that is objectionable in light of policy considerations such as optimal deterrence and the idea of fairness) is explicable on egalitarian grounds. Due to the fact that women are the primary caretakers of children and primary custodians in single-parent families, and furthermore, due to the individual nature of tort liability, such liability, on its financial and symbolic aspects, is borne unequally by women relative to men. Moreover, a less lenient standard of care would cause further encroachment on women's autonomy, and would exacerbate the material and symbolic regressive results of parental liability. Therefore, the standard of care expected from parents (in practice, mainly from women) is lax. Since almost any kind of parental liability regime would impose a greater burden on women (as primary custodians and care takers), the ideal solution from the perspective of egalitarian considerations would be to deny liability altogether. It might be that the very narrow scope of

---

88 See Restatement (Second) of Torts, s. 294 (1965).

89 Ibid., s. 295.

90 Thus the egalitarian approach departs from the rule adopted by the Restatement, ibid. The Restatement postulates that the alternative risk should be 'equal or greater'.

91 Restatement (Second) of Torts, s. 316 (1965).

92 See e.g., *Sun Mountain Prod., Inc. v Pierre*, 929 P 2d 494 (Wash Ct App Div 1 1997). The rule as stated in the Restatement (Second) of Torts, s. 316 (1965) seems to be broader than the similar (or particular) act rule, which the majority of the American courts seem to endorse. See e.g., *Fuller v Studer*, 833 P 2d 109 (Idaho 1992); *Gissen v Goodwill*, 80 So 2d 701 (Fla 1955).

liability, which is based on the idea that the parent is not negligent in the absence of knowledge about the child's proclivity, is the balancing point between non-egalitarian considerations supporting liability and considerations opposing it, when chief among the latter is the egalitarian concern.[93]

Example 9: A decision where to inspect. There are two parks in town, one in an affluent neighbourhood, the other in a poor one. Budgetary constraints allow the stationing of a police officer in only one of the parks. The local municipality has to decide where to place the police officer.[94] This example raises the issue of the limits of the liability of public authorities for nonfeasance. While there are many reasons for courts' deference in this area, the egalitarian concern serves as a factor supporting or opposing a finding of negligence. The initial assumption is that the decision itself to finance only one police officer to patrol the parks is immune from a finding of negligence. Indeed, such an assumption is well established in the case law. On the other hand, a decision as to where to place the police officer is more likely to be scrutinized by the court (than the initial decision to finance stationing only one police officer) and more likely to be subject to a standard of care analysis, although this is by no means certain. Again, there is a tension between the dictates of economic efficiency and those of egalitarian sensitivity. From the efficiency perspective, the expected loss to visitors to the park in the affluent neighbourhood is higher than the expected loss to visitors in the other park. Therefore, a decision to locate the police officer in the 'poor' park would be negligent. A different outcome results under an egalitarian approach. The disutility to the affluent visitors from lack of police supervision in the park is lower than the disutility to the poor from the same lack of supervision. First, the rich can privately hire someone to patrol the park. Such an option is not available to the residents of the poorer neighbourhood. Second, the potential victim's disutility from having to shift to an alternative leisure activity because of the lack of adequate supervision in the park is low, given their resources (they could go to a restaurant). The poor residents have fewer affordable alternatives. Third, due to the diminishing marginal utility of money, the disutility to the rich from the loss caused to them in the park because of the lack of supervision would be lower than the disutility to the poor. In addition, a finding of negligence for not protecting the 'affluent' park would channel the risk of being victimized to the poor, a regressive and undesirable result. Finally, a finding of liability of the public authority toward the rich would increase the amount that has to be paid in damages in comparison to the amount that would be awarded to poor victims. This increased burden would harm the public and would likely cause disproportionate harm to the poor. Note

---

93 Alternatively, another solution exists that reconciles the justification for a broad parental liability and the apprehension of regressive effects of such broad liability from a gender perspective: a regime of strict liability of both parents that is not custody-dependent. The defendant-parent would have a right to contribution from the other parent for half of the amount paid, regardless of comparative fault.

94 This example is an adaptation of the Israeli case of *Groobner*, *supra* note 12, p.158. See also George L. Priest, 'The Current Insurance Crisis and Modern Tort Law', 96 *Yale LJ* (1987) 1521, p. 1586.

that there are three possibilities for a finding of liability: that the municipality is negligent if it placed the police officer in the 'poor' park; that it is negligent if it placed the police officer in the 'affluent' park; or that it is not negligent regardless of where it decides to place the police officer.[95] While other policy considerations might support a no-liability rule, an egalitarian approach ranks the desirability of the solutions in descending order as follows: the second, the third, and finally the first solutions. A determination that neither choice is negligent would still expose the municipality to public choice pressures to have the police officer stationed in the 'affluent' park, with no incentive provided by tort law to counter this pressure. A finding of negligence of the public authority only toward the poor victims would give the municipality incentive to put a police officer in the 'poor' park.

Example 10: Failure to warn women who are at specific risk of being sexually assaulted. A group of white women living in first-floor apartments with balconies in a certain neighbourhood are at specific risk of being sexually assaulted by a serial rapist. The police throughout the investigation avoided warning those women out of fear that such warning might jeopardize the investigation. In the Canadian case of *Doe v Board of Commissioners of Police*,[96] the court imposed liability on the police for a failure to warn. The court's decision revolved around the duty issue, and it did not explore the issue of standard of care in depth. Despite some inconsistencies in the reasoning, the court seemed to ground liability in the fact that giving a warning would not have compromised the investigation. The investigators' professed reason for not giving a warning was that it would have caused the rapist to flee from the area and embark on a spree of rapes in another area. The court rejected this reasoning, based mainly on testimony given by a *defence* expert witness, who conceded that under the circumstances, providing a warning to the women would not have compromised the chances of capturing of the rapist.[97]

While the decision reached by the court is correct, its reasoning is questionable with regard to both duty and standard of care analysis. *Doe* is a further demonstration of the proper ambit of egalitarian considerations in standard of care analysis. First, the concern that providing a warning might divert the risk of being victimized to another group of victims is in itself a legitimate one that should be considered by investigators and therefore should influence reasonableness evaluations. Second, refraining from giving such a warning might in general, although probably not when dealing with sexual assaults, be considered reasonable, even if it increases the total risk posed by the offender, provided however that it brings about a better distribution of that risk from an egalitarian perspective. In the context of sexual assaults however, the goal of reducing total risk should take precedence over the goal of more equitable distribution of that risk, to the extent that egalitarian considerations in this regard

95 Two other possibilities – that the municipality is negligent for not stationing two police officers or that the municipality is not negligent even for not stationing any officer – are excluded under the underlying assumptions of this example.

96 [1998] 39 OR 3d 487 (Gen Div).

97 Ibid., pp. 517–18.

may be irrelevant.[98] Third, the goals of preventing future crimes and apprehending offenders for previously committed crimes may at times be at odds with one another. Assuming that the reasonableness of a trade-off between less prevention and better apprehension varies according to context (meaning that at times the police might decide to further the goal of apprehending offenders even by using potential victims as bait), egalitarian considerations are relevant in the determination of the reasonableness of such a trade-off in each given case. This means that, all things being equal, the use of members of disadvantaged groups as bait would weigh in favour of a finding of negligence, since such a use burdens disproportionately the disadvantaged to the benefit of all of society, which amounts to a form of regressive subsidy.[99]

VI. Incongruity with Existing Tort Law

Arguably, a suggestion to incorporate egalitarianism into the standard of care analysis, for all its normative worth, deviates too far from existing tort law and, therefore, should be opposed on that ground alone. This charge will be termed 'the incongruity challenge'. The first response to this challenge is that the claim defended here is essentially a normative one, while claims of incongruity are applicable mainly, if not only, with regard to positive theories. For the reasons stated above, the standard of care analysis should be attuned to the demands of egalitarianism, and to the extent that it is not so to a sufficient degree, it should be reformulated to correct this failing. It should be noticed, however, that the suggestion put forward here does not dramatically deviate from existing tort law. While it does represent an extension of existing tendencies, its adoption would be more akin to evolution than to revolution. Moreover, adopting a more egalitarian standard of care fits well with, and is supported by, the modern tendency in several jurisdictions to incorporate public values (such as equality) into private law doctrines. Furthermore, the practice of tort law (as opposed to judicial rhetoric) already shows sensitivity to egalitarian considerations in the realm of negligence law, and therefore the adoption of the suggested rule is also supported on the grounds of judicial sincerity.

A. Standard of Care

1. The Definition of Standard of Care can Contain Egalitarian Considerations The first point to be observed is that the test for the standard of care is by nature flexible

98 Still, there might be relevance to other distributive considerations that are neither egalitarian nor efficiency-oriented, such as preferring identified over unidentified potential victims.

99 However, in the sexual assault context, women benefit disproportionately from the capture of the attacker so that using potential victims as bait raises to a lesser extent the problem of regressive subsidy at the inter-group justice level of men and women; it might raise however problems of intra-group justice, that is, certain women rather than others being used as bait.

and amenable, so that it has the capacity to include egalitarian concerns. The test (which varies from one jurisdiction to another) is broad enough conceptually and rhetorically to embrace egalitarian considerations. The test used by courts can quite easily incorporate egalitarianism. It goes without saying that whenever the reasonable person is used by courts to characterize the standard of care,[100] that definition can be filled with egalitarian content. The reasonable person is as capable of being *homo distributus* as she is capable of being *homo economicus*. If the standard of care is defined as what a reasonable person would do, and if a reasonable person is expected to prevent some, but not other, harms from affecting her neighbours, nothing stops that reasonable person from adjusting her level of care to the relative position and status of the parties and taking into account the real burden that prevention and accident costs would have for them. Courts are ready to admit that the standard of care is normative rather than empirical, that the reasonable person is the court, and that the court sets the required standard of care.[101] Nothing stops courts from deciding that a reasonable person should take egalitarian considerations into account.

Furthermore, the prevalent version of the cost-benefit-based standard of care evaluates the social value of the risk-creating activity for purposes of determining whether it is negligent or not.[102] The social value test is a natural vehicle for including egalitarian considerations in the standard of care. In the house-heating examples (Examples 1 and 2), the social value of the heating activity (which creates pollution) derives (or at least can be interpreted as deriving) from the parties' relative status and opportunity costs. The social value of the poor individual using cheap coal is high, since it allows him to increase significantly his quality of life in comparison to the alternative of using much more expensive coal. By contrast, the social value of the rich individual using cheap coal is lower, since her well-being would not be significantly impaired if she were to use the more expensive coal.

In fact, nothing in the original Hand formula prevents courts from making a cost-benefit analysis that is not based merely on absolute amounts or economic efficiency.[103] Accident costs and precaution costs could be understood in a more complex and nuanced way. In Example 1 (the house-heating example), the precaution costs of the poor individual could be understood to be a loss of 60 per cent of his income, which is meagre to begin with. The accident costs could be understood to be a much smaller decrease in the victim's well-being. Therefore, the result of the cost-benefit analysis could be that the poor person's use of the cheaper coal is not negligent. Generally, in resolving the question of negligence

100 See *Blyth v Birmingham Waterworks Co.* (1856) 11 Ex 781, 784; Restatement (Second) of Torts, s. 283 (1965); C.T. Walton, *Charlesworth & Percy on Negligence* (10th edn, London, 2001), p. 365.

101 See e.g., *Glasgow Corporation v Muir* [1943] AC 448, 457 (HL) ('It is still left to the judge to decide what in the circumstances of the particular case the reasonable man would have had in contemplation and what accordingly the party sought to be made liable ought to have foreseen.'); Rogers, *supra* note 12, p. 190.

102 See above, notes 12–13 and accompanying text.

103 Cf. Kenneth. W. Simons, 'The Hand Formula in the Draft Restatement (Third) of Torts: Encompassing Fairness as Well as Efficiency Values', 54 *Vand L Rev* (2001) 901, p. 907; CA 5604/94 *Hamed v State of Israel*, PD 58(2) 498, 518–21 (Israel) (Rivlin J.).

courts often use a broad cost-benefit test. This test should not be equated with a pursuit of efficiency. Value-laden decisions – such as the relative importance of law enforcement – are translated into determination whether the litigated activity was negligent or not.[104] Such determination escapes simple economic analysis since these values are incommensurable with money. As the next section will demonstrate, egalitarian considerations are part of the complex matrix courts use in order to decide whether a given activity is negligent or not.

2. Some Courts Endorse Egalitarian Considerations in Standard of Care Analysis Although it happens rarely, at times courts have explicitly conceded the relevance of the parties' relative resources with respect to the evaluation of the defendant's activity as negligent or not. For example, in *Goldman v Hargrave*,[105] the Privy Council delineated the contours of liability for an occupier's failure to remove or reduce hazards to his neighbours. The court, which explicitly based the defendants' liability on negligence and not on nuisance,[106] decided that one of the factors in evaluating negligence is the scope of the defendant's resources relative to the danger and relative to the plaintiff's resources.[107] A narrow reading of the case could emphasize the fact that the court dealt with an omission to prevent a risk that the defendant did not create, a point that the court was conscious of.[108] Such a reading, however, is unnecessary, and in any event the rationale behind the decision justifies a similar analysis in all cases of negligence. A similar reasoning (and result) was employed in *British Railways Board v Herrington* in which the court opined, '[A]n impecunious occupier with little assistance at hand would often be excused from doing something which a large organization with ample staff would be expected to do.'[109] Courts also take into account the limited resources of public authorities with respect to the need to distribute available income among a number of demanding social functions.[110] In other cases lack of resources coupled with lack of experience and lack of remuneration, led to a finding of no negligence by firefighters.[111] *Paris v Stepney Borough Council* stands as an authority to the proposition that the plaintiff's foreseeable vulnerability (having only one eye), makes the litigated practice (not providing the employee with goggles) a negligent one, even though exposing a two-eyed employee to the same risk would be reasonable.[112] Finally, the power-gap

104 See, e.g., *Hamed*, ibid.; *Priestman v Colangelo* [1959] SCR 615; *Bittner v Tait-Gibson Optometetrists Ltd* (1964) 44 DLR (2d) 113 (On CA).

105 [1967] 1 AC 645 (PC).

106 Ibid., p. 657.

107 Ibid., p. 663.

108 For one such typical reading, see e.g., Rogers, *supra* note 12, pp. 129–30.

109 [1972] AC.877, 899 (HL).

110 See, e.g., *East Suffolk Rivers Catchment Bd v Kent*, [1941] AC 74, 95–6 (HL).

111 See, e.g., *Hammond v Wabana* (1998) 44 CCLT (2d) 101 (Nfld CA); *Killip's Television Service Ltd v Stony Plain* [2000] 3 WWR 702 (Alta QB).

112 *Paris v Stepney Borough Council* [1951] 1 All ER 32 (HL). Note however, that providing goggles to all employees is also much more expensive (cost of precaution) than providing goggles only to one-eyed employees.

between plaintiff and defendant can account (at least partially) to both the existence of duty and the determination of negligence.[113]

3. Court Practice Reveals a Tendency to Take into Account Egalitarian Considerations for Standard of Care Purposes In order to evaluate the adequacy of the incongruity challenge, the proposal should be examined against court practice and not merely against court rhetoric. Several empirical studies show that seemingly deep-pockets defendants are more likely than 'empty pocket' defendants to be found negligent and to pay larger awards.[114] Especially relevant is the work of Valerie Hans. Hans did not find jury verdicts to be correlated directly with perceptions of financial resources, but rather with defendant status, role, size, organizational resources, potential impact, and special knowledge, all of which affect defendants' perceived responsibility so as to justify different evaluations by juries of the same behaviour.[115] Note that the differences in perceived knowledge and control might themselves be influenced by perceived differences of wealth. If this interpretation is true, juries comply with the moral argument underlying the thesis of this chapter: that one's resources affect the moral evaluation of one's conduct. Moreover, given the fact that juries subject different defendants to different standards of care based on their relative positions and status, and given the insight that one's ability to prevent harm depends on one's resources, it would not be a big leap for juries to take into account defendants' wealth for purposes of determining the standard of care expected from them, even if currently juries do not take this data into account.

There is also empirical support for the claim that courts take into account the *plaintiff*'s status. Donald Harris has found that in the United Kingdom, poor plaintiffs have higher success rates in negligence suits than do the rich.[116] It seems, then, that tort practice as applied by juries and judges in different jurisdictions sits well with a theory calling for overt recognition of egalitarian considerations in the standard of care analysis.

Court practice showing sensitivity to egalitarian considerations at the stage of evaluating an activity's reasonableness can be seen also in what courts are *not*

113 See, e.g., *Young v Bella* [2006] SCC 3, paras 33–34 (Professor-student); *Nahum*, *supra* note 59 (lawyer of lender in the grey market – unrepresented borrower).

114 See, e.g., Audrey Chin & Mark A. Peterson, *The Rand Corporation, Deep Pockets, Empty Pockets: Who Wins in Cook County Jury Trials* (Santa Monica, 1985); James K. Hammitt, 'Tort Standards and Jury Decisions', 14 *J Legal Stud* (1985) 751. In reaching this conclusion, the studies took into consideration the facts that deep-pocket defendants and empty-pocket defendants tend to engage in different types of legal cases and to cause different types of typical injuries – which are facts that also influence liability rate and size of awards.

115 Valerie P. Hans, *Business on Trial: The Civil Jury and Corporate Responsibility* (New Haven, 2000), pp. 117–20, 122–7, 212–14; Valerie P. Hans, 'The Illusions And Realities of Jurors' Treatment of Corporate Defendants', 48 *DePaul L Rev* (1998) 327, p. 351.

116 Donald Harris, *Compensation and Support for Illness and Injury* (Oxford, 1984), p. 55. Since then, however, UK courts have undergone procedural transformation; hence the relevance of these findings might have diminished. For different findings in the US see Ch. 4 above, note 11 and accompanying text.

doing and why. Standard economic analysis suggests that courts should view risk-imposing activity as negligent if the risk targets the rich and as non-negligent if it targets the poor. However, no judicial decisions that sanction such a result can be found.[117] This suggests that courts are influenced, consciously or not, by the egalitarian imperative not to employ different degrees of protection for potential victims.

Finally, court decisions occasionally exhibit sensitivity to egalitarian considerations, even if this sensitivity is not explicitly expressed in the reasoning and the rhetoric of the court. For example, in *Matthews v Amberwood Associates Ltd Partnership, Inc.*,[118] the Maryland Supreme Court imposed liability on a deep-pocket defendant landlord for the fatal injury suffered by a tenant's guest from the tenant's dog. While the overall desirability of the result in *Matthews* might be disputed (and its multidimensional distributive results should be more carefully examined), most probably the result was motivated by a distributive-egalitarian concern. Indeed, the dissenting judge faulted the result reached by the majority for 'the implication that rich landlords and sympathetic victims are judged by totally different standards'.[119] As discussed above, the limited tendency of courts to impose a duty of care of lawyers towards unrepresented parties is based to a great extent on egalitarian considerations.[120]

B. Considering Needs and Equality in Tort Law and Private Law

Incorporating egalitarian considerations into standard of care analysis also fits with broader tendencies in tort law and private law that reveal limited attentiveness to needs and equality considerations. Sensitivity to needs is shown by tort law in two ways. First, as mentioned above, distributive considerations concerning loss-spreading and deep pockets have influenced the development of tort doctrine and are helpful in explaining specific results. Thus, for example, vicarious liability, products liability, and liability of public authorities have been explained as partially based on loss-spreading and deep-pocket grounds.[121] Some courts explicitly endorse distributive considerations, mainly loss-spreading ones, as factors in determining liability.[122] While courts in some jurisdictions reject insurance as a relevant factor in liability

117 But see Matthew D. Adler & Eric A. Posner, 'Rethinking Cost-Benefit Analysis', 109 *Yale LJ* (1999) 165, pp. 174, 246 (arguing that, in its cost-benefit analysis, the Environmental Protection Agency did not attach lower values to the lives of migrant farm workers than to the national average, even though migrant farm workers are poorer than average). For rejecting (in dictum) a lower standard toward the poor (while supporting this rejection also on grounds of efficiency), see CA 10064/02 *Migdal v Abu Hanna*, Takdin-Elyon 2005(03) 3932 (Israel), paras 41–2.

118 719 A.2d 119 (Md Ct App 1998).

119 Ibid., p. 138. See also ibid., p. 139.

120 See *Nahum v Dorenbaum*, *supra* note 59 and Example 6 above.

121 See, e.g., Atiyah, *supra* note 25, p. 22; Fleming, *supra* note 21, p. 410.

122 See, e.g., *McConville v State Farm Mut. Auto. Ins. Co.*, 113 NW 2d 14, 19 (Wis 1962); *Escola*, supra note 24, pp. 440–41; *Avellone v St John's Hosp.*, 135 NE 2d 410, 415 (Ohio 1956).

determinations,[123] the existence or absence thereof remains a hidden persuader and an explanation for results achieved by courts and juries.[124] Second, the growing tendency in many jurisdictions to replace classic tort fault-based liability with no-fault plans is itself mainly motivated by distributive considerations. These plans usually trade-off full compensation for a broader basis of entitlement to compensation, which is both motivated and justified by needs-based considerations.

Tort law is also showing some limited sensitivity to equality concerns. First, the formal commitment to an objective standard of care is undermined by the weighing of the circumstances of each case. This amounts to an indirect way of inserting some subjective aspects into the standard of care.[125] In addition to this informal across-the-board inclusion of subjective elements, tort doctrine at times explicitly adopts a subjective standard, or an objective-subjective standard in certain circumstances, especially with regard to the standard of care required of children[126] and in the context of contributory negligence.[127] Hence, allowance is made for children's age; the standard of care required of professionals is higher;[128] and, at times, the parties' disabilities (especially physical disabilities of defendants), are taken into account.[129] This tendency reflects sensitivity to equality considerations, since from a justice perspective the main problem in adopting an objective standard is holding individuals accountable for not meeting the required standard, despite their inability to meet that standard. An objective standard, therefore, overburdens those who cannot meet its requirements.

More broadly, tort law is and should be attentive to the demands of equality by virtue of its being part of legal cultures that endorse equality and are committed to its enhancement.[130] Some jurisdictions are committed to the idea that public law values

---

123 See, e.g., *Hamstra v BC Rugby Union* [1997] 1 SCR 1092, 1108 (Can); *Lister v Romford Ice & Cold Storage Co. Ltd* [1957] 1 All ER 125, 133 (HL).

124 Fleming, *supra* note 21. See, e.g., *Transco Plc v Stockport Metropolitan Borough Council* [2004] 1 All ER 589, para 46.

125 See Rogers, *supra* note 12, p. 190; Page Keeton, *Prosser & Keeton on the Law of Torts* (5th edn, Saint Paul, 1984), pp. 174–5; Walton, *supra* note 100, p. 366.

126 See, e.g., *Mullin v Richards* [1998] 1 All ER 920 (CA) (a test for negligence based on reasonable child of the same age in the same situation); *Gough v Thorne* [1966] 3 All ER 398 (CA) (same test for determining contributory negligence of a minor); *Caradori v Fitch*, 263 NW 2d 649 (Neb 1978); Restatement (Second) of Torts, s. 285 (1965) (test of reasonable person of like age, intelligence, and experience under like circumstances).

127 See, e.g., *De Nartini v Alexsander Sanitarium*, 13 Cal Rptr 564 (Ct App 1961) (allowing for the mental incapacity of plaintiff for purposes of contributory negligence); Keeton, *supra* note 125, p. 178.

128 See, e.g., *Bolam v Friern Hosp. Management Comm.* [1957] 1 WLR 582 (QB); *Heath v Swift Wings, Inc.*, 252 SE 2d 256 (NC App 1979).

129 See, e.g., Rogers, *supra* note 12, p. 253; *Daly v Liverpool Corp.* [1939] 2 All ER 142 (KBD); *M'Kibbon v Glasgow Corp.*, 1920 Sess Cas 590 (Scot 2nd Div); *Haley v. London Elec. Bd* [1965] AC 778 (HL) (implicit); Keeton, *supra* note 125, pp. 175–6; *Fletcher v City of Aberdeen*, 338 P 2d 743 (Wash 1959); Restatement (Second) of Torts, s. 283C (1965) (standard required from the physically disabled is that of a reasonable man under like disability).

130 For example, Ken Cooper-Stephenson and Kate Sutherland have argued that tort law includes and promotes concepts of substantive equality. See Ken Cooper-Stephenson,

in general, and equality in particular, should influence the doctrinal development of private law, including torts.[131] This commitment to equality is not merely rhetorical. Indeed there is a growing body of case law reshaping private law doctrines in accordance with the demands of equality (though, not enough). Examples include the (inconsistent) use of intentional infliction of emotional distress to combat racist and sexist slurs;[132] the growing attentiveness to the symbolic aspects of recognizing certain false statements as defamatory;[133] the continuing resistance to the imposition of a duty of care on pregnant women toward their children for alleged negligence during pregnancy;[134] the reduction of gender inequality in awarding damages in general[135] and damages for lost earnings in particular;[136] and the attentiveness to structural sexist approaches by the police in investigating sexual offences.[137] A similar tendency is noticeable in contract law.[138]

Conclusion

The gist of negligence is the improper balancing of one's interests with the interests of others. Bearing either the risk of accidents or the burden of their prevention creates disutility whose size depends on one's prior resources. From a moral perspective, it is the loss's disutility, rather than its absolute size which should be compared, in deciding whether the behaviour was negligent or not. Accordingly, the means of the defendant and that of the expected plaintiff are relevant for evaluating the reasonableness of the defendant's behaviour. This approach is supported by needs, substantive equality and desert as criteria for distribution and is compatible with notions of fault and corrective justice. Where the burden of precaution is too onerous, given the actors' respective position, the defendants' failure to reduce the risk is justified (the behaviour is reasonable) and not merely excused.

While there is no one ideal way to translate egalitarian commitment into standard of care analysis, several proxies constitute a good starting point. These proxies

'Corrective Justice, Substantive Equality and Tort Law', in Ken Cooper-Stephenson & Elaine Gibson (eds), *Tort Theory* (Toronto, 1993), p. 48; Ken Cooper-Stephenson, 'Economic Analysis, Substantive Equality and Tort Law', in ibid., p. 131; Kate Sutherland, 'The New Equality Paradigm: The Impact of Charter Equality Principles on Private Law Decisions', in David Schneiderman & Kate Sutherland (eds), *Charting the Consequences* (Toronto, 1997), p. 245.

131 See, e.g., Sutherland, ibid., pp. 253–8; CA 294/91, *Jerusalem Chevra Kadisha v Kestenbaum*, PD 46(2) 464, 530 (Israel); Aharon Barak, *Interpretation in Law* (vol. 3, Jerusalem, 1994), pp. 680–85. For comparative law solutions, see ibid., pp. 667–78.

132 See Ch. 7 below, note 5.

133 See Ch. 4 above, note 36.

134 See Ch. 6.II below.

135 See, e.g., CA 64/89 *Gabay v Luzon*, PD 48(4) 673 (Israel).

136 See, e.g., *Reilly v United States*, 665 F Supp 976, 997 (RI 1987), *aff'd*, 863 F 2d 149, 167 (1st Cir 1988). Of course, some courts do take this fact into account. See e.g., *Shows v Shoney's, Inc.*, 738 So 2d 724 (La App 1st Cir 1999). See Ch. 8 below.

137 *Doe*, *supra* note 96.

138 See Zamir, *supra* note 38, pp. 1751–3, 1783–5.

include proportionality, calculating the pecuniary loss of the average victim, and that of a victim similarly situated as the defendant. Egalitarian sensitivity is relevant in a broad spectrum of situations: active risk creation, channelling risk from one group of potential victims to another, and failure to prevent risk created by a third party. It pertains to both financial and social vulnerability of victims. Inculcating egalitarian sensitivity into the notion of reasonableness exceeds the issue of standard of care, as the concept of reasonableness is relevant to other doctrines as well. Finally, the analysis offered in the chapter is compatible with the prevalent definition of standard of care in common law jurisdictions, with some court decisions from several jurisdictions and with courts' practice, which is not always articulated explicitly.

Chapter 6

Duty of Care

Introduction

This chapter addresses the role of egalitarianism in duty of care analysis. It begins, in Part I, with a general exposition of the ways in which egalitarian sensitivity can and should affect duty of care analysis. The last three parts are dedicated to the case study of maternal prenatal duty. The analysis shows how the egalitarian concern, which seemingly operates to curb liability of women as a disadvantaged group, in fact supports the imposition of a duty that is conditional on the existence of liability insurance covering the activity leading to the tort litigation, and is limited to the scope of the coverage ('conditional duty' or 'the suggested rule'). Part II presents the problem, the possible solutions to it and the approaches taken in several common law jurisdictions. Part III presents the arguments against unconditional duty, explains that the rejection of such duty is best justified by the duty's equality effects and defends this view notwithstanding the existence of disadvantaged plaintiffs – newborns with physical injury. It also examines the desirability of imposing a general duty. Part IV, the heart of this chapter, defends from egalitarian-feminist perspective the adoption of a rule of conditional duty. Conditional duty promotes women's interests and autonomy, by benefiting the women who are to be found liable without hurting women's collective interests.

I. The Effects of Egalitarianism on Duty of Care

As is true in general, egalitarianism can work in two opposing directions with respect to the scope of duty: as a reason to narrow it when it burdens the disadvantaged and as a reason to expand it when it benefits the disadvantaged. Analytically, the former alternative is fitting with the understanding of duty as a filter of liability. Duty is rejected when there are good reasons to avoid imposing liability on those who acted negligently. These reasons include: the fear of over-deterrence of non-negligent activity by potential tortfeasors; the sense that liability might be too burdensome and hence unjust even when imposed on a negligent tortfeasor; and the concern that imposing a duty will have an adverse effect on potential plaintiffs, third parties, society as a whole, or on the courts.[1] In sum, liability should not be imposed if it would

1 See Richard A. Buckley, *The Modern Law of Negligence* (3rd edn, London, 1999), pp. 15–26; Jane Stapleton, 'Duty of Care Factors: A Selection from the Judicial Menus', in Peter Cane & Jane Stapleton (eds), *The Law of Obligations: Essays in Celebration of John Fleming* (Oxford, 1998), p. 59; W.V.H. Rogers, *Winfield and Jolowicz on Tort* (16th edn, London, 2002), p. 106.

bring about undesirable results that outweigh the undesirability involved in leaving negligent behaviour undeterred and those harmed by this behaviour uncompensated. One of the reasons to avoid imposing a duty might be its inegalitarian effects. When potential defendants are typically disadvantaged, narrowing the scope of liability or denying it altogether might be desirable from an egalitarian perspective. The case for denying an unconditional duty of maternal prenatal care is based on such a rationale. Chapter 5 suggested that the narrow scope of the duty imposed on parents for negligent supervision can be explained (or justified) based on the inegalitarian effect of such duty in gender terms. The inegalitarian effect, then, serves as a reason to oppose liability despite the possible existence of considerations supporting liability such as fairness, deterrence and desert which often support the imposition of liability for negligent behaviour. When deviation from the required standard is set, using the concept of duty to deny liability might operate as an excuse: while the defendant's activity is not justified, avoiding the imposition of liability is justified, based on the surrounding circumstances, which include the parties' status and the effects of imposing liability. For an instrumentalist, the role of the duty might be understood as (1) conducting a cost-benefit analysis of the results of imposing liability for negligent behaviour and (2) denying liability if the costs outweigh the benefits. While at the standard level, the defendant's conduct is being evaluated, at the duty level, the results of imposing liability for such negligent conduct are being evaluated. At both levels, cost-benefit analysis should not be (and in practice is not) equated with efficiency or wealth maximization. Rather, it should take into account all the relevant factors, including the relative status of the affected parties and the rule's effect upon them.

Egalitarianism can also serve as reason for *expanding* the scope of duty towards the disadvantaged. Typically, it would serve as a reason to recognize a duty, despite the fact that other policy considerations militate against such recognition. One way egalitarianism helps tip the scales in favour of liability is by making the benefits from liability – compensation and deterrence – more valuable, given the identity of the rule's beneficiaries. Compensating the disadvantaged is important, since it decreases the wealth-holding gap in society and since the amount received is crucial for preserving the victim's well-being. Deterring behaviour that harms the disadvantaged is important, since the disadvantaged lack the political and economic muscle to prevent or minimize the risk.

Another way egalitarianism helps tip the scales in favour of liability is by putting a check on the scope of liability. Indeterminate liability is a recognized consideration opposing recognition of duty.[2] By restricting the duty – in circumstances in which there are good reasons to curtail it – to situations in which the rule's beneficiaries are disadvantaged, the scope of potential liability decreases, and, accordingly, the fear from indeterminate liability recedes. The following examples will clarify the discussion.

In the context of a lawyer's duty toward an unrepresented opposing party, there are weighty considerations against recognizing such a duty, chief among them the fear that such a duty would undermine the lawyer's duty toward her client.

---

2 *Ultramares Corp. v Touche*, 174 NE 441 (NY Ct App 1931).

Nonetheless, the fact that the opposing party is unrepresented and as such is likely to be at a disadvantage, might support the imposition of duty. Indeed, in the Israeli case of *Nahum v Dorenbaum*[3] whose facts are summarized in Chapter 5 above,[4] it is clear that the disadvantage in the specific case – of an unrepresented borrower in the grey market – was a significant factor behind the majority's alternative reasoning, that the lender's lawyer owed a duty to the borrowers, even if in the specific transaction at issue, he did not represent both sides.

Another example of a situation in which egalitarianism supports expansion of liability is that of failed vasectomy operations. At times, the negligence may be manifested in the level of care in which the operation was conducted. At other times, it may be manifested in the explanation given to the patient regarding the risk of spontaneous reversal. The latter situation was the one litigated in *Goodwill v British Pregnancy Advisory Service*.[5] The court in *Goodwill* rejected the existence of a duty towards future sexual partners of the patient out of the concern of creating indeterminate liability. Such a broad holding is problematic,[6] based *inter alia* on egalitarian approach. To begin with, and regardless of egalitarian considerations, denial of duty creates a serious problem of externalization. Most of the damage from the unwanted pregnancy resulting from negligence surrounding vasectomy is borne by the woman and not by the patient. A rule denying a duty might leave the person damaged (the woman) without a cause of action and the person with the cause of action (the patient) without damage.[7] Such a split was a reason for recognizing a duty of the testator's lawyer towards the beneficiaries of the will for negligence in drawing up the will which led to the loss of legacy.[8] The inefficiency of a rule denying duty towards the sexual partner in the vasectomy context is exacerbated due to the regressive equality effect of the rule. The relational loss is borne by potential plaintiffs (women) who are disadvantaged in comparison both to men who undergo a vasectomy and the physicians who operate on those men. Therefore, the denial of duty is both inefficient and overwhelmingly regressive.

The equality effects of imposing or denying a duty on potential plaintiffs, defendants and third parties should be a factor in deciding the scope of liability for negligent supervision, both generally and in the case of public authorities in particular. In the context of public authorities, the relevant considerations should be the relative strength of typical plaintiffs in comparison to the average taxpayer (or, if possible, given the alternative use of the money paid as compensation). When

3 CA 2625/02 *Nahum v Dorenbaum*, PD 58(3) 385 (Israel).

4 Ch. 5.V.A, Example 6 above.

5 *Goodwill v British Pregnancy Advisory Service* [1996] 2 All ER 161 (CA).

6 Liability can still be denied if the physician was not negligent or if there was no causal connection between the negligence and the damage. Moreover, the plaintiff in *Goodwill* had an independent consultation with her physician who alerted her of the small chance of spontaneous reversal.

7 While the woman is likely to have a right to child support from the father regardless of the father's fault, these amounts do not compensate her in full for the damage from the unwanted pregnancy.

8 *White v Jones* [1995] 2 AC 207; [1995] 1 All ER 691, 708 (HL). Judge Gibson in *Goodwill* rejected the analogy to *White v Jones*.

potential plaintiffs are stronger than average, the justification to burden the public with the expense of compensating the plaintiffs lessens. Thus, for example, a negligent inspection by a securities regulator presents a less compelling case for recognizing a duty than a negligent inspection by a labour relations regulator. Needless to say, the rule's equality effect is only one consideration. Examples of other important considerations are the type of interest harmed, the degree of fault of the public authority and the extent to which it is a peripheral party, the extent of reliance by the plaintiff, and the likelihood that imposing liability will improve or hinder the public authority's incentives. Nonetheless, the equality effects of liability might serve as *partial* explanation for a tendency to curtail the scope of duty of public authorities toward plaintiffs who are typically strong. A case in point is the limited scope of duty toward real estate owners for negligent supervision of developers.[9]

II. Possible Solutions to the Problem of Maternal Prenatal Duty

While it is well established that third parties owe a duty of care to a child born with an injury from their prenatal negligence,[10] the equivalent question with respect to maternal prenatal negligence receives different answers in different jurisdictions. A basic distinction is drawn between a general duty and a duty with respect to lifestyle choices that may injure the future child.[11] A general duty involves injuries to the foetus from negligent activities that may not directly implicate the unique relationship between mother and foetus;[12] Rather, the pregnant woman is requested to meet the standard of care that is imposed on all members of society in order to avoid harm to third parties. A classic example is negligent driving, where the driver already owes a duty of care towards any other user of the road, and the question then arises whether she owes a duty to the child. A general duty can be imposed when the activity in question risked potential plaintiffs other than the child born, or when such activity injured another plaintiff. In contrast to general duty, in which the pregnant woman is seemingly not subjected to a special burden because of her pregnancy, duty with regard to lifestyle choices imposes on the mother a duty to behave in a way

9 For rejection of duty see, e.g., *Murphy v Brentwood District Council* [1990] 2 All ER 908 (HL). For a reasoning similar to that offered in the text, emphasizing fairness considerations see Kevin Woodall, 'Private Law Liability of Public Authorities for Negligent Inspection and Regulation', 37 *McGill LJ* (1992) 83, p. 134. For a summary of the different approaches in common law jurisdictions see Bruce Feldthusen, *Economic Negligence* (4th edn, Toronto, 2000), p. 263 n.7 and ibid., pp. 165–8.

10 *Montreal Tramways Co. v Leveille* [1933] SCR 456 (Can); *Payton v Abbott Labs,* 437 NE 2d 171 (Mass 1982).

11 For the terminology and the distinction see *Dobson v Dobson* (1997) 148 DLR (4th) 332, 336 (NBCA). For reasons of style the pregnant woman will be referred to as 'mother', the foetus or the future child as 'child', duty of care as 'duty' and maternal prenatal duty as 'the duty'.

12 *Bonte v Bonte*, 616 A 2d 464, 468 (NH 1992) (Brock CJ and Batchelder J, dissenting).

that does not unreasonably risk the child. Consumption of alcohol, drugs and cigarettes are the classic examples, but this duty can be extended to matters of nutrition, medication, sports activities and many other areas of life. The possible solutions that have been presented thus far range – from the most limited to the most expansive – from a no-duty rule rejecting duty altogether, through a general duty when another plaintiff has been injured, to a general duty when the activity risks other potential plaintiffs, and finally to a duty for lifestyle choices (a 'specific duty'). Liability for lifestyle choices, in turn, can either be limited to choices that are illegal according to a norm which is external to the tort of negligence (such as the use of drugs, which is a criminal offence), or else not be so limited. 'Unconditional duty' is a rule recognizing both general and specific duty.

Theoretically, it would be possible to insure any activity which is viewed as negligent and which might subject the defendant to general or specific duty. In practice however, not only is liability resulting from illegal activity not covered, but many policies also exclude from coverage deliberate or other conduct that courts a particular risk, such as, for example, consumption of alcohol.[13] The potential availability of insurance increases the range of solutions. Duty could be imposed with respect to activities that the liability insurance market is likely to insure. Such a rule is likely to reject specific duty, on the assumption that lifestyle choices are not likely to be insured. Alternatively, one could condition duty on the existence of coverage of the specific event leading to tort litigation, and limit the scope of liability to that coverage. Under such a solution, if a certain lifestyle choice injured the plaintiff, liability would only be imposed if the activity was insured, and the extent of such liability would not be greater than the extent of coverage. Another possible solution is to impose only a general duty (and, it should be recalled, there are two versions of general duty) which is conditioned upon the existence of liability insurance. Under this approach, even if a lifestyle choice was insured, duty will not be imposed; in addition, activity that risked or harmed third parties would not lead to a duty towards the child, if the liability towards the child was not insured.

There are three major ways to resolve the issue of the scope of maternal duty. At one extreme there is the solution that categorically denies any duty. At the other extreme, one could impose an unconditional duty. The intermediate solution is to impose a duty when the liability is insured (or is likely to be insured). In practice, courts adopt either the first or the third solution, but not the second. Cases denying the existence of duty are *Stallman v Youngquist* (1988, Illinois, majority),[14] *Dobson v Dobson* (1999, Canada, majority),[15] and *Remi v MacDonald* (2004, Massachusetts),[16] all three in the context of road accidents, and *Chenault v Huie* (1999, Texas CA),[17] in the context of drug abuse

---

13 E-mail from Ms Deirdre Martin from the Insurance Bureau of Canada, 6 October 1999, on file with the author.

14 *Stallman v Youngquist*, 531 NE 2d 355 (Ill 1988).

15 *Dobson v Dobson* [1999] 2 SCR 753 (Can).

16 *Remi v MacDonald*, 801 NE 2d 260 (Mass 2004).

17 *Chenault v Huie*, 989 SW 2d 474 (Tex Ct App 1999).

during pregnancy. Cases imposing duty when insurance was available are *Lynch v Lynch* (1991, New South Wales),[18] *Bowditch v McEwan* (2002, Queensland),[19] *Nat'l Casualty v NTB* (2002, Florida),[20] all three in the context of road accidents, *Bonte v Bonte* (1991, New Hampshire, majority),[21] (the insured defendant, a pedestrian, was hit by a car while crossing the road outside a designated pedestrian crossing), and *Grodin v Grodin* (1980, Michigan)[22] when the mother took medicine during pregnancy and the child was born with discoloured teeth. In the United Kingdom, section 1(1) of the Congenital Disabilities (Civil Liability) Act 1976 creates a rule of immunity of the pregnant woman, with an exception for road accidents.

The main characteristics of the case law are that these cases are relatively few and recent, and they involve relatively many dissents. The question is being raised mainly in the context of road accidents: only *Grodin*[23] and *Chenault*[24] dealt with specific duty. Liability was never imposed in the absence of insurance (although the existence of insurance is not always mentioned in the decision[25]) and only in one case – *Chenault* – was sought. The relevance of insurance was discussed in some of the cases; in some it tipped the scales in favour of liability[26] and in others it was held to be an irrelevant factor.[27] Only one case, *Nat'l Casualty v NTB*,[28] adopted the solution of condition duty, without, however, providing a reasoned explanation for this position.

III. The Egalitarian Case Against Unconditional Duty

In answering the question of what should be the scope of the duty, distributive sensitivity and an egalitarian-feminist commitment are the key elements of the analysis. The rule should adequately balance the interests of children in their physical integrity and the interests of mothers and women in respecting their autonomy, well-being and status. Such a rule would impose on women the minimal burden required in order to effectively promote the bodily integrity of potential plaintiffs, while giving adequate consideration to women's well-being and examining the appropriateness of the burden imposed on women in light of the relative status of those being burdened and those benefited from the rule.

18 *Lynch v Lynch* (1991) 25 NSWLR 411.

19 *Bowditch v McEwan and Ors* [2002] QCA 172.

20 *National Casualty Company v Northern Trust Bank of Florida*, 807 So 2d 86 (Fla Ct App 2002).

21 *Bonte*, *supra* note 12.

22 *Grodin v Grodin*, 301 NW 2d 869 (Mich Ct App 1980).

23 Ibid.

24 *Chenault*, *supra* note 17.

25 For the *Grodin* litigation, see John A. Robertson, 'Procreative Liberty and the Control of Conception, Pregnancy, and Childbirth', 69 *Va L Rev* (1983) 405 n.114 (based on telephone interview with John Kunkel, plaintiff's attorney (15 October 1982)).

26 See e.g., *Lynch*, *supra* note 18, pp. 415–16.

27 See e.g., *Dobson*, *supra* note 15, pp. 794–6 (Cory J), 801–2 (McLachlin J).

28 *Nat'l Casualty v NTB* , *supra* note 20.

A. The Arguments

In the absence of insurance, imposing the duty is undesirable, since the main two goals justifying the imposition of liability in torts – deterring potential tortfeasors and compensating victims – are not likely to be achieved.[29] The compensatory goal will not be achieved since in the vast majority of cases the injured child stays with her mother, so that the effect of liability is to transfer money from one pocket to another within the same economic unit, namely, the family. For the same reason, deterrence is not promoted. If the mother has the financial resources, she would use them anyway in order to take care of her child (and she is under a legal duty to do so even if maternal prenatal duty is not imposed). If she does not have the resources, imposing liability would be futile. Moreover, women have much stronger incentives than those provided by legal rules in general and tort law in particular to avoid unreasonably risking their future children.[30] If these incentives fail, it is doubtful whether the threat of civil liability will deter those women who are not adequately cautious during pregnancy.

Furthermore, imposing a duty may have several negative results which pertain mainly to women's status and well-being.[31] First, it may over-deter conforming women – those women who are in any case unlikely to act negligently while pregnant. Their fear that with time the scope of the standard of care imposed on pregnant women would be excessively broadened might cause them unnecessarily to avoid certain activities. Second, women's disempowerment in society and the tendency of society to over-regulate their reproductive functions raise the spectre of adopting, with time, an excessively burdensome standard of care.[32] Third, despite the fact that logically, a duty towards a child who was born alive has no bearing on the question of a duty towards the foetus,[33] imposing the duty might weaken women's control over their reproduction, threaten the right to abortion and increase the incidence of forced

29 See *Dobson*, *supra* note 15, pp. 767, 772, 781–2; Note, 'The Impact of Medical Knowledge on the Law Relating to Prenatal Injuries', 110 *U Pa L Rev* (1962) 554, 584; Lynn M. Paltrow, 'Pregnant Drug Users, Fetal Persons, and the Threat to *Roe v Wade*', 62 *Alb L Rev* (1999) 999, p. 1045 n.272.

30 See notes 70–72 below (non-conforming women typically do not risk their future children voluntarily).

31 Paltrow, *supra* note 29; Sheilah Martin & Murray Coleman, 'Judicial Intervention in Pregnancy', 40 *McGill LJ* (1995) 947; Dawn E. Johnsen, 'The Creation of Fetal Rights: Conflicts with Women's Constitutional Rights to Liberty, Privacy, and Equal Protection', 95 *Yale LJ* (1986) 599.

32 *Dobson, supra* note 15, pp. 782–90; *Winnipeg Child and Family Services (Northwest Area) v G (DF)* [1997] 3 SCR 925 (Can); (1998) 152 DLR (4th) 193, 210–11 (Can) [*WCFS*, cited to DLR]; Ian R. Kerr, 'Pre-Natal Fictions and Post-Partum Actions', 20 *Dal LR* (1997) 237, p. 266; Johnsen, ibid., pp. 606–7; Janet Gallagher, 'Prenatal Invasions & Interventions: What's Wrong with Fetal Rights', 10 *Harv Women's LJ* (1987) 9, pp. 44–5.

33 In fact, the availability of abortion is morally necessary in order to impose a duty on the pregnant women towards the future child. When bringing the pregnancy to term is not a voluntary decision, the *prima facia* case for supporting the imposition of a moral duty on the woman towards her future child becomes very contentious.

medical intervention for the foetus' sake.[34] Although as far as tort law is concerned, when there is no insurance there is no point in suing, forced medical intervention is likely to occur regardless of the existence of insurance, so that imposing the duty (which is futile in terms of promoting deterrence and compensation) might increase the excessive social regulation of women's reproduction. Fourth, the litigation and findings of liability resulting from a rule that imposes such a duty contain several objectionable symbolic messages, of which the two principal ones are: (1) the bad-mothers discourse, namely attributing selfishness and irresponsibility to pregnant women (or to women in general), and (2) treating women merely as means of reproduction rather than as ends in themselves.[35] Such instrumental perception of women may contribute to their exclusion from equal participation in the community, the public sphere and loci of power. Fifth, the possibility to sue, under a regime imposing a duty, could be abused, particularly by aggrieved and vengeful ex-partners filing suits for their nuisance value.[36] Sixth, imposing a duty unduly focuses on the nonconforming behaviour of a minority of women, rather than on the social and economic infrastructure that leads these women to act in this way. By this, imposing a duty falsely presents an illusion of an instant solution to a painful social problem, and might delay the adoption of a more comprehensive and effective (if expensive) solution to this problem. Imposing duty is the easy and cheap solution to the problem, but the wrong one, both overall and from the perspective of children's interest to be born whole.[37]

---

34 See e.g., Paltrow, *supra* note 29 (noting the connection between prosecuting pregnant drug users and the right to abortion and arguing that anti-choice groups concentrate, as a tactic, on foetal rights in the context of drug abuse, since drug users are an unpopular group).

35 See e.g., *Dobson*, *supra* note 15, p. 759 ;Johnsen, *supra* note 31, p. 622; Sheilah L. Martin, 'The Control of Women through Gender-Biased Laws on Human Reproduction', in Richard F. Devlin (ed.), *Canadian Perspectives on Legal Theory* (Toronto, 1991), p. 291; George J. Annas, 'Pregnant Women as Fetal Containers', 16 *Hastings Cent Rep* (1986) 13.

36 See *Dobson*, ibid., p. 781. Another version of this argument which was also endorsed in *Dobson* – that the possibility to file a suit will disrupt family harmony between spouses and between parents and children – is unconvincing. In the absence of insurance, tort litigation is the symptom of family dysfunction, not its cause. Other unconvincing arguments against imposing a duty are that such imposition might induce abortion and that it would have a boomerang effect, since women would avoid undergoing medical examination during pregnancy. See *WCFS*, *supra* note 32, p. 213. First, scepticism is due with respect to tort law's potential to influence a woman's decision whether to have an abortion or to seek medical care. This scepticism is especially warranted with respect to significant aspects of the conduct we would like to deter, such as drug abuse during pregnancy. This scepticism is warranted at least with respect to the hollow threat of damages award as opposed to the injunction remedy, which was sought in *WCFS*, and which might – perhaps – affect women's decisions regarding abortion and medical care. Second, assuming that tort law could affect women's decisions during pregnancy, it is far from clear that abortion is an undesirable result from a social perspective when the alternative is a high likelihood of giving birth to a seriously injured child.

37 For support of the desirable solution of education and investing resources to treat women at risk see, e.g., Royal Commission on New Reproductive Technologies, *Proceed with Care: Final Report* (vol. 2, Ottawa, 1993), pp. 961–5 (advocating a response to lack of proper

B. Egalitarian Framework

Elsewhere I argued that these considerations justify a rejection of solutions imposing unconditional duty and that it is the distributive consequences of such rules that justify this conclusion.[38] This section will not repeat that discussion in full, but rather will outline its main points. One should distinguish between burdens that are excessive *per se* – regardless of the way they are borne in society – and burdens that are problematic given the identity of those who bear them.[39] Maternal prenatal duty belongs to the second group.[40] In circumstances in which the decision to bring the pregnancy to term is voluntary and the risk from the negligent behaviour is foreseeable, the expectation that the mother should avoid unreasonable risks in order to prevent injury to her future child cannot be easily considered as excessive *per se*. It is the fact that the burden is imposed only on women – a disempowered group in society – which renders the adoption of unconditional duty problematic. Accordingly, the main arguments militating against the imposition of a duty can be better understood and defended in an egalitarian framework. The first three concerns (over-deterrence, excessive broadening of the standard, and excessive regulation of reproduction) are especially convincing *since* the rule targets a disadvantaged group. First, there is greater likelihood that these negative results will occur, when those burdened by the rule are disadvantaged, even if for the epistemological gap between the experience and ethics of the advantaged – who create and apply the rules – and the disadvantaged.[41] Such a gap results in a failure of the former to appreciate the interests of the latter. Second, the identity of those burdened by the rule as disadvantaged makes the results discussed in the first three concerns more problematic, even if that identity does not affect the likelihood that the results will occur. This is so, since society should protect more vigorously the little that the disadvantaged have, and since the rule's result – burdening the disadvantaged – is an undesirable result in itself. It follows, then, that the special weight that should be given to the interests of the potential defendants as disadvantaged should lead to a rejection of unconditional duty.

Similarly, the sixth concern (choosing the easy solution) is convincing, since it is easier to burden the disempowered and harder to generate the political power required to embark on large-scale expenditures aimed at benefiting the disempowered.

---

maternal care which is based on support and care rather than on legal intervention); *Dobson*, *supra* note 15, p. 773; Carolyn Coffey, 'Whither v State: Aberrational Judicial Response or Wave of the Future for Maternal Substance Abuse Cases?', 14 *J Contemp Health L & Pol'y* (1997) 211; Paul H. Wise, 'Child Beauty, Child Rights and the Devaluation of Women', 4(1) *Health and Human Rights* (1995) 470.

38 Tsachi Keren-Paz, 'On Mothers, Babies and Bathwater: Tort Law, Distributive Justice and Prenatal Duties', 14 *Social & Legal Studies* (2005) 179.

39 Ibid., pp. 183–4.

40 Ibid., pp. 184–7.

41 Cf. Duncan Kennedy, 'Distributive and Paternalist Motives in Contract and Tort Law, with Special Reference to Compulsory Terms and Unequal Bargaining Power', 41 *Md L Rev* (1982) 563, pp. 646–8.

Likewise, the fifth concern (abuse of the process by ex-partners) becomes more convincing when the defendants in these suits are typically weaker than the plaintiffs, so that by imposing a duty the legal system increases both women's vulnerability and the gender power gap in domestic settings.

Finally, with respect to the fourth concern, that of the symbolic ramifications of the rule, these ramifications are created due to the fact that women bear the rule's burden disproportionately. It is the lack of reciprocity that allows the reasonable conclusion that women are treated as means.[42] When the duty is imposed generally and all individuals are equally potential plaintiffs and defendants, restricting their autonomy for the benefit of others while using them also as means, is offset by treating them as ends in themselves. In other words, they are also potential plaintiffs for whose benefit others are subject to duties. Under such circumstances, using these potential defendants as a means does not carry the demeaning message that those bound by duties are not important in themselves or that they are less important than those holding the correlative right.

The situation is different when a disadvantaged group is subject to a duty to others. In that case, we can impute from the existence of a selective duty that those subject to the duty are not appreciated for who they are, and are not considered equal to other members in society. First, by subordinating women's interests to children's interests, women are devalued in comparison to children. Such a devaluation would not occur, or at least would be greatly attenuated, were parental duties to children not gender-biased. Second, by imposing a selective duty on women towards children while men are not made subject to any equivalent duty, women are devalued in comparison to men. Since only women are subject to such a duty to children, only women are regarded as means rather than as ends.

C. Newborns with Disability as Disadvantaged Plaintiffs?

1. Newborns An egalitarian analysis of prenatal duty has to account for the fact that an unconditional duty is seemingly warranted since potential plaintiffs – newborns – are weaker than potential defendants, and therefore the distributive result of the rule is progressive. For argument's sake, let us accept the underlying assumption, which is by no means obvious, that newborns are more disadvantaged than women. Still, imposing a duty is undesirable from an egalitarian perspective for three reasons which are explained below. All of these reasons are based on a common understanding: that the overall equality effect of a given rule should be taken into account. When the long-term effects of a rule that imposes a duty on the status of women, men and children are taken into account, egalitarianism opposes the imposition of duty.

(a) Narrowing the gap between women and children is not necessarily desirable. An egalitarian inquiry should compare the existing holdings of

42 For another theoretical approach to tort law, one that emphasizes reciprocity of burdens and benefits within a Rawlsian framework, see Gregory C. Keating, 'Distributive and Corrective Justice in the Tort Law of Accidents', 74 *S Cal L Rev* (2000) 193.

different groups in society against their holdings according to the ideal distributive scheme. The fact that one group has more than another is not necessarily problematic. The question is whether the suggested rule brings the affected groups closer to the desired result. A rule that decreases the gap between women and children is therefore not necessarily desirable. Moreover, even if the distribution of holdings between women and children under a no-duty rule tilts too much toward women, a rule decreasing the gap between the two groups will not be necessarily closer to the ideal distributive scheme.[43] It should be recalled that, for reasons explained above, the effectiveness of an unconditional duty in preventing injury and compensating for it is meagre. By burdening women without benefiting children in practice, an unconditional duty is likely to bring about a result that is further from the ideal distribution than a no-duty rule.

(b) The distributive triangle: women–men–children. The negative effects of the rule can be summarized as entrenching patriarchy in society. This means that in the triangle of women, men and children, imposing a duty burdens women and benefits men without benefiting children. Moreover, since patriarchy harms children as well, the likely result of imposing a duty is to increase the gap between women and men (the most powerful) and to increase the gap between men and children (the least powerful). Even if the gap between women and children is decreased, and even if such decrease is warranted from an egalitarian perspective, it is likely that the overall equality effect of the rule is undesirable.

(c) Children's interests as men's interests. The interests of children might be revealed to be those of men; accordingly we might deal not with a triangle of women–men–children but with a rule shifting power directly from women to men. The children born are not sexless. They are girls and boys who will become adult women and men. When the temporal aspect is taken into account, the rule's effects on women and men become clear. Women bear disproportionately (if not solely) the burden of an unconditional duty as pregnant women. The benefit to children (assuming it exists at all) is spread among boys and girls alike. The newborn girls, when they become adult women, will themselves be subjected to the duty. The boys will not, and as grown men, they will benefit from the patriarchal nature of the rule.

This analysis exemplifies a point made in Chapter 3, that there is no necessary tension between egalitarianism and efficiency. The rule of an unconditional duty is inefficient, in that it imposes a significant burden on mothers without benefiting children. From a distributive perspective this inefficiency is translated into an inegalitarian distribution, in which men benefit from the rule at the expense of women, and arguably at the expense of children as well.

---

43 If, for example, the ideal distributive scheme allocates 10 units to women and 5 to children, a distribution under a no-duty rule which is 12:4, is preferable over a distribution under unconditional duty of 7:6, despite the fact that the latter distribution decreased the gap between the two groups. The magnitude of the deviation of the no-duty distribution from the ideal distribution is 3 ((12 – 10) + (5 – 4)), and that of the unconditional duty is 4 (10 – 7) + (6 – 5)).

2. The Disabled as Disadvantaged Similarly, an egalitarian account should respond to the charge that it ignores the interests of potential plaintiffs with physical (or mental) injury who are arguably worse-off than women. The response follows the one outlined above with respect to the interests of children as a disadvantaged group. While such disadvantage should not be ignored, and while the interest in physical integrity should receive more protection than other interests protected by tort law, in the model advocated in this book this disadvantage or interest should not override other interests. The overall equality effects of the rule should be evaluated. Therefore, the scope of liability with respect to risks of physical injury should also take into account other disadvantages, such as gender. Given the fact that an unconditional duty is unlikely to reduce the number of injuries, the analysis does not change when the interests of the disabled are taken into account.

D. General Duty?

Elsewhere I argued that even imposing a general duty – the least problematic option from an egalitarian perspective – is undesirable.[44] Even when liability is conditional upon injuring another victim (and this requirement minimizes the material and symbolic negative effect of the rule), the rule nonetheless has a disparate impact on women who are potentially liable for the future child during the 40 weeks of pregnancy. Recall that according to the model, the rule's equality effect has to be balanced against its other effects, so the lesser the disparate impact of the rule, the weaker the case against adopting the rule. Assuming the added burden is not significant from a practical perspective,[45] and given the fact that pregnant women are not subject to a special duty, the negative symbolic aspects of the rule are also insignificant. Under these circumstances the negative inference from adopting the rule – devaluing the disadvantaged and their interests – can be made to a lesser extent.[46] However, since in the absence of insurance the benefits from the rule are meagre at best, even the case for adopting the least objectionable version of an unconditional duty remains dubious.[47]

44 Keren-Paz, *supra* note 38, pp. 187–92.

45 See Part IV.C below.

46 See Keren-Paz, *supra* note 38, pp. 189–90.

47 The following three points complete the analysis. First, the rejection of an unconditional duty faces the problem of any protectionist rule, that of a double bind or, in this case, undermining women's agency. Nonetheless, the dangers involved in recognizing an unconditional duty outweigh the price paid for this protectionist approach. Second, some believe that imposing a duty might affect not only the level of care taken by pregnant women but also the number of pregnancies carried to term. For the claim and its critique see note 36 above. Third, parental postnatal liability to children also raises issues from an egalitarian perspective. While the possible gender bias should be taken into account – for initial and partial discussion see Chs 3 above, notes 101–2 and accompanying text, 5 above, Example 8 – the unique biological nature of pregnancy should not be ignored, and accordingly no hasty analogies should be drawn from the analysis in this chapter to post-natal maternal care.

IV. Conditional Duty

This part defends a claim which at first sight is both radical from the perspective of tort law's history and logic and counterintuitive from an egalitarian-feminist perspective: that the egalitarian concern supports the imposition of a conditional duty. Focusing on an abstract concern for autonomy and neglecting to conduct a nuanced and full egalitarian analysis led some courts, despite their best intentions, to arrive at undesirable results from a feminist-egalitarian perspective.

A comprehensive distributive analysis of maternal prenatal duty should take into account the following points: (1) the unity of interests among potential plaintiffs and defendants as a result of the existence of liability insurance; (2) the tension between the practical and symbolic results of the rule; (3) the issue of inter-group justice among men and women with respect to the way premiums are collected; (4) the issue of intra-group justice resulting from the fact that one group of women (the conforming women) subsidizes another group of women (the non-conforming women); and (5) balancing gender equality with other distributive criteria, such as desert, as well as other egalitarian dimensions, such as class and race.

A. The Unity of Interests Among Pregnant Women and their Children

Recognizing a duty seemingly creates rivalry between the group of pregnant women (the potential defendants) and the group of children who are born injured (the potential plaintiffs).[48] However, when liability insurance exists the true rivalry is between, on the one hand, the mother and child, and, on the other, the mother's insurer.[49] In the vast majority of cases in which a child is born with an injury due to its mother's behaviour during pregnancy, the child will remain with the mother, with the result that the financial and other costs of the injury will be borne mainly by her. The same-pocket reality, it should be recalled, is offered as a reason for the futility of imposing a duty in the absence of liability insurance. The possibility that the child would sue the mother after he or she reaches majority, and the existence of situations in which the mother does not take care of the injured child, do not change this conclusion. Often, courts assume the existence of parental care for injured children even after the child reaches adulthood, and a duty to support a destitute adult child might be imposed by law.[50] Similarly, there is no ground for a sweeping assumption that if the child is kept in an institution, the mother will not finance the cost, if she has the means. Even in the rare cases that she will not, legal duty to pay these costs may exist, based on the duty of a parent to provide for her child (rather than on the duty to

---

48 The existence of such rivalry is the premise – and the result – of the adversarial model. This model is criticized by the feminist literature. See, e.g., Cynthia R. Daniels, *At Women's Expense: State Power and the Politics of Fetal Rights* (Cambridge, 1993), p. 138 – the discussion in the text should not be understood as endorsing the adversarial model when no insurance exists.

49 Cf. Allan C. Hutchinson, 'Birth Rights: The Burden of Caring For Unwanted or Seriously Injured Children', 4(2) *National* (1995) 40.

50 See e.g., *Turpin v Sortini, 643 P 2d 954,* 965 (Cal 1982); CA 283/89 *Municipality of Haifa v Moskovitz*, PD 47(2) 718, 725 (Israel).

compensate the child for prenatal injuries inflicted negligently). Given that existing law can adequately resolve the problem of those rare cases in which (1) the injured child is not in the mother's custody, (2) the mother has adequate financial means, and (3) the mother abandons the child, it is highly doubtful whether it is justified to recognize a maternal prenatal duty just for the purpose of resolving such situations.

The same-pocket reality explains why it is in the mother's interest to be found liable, in order that her child will receive compensation for the child's injury. Over and above parents' natural interest in their children's well-being, mothers, as those overwhelmingly responsible for providing care to children, both healthy and injured, will be those most benefited from the existence of funds to compensate the child. One's positive liberty and obviously one's well-being are significantly affected by one's available resources. *Ex post* then, women who have injured children (and of course the injured children themselves) would fare better under a regime of conditional duty. Moreover, a conditional duty regime might also increase pregnant women's *ex ante* autonomy.[51] A no-duty rule would have the effect of increasing the tendency of pregnant women to limit risky activity (such as driving), out of the fear that if the risk materialized, then their child would not be compensated, in the absence of liability. Thus, for example, the *Dobson*[52] case, whose reasoning is rife with rhetoric of women's autonomy and equality, brings about the opposite result – harming Ms Dobson, harming her injured child and impinging upon the autonomy of pregnant potential drivers. For this reason the court in *Dobson* threw out the mother and the baby with the patriarchal bathwater.

Ignoring the unity of interests of the pregnant woman and her child in finding the mother liable and focusing the debate on women's abstract interest in autonomy and equality ignores the fact that the real rivalry in cases such as *Dobson* is between the insured (and her child) and the insurer. Behind the feminist rhetoric of the decision hides an insurer seeking to avoid paying insurance benefits to those injured as a result of the negligence of the insured. It should be mentioned that one of the pragmatic arguments against imposing duty is the fear of collusion between plaintiffs and defendants.[53] While such an argument is unconvincing on the merits,[54] it attests to the fact that the real battleground in cases where insurance exists is between the insured-defendant and the insurer, and not between the insured mother and her future child.

The unity of interests between potential defendants-mothers and plaintiffs-children in holding the former liable distinguishes this situation from the paradigmatic tort case. Usually, potential tortfeasors do not have a strong interest in the victims

51 The analysis is based on the assumption, which is by no means simple, that tort rules can direct pregnant women's behaviour.

52 *Dobson*, *supra* note 15.

53 See David E. Koropp, 'Setting the Standard: A Mother's Duty During the Prenatal Period', 2 *U Ill L Rev* (1989) 493, p. 501 n.68.

54 The collusion argument has been invoked in the past as a consideration supporting parental and spousal immunity. It served patriarchal order, and as such is problematic in itself from an egalitarian perspective. Moreover, on the merits, the apprehension of collusion seems to be overstated, especially given the fact that in practice the defendants' lawyers would be appointed by the insurer. In modern American law, the weight given to the collusion argument decreases.

being compensated for their loss. Therefore, hinging the defendant's liability on his purchase of liability insurance might cause a serious disincentive to purchase insurance. Such a disincentive does not exist with respect to pregnant women. On the contrary, such liability regime gives the pregnant woman an incentive to purchase liability insurance, which might be the only available or affordable insurance for prenatal injuries.[55] At first glance, a conditional duty regime might create a moral hazard problem: it could be argued that the pregnant woman would not take adequate care during pregnancy in order to receive compensation. This fear is highly unfounded. First, the compensation is given for real damage that was caused; given the same-pocket reality in the mother–child unit, receiving the insurance award cannot improve the lot of the mother compared to the alternative of no injury and no award. Second, the natural incentive the mother has to protect the health of her future child reduces the concern regarding moral hazard. If there is one field in which one can expect risk aversion, this is the field, and in this respect one should also recall that serious injuries are not fully compensated for by tort law.

B. The Tension Between the Practical and Symbolic Results of the Rule

A conditional duty rule benefits non-conforming women by increasing their autonomy during pregnancy, and it benefits women who have a child who is born injured due to their negligence by providing compensation for these injuries. From a practical perspective, then, imposing duty is justified from an egalitarian-feminist perspective.[56] However, such a rule apparently involves negative symbolic and long-term practical ramifications which were introduced above and include mainly valuing women merely as means, the bad-mothers discourse, increasing forcible medical intervention during pregnancy and threatening the right to abortion. These consequences are also partially borne by non-conforming women. Hence, imposing duty simultaneously improves their lot (mainly from a practical perspective) and worsens it (due to the duty's symbolic and long term effects). For the women who are sued, the negative consequences from recognizing a duty cannot support rejection of such duty. The existence of such litigation attests to the fact that the relevant defendants are interested in being found liable. This was evident in the *Dobson* and *Grodin* cases.[57] Denying a duty based on the interests of non-conforming women amounts to paternalism. While a sweeping anti-paternalist approach is unattractive, paternalism is especially problematic when it is directed at members of disadvantaged groups. It is problematic from a practical perspective for two reasons. First, there is a greater chance that the paternalistic rule will not achieve its purported result due

55 First party insurance covering all risks to the child while still *in utero*, might be too expensive and might not be offered by insurers.

56 This conclusion holds true even when the costs of financing are taken into account. See Section C below.

57 For *Grodin* see Robertson, *supra* note 25. For *Dobson* see Chris Morris, 'Family Believes Ryan Forgotten', *The Toronto Sun* (10 July 1999); Janice Tibbetts, 'Mother Attacks Pro-Choicers After Son Loses Foetal Rights Case: Expresses Anger in Letter Sent to Several Newspapers', *National Post* (15 July 1999) A5.

to the inability of those making the rules to appreciate the priorities, preferences and interests of those regulated by the rule. Second, paternalistic motives might serve as a pretext in order to marginalize the disadvantaged and perpetuate their subordination.[58] Paternalism which is directed at the disadvantaged is also problematic ideologically, since it does not recognize the ability of the disadvantaged to determine for themselves what is best. This message is insulting when there is a gap between those who decide and those on whose behalf decisions are made, and it is especially insulting when the former are ranked the top of the social ladder and the latter are ranked at the bottom. If there is a good reason to oppose a conditional duty, then, this reason should lie with the interests of others who are harmed by imposing the duty. The inquiry will turn now to this question.

C. The Ways Premiums are Collected: Questions of Inter- and Intra-group Justice

Imposing conditional duty involves two types of costs. One type, which will be discussed below, is the symbolic ramifications of imposing liability and its long term effects on women's status in society. The other type of cost is the increase in premiums needed in order to cover the insurers' exposure to children-plaintiffs. There are three ways to finance this increase. One way is to spread the cost uniformly among women and men alike. Another way is to spread the cost uniformly solely among all women, or exclusively among women of child-bearing age. A third way is to try and price individually the risk posed by any woman seeking prenatal liability insurance. Given the costs involved in gathering the relevant information and the low expected scope of liability, the third solution is unlikely to be adopted.[59] Each of the other two solutions involves an element of subsidy. Under the second regime (spreading the cost among women) conforming women subsidize non-conforming women. The rise in premiums the former group pays is the lion's share of the amount collected from the insured and given as compensation to the injured children of non-conforming women. Under the first solution (spreading the costs among male and female insured), while conforming women continue to subsidize non-conforming women, they do so to a lesser extent, since men participate in the subsidy.

This analysis reveals the tension between the egalitarian concern and other considerations. From an egalitarian perspective it is clear that the first solution (and, for reasons explained below, the second solution as well), is preferable to a solution denying a duty. However, the criterion of desert opposes a solution according to which the careful subsidize the non-careful. The first two solutions involve exactly such subsidy.[60] By contrast, the second solution, and even more so the first one, are

58 For example, it has been argued that paternalism towards women in the context of protectionist labour legislation was intended to exclude women from significant participation in the labour market. See Heidi Hartmann, 'Capitalism, Patriarchy and Job Segregation by Sex', in Elizabeth Abel & Emily K. Abel (eds), *The Signs Reader: Women, Gender and Scholarship* (Chicago, 1983) 193, pp. 215–23.

59 Phone conversation with Peter Thurton, Director Market Conduct, RBC Life Insurance Company, 2 February 2000, Toronto. See also notes 66–7 below.

60 Cross-subsidy is usually problematic from an efficiency perspective as well, by causing under-deterrence of high-risk insured and over-deterrence of low-risk insured. The

supported by a loss spreading policy. Moreover, the first solution is a rare example of progressive cross-subsidy. As discussed in previous chapters, collecting uniform premiums usually results in the poor subsidizing the rich. Spreading the costs of liability for children born injured among all the insured is progressive, since men who do not contribute to the creation of this injury participate in financing the redress, and since men's income is higher on average than women's.[61] The objection to the first solution – on the grounds that it is unfair to impose liability on those who did not create the risk – should be rejected. First, the cross-subsidy effect is endemic to liability insurance and an attempt to create an exception, especially in the rare situation where the subsidy is progressive, is inappropriate.[62] Second, it is most likely that even if the first solution were adopted, the general regressive effect of liability insurance (caused by the fact that women and men are insured together) would still overshadow the progressive effect caused by men's participation in financing compensation for prenatal injuries.[63] Third, considerations of fairness, according to which those benefiting from an activity should bear its costs strongly support a solution that spreads the increase in premiums to men as well. Bringing children into the world is in men's interest as well; the fact that biological constraints impose the physical burden of pregnancy exclusively on women does not mean that the financial results of pregnancy, including the materialization of risks involved in the pregnancy, should be borne solely by women.[64]

Naturally, a loss-spreading policy is at tension with desert as criteria for distribution. The former supports subsidy while the latter opposes it (as does deterrence). Loss-spreading is commonly given preference in many legal systems in the sense that potential defendants are allowed to purchase liability insurance. It is hard to see a reason why in the context of prenatal injuries, willing women should be deprived of the opportunity to submit themselves to a negligence liability regime accompanied by, and conditional on, the existence of liability insurance. In any event, a desert-based claim against such a solution is no more convincing in the maternal prenatal context than in any other negligence litigation.[65] More generally, striking the balance between desert and

---

latter might drop out of the market and consequently the insurance market might collapse. Maternal prenatal duty does not involve this adverse selection problem for two reasons. First, it is doubtful whether the spectre of tort liability will change pregnant women's behaviour. Second, since the scope of liability is relatively small (see notes 66–7 below), the increase in premiums will be small and will not cause market collapse.

61 In fact, the progressive effect of the first solution is not so significant since in many cases when a child is born injured, his father, or the mother's partner, participates in bearing the financial costs of caring for the child.

62 Cf. note 80 below and accompanying text, Ch. 7 below, note 47 and accompanying text.

63 Cf. Tsachi Keren-Paz, 'Private Law Redistribution, Predictability and Liberty, 50 *McGill LJ* (2005) 327, p. 339 n.38.

64 For a similar claim see Sylvia A. Hewlett, *A Lesser Life: The Myth of Women's Liberation in America* (New York, 1986), Chs 3, 4, 6, 7.

65 Below it is suggested that desert considerations are less convincing in the prenatal context. See notes 70–72 below and accompanying text.

loss spreading considerations depends on the magnitude of the subsidy involved. If the premiums paid by conforming women (in the first and second solutions) and men (in the first solution) are significantly greater in order to cover a risk they did not create, the case against the suggested rule becomes stronger. If, on the other hand, the additional burden is insignificant, the advantages derived from spreading the loss significantly outweigh the injustice of burdening the subsidizers 'unjustly'. In the context of prenatal duties, both common sense[66] and estimations of tort scholars, tort practitioners and insurers suggest that the increase in premiums would not be significant.[67] This would be especially true if only a general, as opposed to a specific, duty is recognized.

There appears to be a difference between the first two solutions. While the first solution is also supported by egalitarianism (in addition to fairness and loss-spreading), the second solution is supported only by fairness and loss spreading considerations but is not supported by the egalitarian-feminist concern,[68] since the financial cost of providing compensation is borne by women alone. Nonetheless, if it is true that a conditional duty enhances women's autonomy and well-being (due to its *ex ante* and *ex post* effects), such a solution is desirable from a feminist perspective even if only women bear the costs of financing it. To take an example, if indeed pregnant women will avoid driving under a no-duty rule but will take the risk under a conditional duty rule, women's well-being will increase even if the second solution is adopted. There is no clear answer to the question which of the two regimes is likely to be adopted; the answer depends also on the structure of the insurance market. It is doubtful whether the market will offer policies covering only prenatal liability. Likewise, malpractice coverage is not likely to cover prenatal injuries. As to other types of liability insurance, it is more likely that administrative considerations will lead to spreading the increase in premiums among men and women alike. The fact that the amount in question is relatively small increases the chances that individual or selective pricing would be rejected. In any event, the outcome of the analysis is that even if the second solution is adopted, the suggested rule is still desirable from an egalitarian-feminist perspective.

D. *Intra-group Justice: Class and Race*

The analysis so far has suggested that conditional duty involves two types of costs, financial and symbolic, which are borne mainly by conforming women. The answer to the question whether this subsidy is desirable depends partially on answering the

---

66 One should bear in mind, that, assuming an average 40 years of driving and a birth rate of around 1.5 children per woman, the potential risk of a future child as plaintiff exists for only around 2.5 per cent of the duration of women's driving years.

67 For correspondence supporting this conclusion see Keren-Paz, *supra* note 38, n.7.

68 The second solution may have a progressive equality effect along the lines of race and class, if conforming women are *stronger* than non-conforming women. As the discussion in the next section suggests, there is no reason to assume that conforming women are *weaker* than non-conforming women.

question whether we have reason to believe that within the group of women, those who subsidize are stronger or weaker than those being subsidized. A progressive subsidy would provide further support for a conditional duty, while a regressive subsidy would weigh against such a solution. If the subsidy is progressive, there is an apparent tension between considerations of desert which oppose such a subsidy and egalitarian considerations which support it. The discussion begins by critically examining the notion of desert and its proper weight in our context. It continues by offering an intra-group equality effects analysis. Finally, it examines whether we have reason to believe that the group of non-conforming women, those being subsidized, is indeed weaker than the group of conforming women.

Proper weight of desert. The idea that desert considerations justify imposing liability on pregnant women who negligently injured their children merits critical examination. First, with respect to lifestyle choices, these choices are so fundamental and culturally based[69] that the notion of an objective standard, deviation from which should invite blame, is contestable. This problem is exacerbated by the well-founded fear that the interests of women as a disadvantaged group would be disregarded. Moreover, while at first glance it is possible to attach moral blame to pregnant women who make lifestyle choices that harm their children, we have, arguably, reason to doubt the appropriateness of such moral condemnation. Some harms are created in circumstances (such as addiction) that, even according to mainstream moral philosophy, prevent or greatly complicate desert-based moral condemnation.[70] Research shows that most women who are addicted to drugs or alcohol do whatever they can to take responsibility for their lives during pregnancy and attempt to overcome their addiction. There is also data suggesting that some of these women attempt to be admitted into drug treatment centres but are turned away.[71] Under these circumstances, ascribing responsibility to them largely ignores the social conditioning that led these women to act as they did and the fact that almost no woman will consciously risk her future child.[72]

Intra-group equality effects analysis. If non-conforming women are weaker than conforming ones, the practical results of the rule would be a progressive subsidy given by conforming women with respect to the costs of providing compensation to the injured children. Under such assumption, one might think that the ideological and long term effects of the rule involve less externalization since part of these costs (such as the bad mothers discourse and increasing regulation on pregnant women) will anyway be borne disproportionately by non-conforming women. On the other hand, one could argue that symbolically the suggested rule is problematic, precisely

69 *Stallman, supra* note 14, p. 360; *Chenault, supra* note 17, pp. 477–8. ('Yet, religious beliefs, social and economic status, age, maturity, and educational level differ significantly among women. Each of these factors may affect a woman's decisions with respect to prenatal care.')

70 Cf. McLachlin J in *WCFS, supra* note 32, p. 212.

71 Wendy Chavkin, 'Mandatory Treatment for Drug Use During Pregnancy', 266 *JAMA* (1991) 1556, p. 1557; Paltrow, *supra* note 29, pp. 1026–7.

72 See Paltrow, ibid. (correlation between drug abuse and being physically abused, and encountering barriers to getting help).

because it produces the bad-mothers discourse with respect to members of groups that are disadvantaged in terms of race and class.[73]

Are non-conforming women weaker? It is hard to identify one group as stronger than the other. In the adjacent context of forced medical treatment given to pregnant women for the foetus' sake, the American and Canadian experience teaches that such measures are suffered disproportionately by poor women of colour.[74] For the purposes of egalitarian analysis it does not matter whether this is the result of discriminatory enforcement or the result of a social infrastructure that makes these women more likely to injure their future children. The rule's disparate impact is in itself reason enough not to adopt such a rule. In any event, in the tort context there is no reason to assume that the group of women who would be sued is weaker than average, and one can assume that they are stronger than the average. As long as the remedy is limited to damages, suing the mother is worthwhile only if she carries insurance. Women who can afford to purchase liability insurance are likely to be stronger than those who cannot, so it is hard to see a convincing egalitarian argument against imposing such duty. Since the financial burden is borne only by those who are insured, there should be no serious concern regarding regressive redistribution.

As for conforming and non-confirming women (whether they purchase insurance or not) there are no strong indications regarding their relative strength. This being said, assuming that external constraints – financial and other – rather than free will are the cause for behaviour during pregnancy which unduly risks the future child, one can assume that the level of conformity increases among women of high socio-economic status.

E. The Symbolic Aspect of Liability

The symbolic costs and long term effects of imposing a duty on the status and rights of women are borne by all women and not only by non-conforming women. Do these costs justify rejection of such a duty? The answer to this question depends on the magnitude of these costs. Significant costs make the adoption of a conditional duty undesirable, despite the rule's advantage in terms of loss-spreading. When symbolic costs exceed a certain level it becomes unfair – as a matter of intra-group justice and from a desert perspective – to impose on conforming women considerable burdens despite the fact that their behaviour is faultless. When symbolic costs exceed a certain level, the duty becomes undesirable as a matter of inter-group justice as well: the rule harms women as a group by lowering their status relative to men. If, alternatively, the rule's symbolic costs are insignificant or speculative, the rule's advantages in terms of protecting the well-being of women who have injured children (and of the children themselves) and the rule's advantages in terms of protecting pregnant

73 Such argument, however, raises the problem of paternalism, assuming non-conforming women prefer being subject to a duty so that their children will receive compensation.

74 See, e.g., Veronica E.B. Kolder, Gallagher & Parsons, 'Court-Ordered Obstetrical Interventions', 316 *New Eng J Med* (1987) 1192, p.1193. For the similar Canadian experience see Martin & Coleman, *supra* note 31, n.81.

women's autonomy during pregnancy should tip the scale to adopting conditional duty.

Most of the negative symbolic and ideological consequences of the suggested rule are the product of the rule itself rather than of the underlying behaviour that results in a finding of liability. Granted, the bad mothers discourse is likely to be created when the defendant's conduct is known in public, but the tort litigation process is likely to increase this discourse. In the absence of a duty of care, a zone of immunity is created so that tort law will not evaluate the concrete behaviour and will not pass judgment on it as negligent or not. Other consequences – treating women as means, increasing the likelihood of regulating women's reproduction and curtailing the right to abortion – are to an even greater extent almost entirely the consequence of the legal process and the liability it produces, as distinct from the underlying behaviour of the women. This insight – that the legal process and legal liability have social meaning and ramifications that exceed the direct costs involved (litigation costs and damages) – is important. This insight is well known in the context of the duty of care – the purpose of the duty is to filter out situations in which imposing liability would bring about socially undesirable results.

A correct understanding of the suggested rule and the rationale behind it should cause its adoption to be almost free of problematic symbolic and ideological negative results. The suggested rule should be understood as a tool (admittedly a partial and limited one) to ensure compensation to injured children, and by this improving, in addition to the children's well-being, the well-being and autonomy of their mothers as well. Understanding the unity of interests of mother and child in this context and the rivalry between insured-mothers and insurers (rather than between defendant-mothers and plaintiff-children) should lead to the conclusion that the imposition of liability would be desired by those women found liable. Imposing liability should not be interpreted as a patriarchal act of supervising pregnant women's behaviour and as an attempt to interfere with women's autonomy. On the contrary, imposing a duty should be understood as a required step which is necessary in order to advance the interests of women (and their children). Obviously, such understanding neutralizes the symbolic impact of the bad mothers discourse, viewing women as means, increasing regulation and curtailing the right to abortion. The bad mothers discourse is unlikely to result, once it is understood that a finding of negligence is required in order to ensure compensation that the mother is interested in receiving (or formally, in giving).[75] A conclusion that women are treated as a means for ensuring the well-being of their children becomes untenable when one recalls that the women found liable are interested in being found liable and that the litigation is (substantively if not formally) initiated by them. The fact that imposing liability is desired by the women and that liability is limited to the existing insurance coverage curb the fear of unwanted intervention in women's reproduction, since such intervention cannot be justified in the same

75 The motivation to compensate the victim explains a common tendency to stretch the definition of negligence when the defendant is insured. Once it is understood that liability is stretched for distributive reasons, the symbolic meaning of being found liable changes and the ensuing social opprobrium from such a finding is reduced.

way as it would in the case of a conditional duty. Finally, understanding that it is in the interest of both mother and child that liability be imposed, prevents the potential use of imposing duty for purposes of limiting women's autonomy in the context of abortion in which (at least arguably) there is conflict of interests between the interests of the woman and the foetus.

Moreover, understanding that women are likely to prefer a conditional duty rule might cause its adoption to produce desirable symbolic results. A solution reflecting women's real preferences empowers them, and the willingness to stick to a solution that clearly distinguishes between an undesirable imposition of liability (in the absence of insurance) and a desirable one emphasizes the respect the legal system accords to women's interests. Conversely, a solution denying imposition of liability despite women's probable preference for such a rule, and reasoning that is based on the inability to support such a rule in general principles of the law[76] reflect formalist reasoning which is problematic for the following three reasons: (1) the reasoning does not respect women's interests by subordinating these interests to considerations of coherence; (2) the reasoning refuses to see women's well-being and preferences as relevant or decisive for delineating the contours of the legal rule, by refusing to distinguish between liability that is desirable to the women and liability that is not; and (3) the reasoning is paternalistic in that it determines that the real interest of women is not to be held liable. The beauty of the suggested rule is that it allows any individual woman to choose voluntarily and ahead of time, by deciding whether to purchase liability insurance or not, whether or not she subjects herself to liability. This empowers women as a group and respects their preferences and wishes optimally.

F. Supplementary Comments with Respect to the Suggested Rule

The suggested rule makes liability conditional upon the existence of liability insurance and limits liability to the scope of coverage. Not the availability of insurance, but rather its existence is determinative for purposes of liability. At first sight, conditioning liability on the existence of insurance seems problematic, since it places too much power in the hands of insurers. Those who care about women's interests, the argument goes, would do better not to entrust women's interests in the hands of giant corporations interested in profit maximization and who happen to represent a fairly conservative business. While it is a reasonable assumption that insurance companies would tend to be even less concerned about women's status in society than courts and legislators, limiting liability to the extent of existing insurance coverage cannot impede women's interests, compared to a no-duty rule. As will be recalled, liability would be conditional upon the purchase of insurance coverage. This means that women are in fact given an option to purchase insurance that might entail liability or else avoid purchasing insurance. If the terms of coverage (such as intrusive attempts to regulate women's behaviour during pregnancy) or any increase in premiums are not to the liking of those potentially insured, they can

76 For such reasoning see *Dobson*, *supra* note 15, p. 801 (McLachlin J).

forgo coverage, and in such case they would be no worse off than under a sweeping no-duty rule.[77]

Another unpersuasive argument against conditional duty is that of unpredictability. Arguably, conditioning liability upon the existence of insurance introduces an element of randomness and unpredictability with respect to the existence of liability. However, the suggested rule does not hamper the predictability of any of the three actors in this interaction: potential plaintiffs, defendants and insurers. With respect to women and insurers, the suggested rule increases predictability, since in the absence of insurance there is no liability, and when insurance exists, defendants would be liable if negligent. Since the decision whether or not to purchase insurance is in the hands of women, the suggested rule increases predictability. The same is true for insurers. Their liability and its scope depend on the terms of the policy, which are under the control of the insurer. As to potential plaintiffs, as infants they are incapable of developing reliance and therefore have no stake in a predictable legal rule regarding their entitlement for damages. In any event, the rule is clear so plaintiffs can know, *ex post*, if they have a right to sue.

The suggested rule expressly limits possible remedies to monetary damages, and excludes injunctions. The fact that the behaviour during pregnancy might be continuous might bring about attempts to issue injunctions in order to regulate the woman's conduct. Indeed, in *WCFS v G*,[78] the plaintiff attempted to confine the woman in order to prevent her from sniffing glue throughout the pregnancy. An injunction remedy is highly dangerous, since it excessively encroaches on women's autonomy. It also broadcasts the problematic message that women are merely means to bringing healthy children into the world. This might lead to a slippery slope, the last stage of which is described in *The Handmaid's Tale*.[79] The remedy of injunction is problematic because it lacks the built-in mechanism that

77 One qualification is needed. A problem might arise in situations in which the added burden on women through premiums or intrusive regulation is substantial, but is not high enough to set off the woman's risk aversion, leading her to buy insurance intended to cover her liability to third parties in general. This would happen if the market does not offer separate coverage for prenatal liability, so that women face the choice of not purchasing any liability insurance or purchasing an unfavourable insurance package, which put women at disadvantage in comparison to a no-duty rule. Nonetheless, this problem probably does not render the suggested rule inferior to a no-duty rule for three reasons. First, the chances that insurers will include such provisions is not high, due to the fact that the added risk is relatively small and because of the administrative costs of pricing the risk and including it in the policy (and perhaps also due to competition in the market). Second, insurance contracts are subject to consumer protection regulation. If draconian provisions appear, they should be dealt with at this level. Finally, the problem of insurers' discretion to refuse to insure certain risks is a general one and is not unique to the context of liability insurance or the question of whether to impose liability. To the extent that the insurer's discretion is uninhibited, it can also exclude coverage for first party insurance sought by the mother for her loss from giving birth to an injured child.

78 *WCFS*, *supra* note 32.

79 Margaret E. Atwood, *The Handmaid's Tale* (New York, 1986).

exists in suits for damages and which serves as a check on excessive liability. Suits for damages are futile in the absence of insurance, and this reduces the risk of abuse of the right to sue. Basing the suggested rule on the rationale offered will provide an effective barrier to adoption of injunctions, and the rule can state expressly that the duty is limited to compensation for injuries observed after a child is born.

The analysis so far has not directly evaluated the desirability of the suggested rule, on the assumption that insurers will collect premiums based on individual pricing of the risk. Under such an assumption, the group of non-conforming women alone would bear the financial costs of the increased premiums. No doubt such a solution (which is unlikely to be adopted) is inferior to the other two alternatives of premium collection, and it obviously involves a greater degree of intrusion by the insurer into the conduct of women. However, imposing liability is still dependent upon purchasing insurance, so that the option not to purchase coverage will check excessive regulation, and it guarantees that liability is the solution preferred by each woman who purchased insurance. The combination of the voluntary nature of purchasing the insurance and conditioning liability on the existence of liability insurance creates a rare solution in which the legal rule promotes the actual preferences of (almost) all women.

Should conditional duty be imposed also with respect to injuries resulting from lifestyle choices? As a preliminary issue, such injuries are not likely to be insured. If they can be insured, an affirmative answer is warranted, although the considerations opposing the suggested rule are more convincing. The answer to the fear of a slippery slope – namely, that recognizing a duty will lead with time to demanding of pregnant women too stringent a standard of care – is women's control over the scope of coverage they seek to purchase. Choosing to purchase coverage attests to the fact that these women would like liability to be imposed, and the negative symbolic result from liability is negligible when liability is understood to be a compensation mechanism that women embrace voluntarily. If the insurance market offers interested women the possibility to insure the risk of having a child injured due to alcohol consumption during pregnancy, there are no convincing reasons to prevent interested women from ensuring compensation to their children should this risk materialize. To this one might respond that if indeed insurance causes the woman to take the risk, a no-duty rule might cause the woman to avoid the risk, and, arguably, that this is the desirable result from a social perspective. As a preliminary issue, note that this argument proves that a conditional duty rule increases women's autonomy. On the merit the argument is problematic. Generally, insurance undermines deterrence. Nevertheless, we allow potential tortfeasors to purchase liability insurance, despite the fact that absent the availability of insurance many risky (and negligent) activities would have been prevented. Against this background, creating a specific exception to pregnant women which prevents them from taking the risk and insuring against it seems discriminatory and unjustified.[80]

80 Cf. note 62 above and accompanying text.

G. *The Analytical Aspect: Insurance, Standard, and Duty of Care*

The suggested rule appears to diverge from the conventional understanding of the tort of negligence by combining the existence of fault with insurance coverage as a reason to impose liability. According to this critique, the mother's fault is the pretext for compensating the injured child. Furthermore, a solution according to which a negligent woman 'receives' compensation while a non-negligent woman does not, seems to contradict intuitions of both morality and common sense. In fact, the suggested rule can be easily squared with the analytical structure of the tort of negligence, its internal logic and its basic distributive policy. The suggested rule should be defended from attacks coming from two opposite directions. First, it should be explained why compensation is not given to a child injured by its mother's prenatal negligence, when the mother was not insured, and hence no duty exists. Second, it should be explained why no compensation is given to a child whose injury was not caused by its mother's (or anyone else's) negligence.

As regards the first question, the purpose of a duty of care is to filter out from all cases in which one's negligence caused harm the cases in which we would not like to impose liability for various policy considerations. When the mother does not carry insurance, imposing liability on the negligent mother is undesirable, since the benefit to the plaintiff and to potential plaintiffs is limited while the burden on women as a group is substantial. In contrast, when the liability is insured, the benefit to the plaintiff from imposing liability is substantial and the burden on women significantly decreases (and in fact might be lesser than the burden imposed on them under a no-duty rule when insurance is available). Therefore, there is no justification to filter out cases in which the mother's negligence occurred when she was insured, but it is justified to filter out the cases when negligence occurred when the mother was not insured.

As regards the second question, the basic distributive decision of the tort of negligence is that those who injure others without fault are not liable. In this respect, there is no difference between the child who was injured *in utero* not as a result of her mother's fault and any other plaintiff who was injured from a reasonable risk created by the defendant's activity. The suggested rule no longer contradicts one's intuition when one bears in mind that it is the injured child who indeed was injured due to his mother's negligence (and not his mother) who receives the compensation. By contrast, the child who is injured not as a result of his mother's fault will not receive damages according to the tort of negligence. The fact that the mother has an interest in being found liable when she is insured, does not undermine the structure and logic of the tort of negligence, provided that we can identify a behaviour of the mother that deviates from the required standard of care.

To conclude: children injured as a result of negligence when there is no insurance would not receive compensation since policy considerations which are examined at the duty level militate against liability, despite the fact that the mother was negligent. Children who are injured as a result of causes other than the mother's negligence (whether the mother is insured or not) would not receive compensation, since the requirement for deviation from the required standard of care was not met. A plaintiff's entitlement to compensation according to the tort of negligence is conditional upon cumulative proof of the existence of both duty and breach. Only when the mother is negligent and insured are the two requirements met, and, accordingly, imposition of liability is justified.

Nevertheless, in examining the desirability of the suggested rule, what matters is not only the rule's theoretical compatibility with the analytical model of the tort of negligence but also the way in which the rule is implemented in practice. The concern is that the suggested rule will cause liability to be expanded beyond its proper scope out of a desire to compensate plaintiffs who would otherwise remain without recourse. This in fact is the collusion argument in disguise. The fear of excessive burden on insurers is unconvincing, since insurers will likely price adequately (if not excessively) the cost of coverage. The real question is one of loss-spreading. Expanding the scope of liability will trigger increase in premiums. In fact, such an expansion will shift the liability insurance market to a regime resembling first party insurance. Whether such a result is desirable is unclear, and in order to answer this question empirical data is required. In any event, to the extent that expansion of negligence liability out of distributive considerations is indeed problematic, this is not unique to the context of maternal prenatal duty, and it is hard to see why pregnant women and their future children should be treated unfavourably[81] The fear of expanding the scope of liability is a kind of slippery slope argument. In the absence of suspected regressive equality effects, it should not be viewed as a convincing argument against the adoption of a solution which is otherwise desirable.

H. The Pragmatic Aspect: Much Ado About Nothing?

The analysis conducted above predicts that, as a practical matter, suits based on a theory of maternal prenatal negligence would be brought forward only if the mother is insured. In the absence of insurance, liability is unlikely to promote either deterrence or the compensatory goal of tort law. Indeed, the case law supports this prediction. That it is impossible to find cases imposing liability in the absence of insurance can be explained on two alternative (and possibly partially overlapping) grounds. One explanation is ideological, according to which courts are reluctant to impose liability due either to the fear of encroaching excessively on the autonomy of women or to feminist-egalitarian considerations.[82] Another explanation is pragmatic: in the absence of insurance it is pointless to bring suit. According to this explanation, it is the absence of motivated plaintiffs, rather than the sensitivity of judges, that accounts for the fact that there are no cases in which duty was imposed in the absence of insurance. The small number of suits filed when no insurance exists, coupled with the relatively frequent use of criminal law and other regulative measures directed at pregnant women who took drugs during pregnancy and gave birth to injured children,

81 As the dissenting judge in *Dobson* noted, the fact that Cynthia Dobson owed a duty of care to all those who might be injured from her negligent driving with the exception of her child, and the fact that any other road user, but not herself, owes a duty of care to her future child are an anomaly. See *Dobson*, *supra* note 15, pp. 764, 811–12.

82 Such reasoning can be found in *Chenault*, *supra* note 17 which is the only located case in which a suit was brought in the absence of insurance.

suggests that pragmatism rather than feminist ideology is the likely explanation for the absence of liability when no insurance coverage exists. Moreover, the fact that courts recognize a duty when the mother is insured without explicitly mentioning that the holding is limited to circumstances when insurance exists, might be interpreted as insensitivity to the egalitarian concern and as an opening for future recognition of an unconditional duty.

One might ask whether there is a need for a rule that formally makes duty conditional upon insurance. If suits are not filed when liability is not insured, why should a conditional duty rule be adopted? To begin with, one might wonder why we should *avoid* formally adopting the desired rule. The only reason that comes to mind is unconvincing. This reason, which was offered by the majority in *Dobson*,[83] emphasizes the irrelevance, from the plaintiff's perspective, of whether the defendant is insured or not, as a basis for the imposition of liability. This reasoning is unconvincing since, first, from the perspective of the typical plaintiff in the prenatal context, it is highly relevant whether the defendant is insured since if the answer is in the negative there is no point in suing. Second, tort liability balances the interests of potential plaintiffs and defendants. That the plaintiff is indifferent as to whether the defendant is insured, should not be decisive. Insurance matters to the defendant; therefore, balancing the plaintiff's interests in receiving compensation and the defendant's interest in preserving her autonomy should lead to conditioning the duty on insurance. The fact that we cannot provide a remedy to all potential plaintiffs without excessively encroaching upon the autonomy of potential defendants, should not lead to the conclusion that we should withhold a remedy in cases in which imposing liability would not negatively affect defendants' autonomy.

Moreover, despite the fact that the nuisance value of a tort suit against pregnant women is not significant, it cannot be ignored altogether. The suggested rule will separate legitimate suits from the rest. Third, there is a difference between the symbolic meaning of the suggested rule and that of an unconditional duty rule which is limited in practice to situations when insurance exists. The former sends the message that women's interests are being valued by society and courts. This message is absent under the latter rule. Finally, an unlimited duty rule might lead more easily in the future to injunctions as available remedies, than does the suggested rule.

Even if the suggested rule is supported by the egalitarian consideration and is desirable on the merits, it is still open to criticism as being partial and under-inclusive. If imposing duty is a mechanism whose purpose is to afford compensation to injured children and their mothers, it is a highly partial mechanism, since it would not benefit children injured not as a result of their mothers' negligence. In addition, to the extent that coverage is capped, even those injured due to negligence would receive only partial compensation. The fact that the suggested rule is only a partial step towards the ideal solution is not a convincing argument against its adoption. The only convincing reason against adopting partial solutions is a grounded fear that the partial solution would decrease the chance that the more comprehensive solution would be adopted. Such a fear in our context is ungrounded. It is hard to see how the call for the judiciary to adopt a conditional duty rule would undermine either the

83 See note 27 above.

developing of a first party insurance market covering all prenatal risks of injury or changes in the state's social insurance legislation and welfare programmes.

The extent to which the suggested rule will have significant practical effect depends on the relative availability of liability insurance for prenatal injuries as opposed to first party insurance schemes covering the same risk. Since only a small fraction of congenital injuries are the result of maternal prenatal negligence, the difference in premiums might be significant, so that the suggested rule might have practical effect which is not negligible. In any event, in jurisdictions in which liability for road accidents is fault based, the suggested rule has significant ramifications, given the ubiquity of mandatory liability insurance on the one hand, and the centrality of driving in modern societies on the other.

Chapter 7

Discrimination as Negligence

Introduction

This chapter continues the delineation of the role of egalitarianism in shaping the tort of negligence. It accomplishes two tasks. One is defending the claim that discriminatory behaviour can and should be covered by the tort of negligence, and that such a complementary response is desirable notwithstanding the existence of alternative responses to the problem. The second task is to show, by using the example of discrimination as negligence, the ramifications of the choice between standard and duty as the proper locus for egalitarian sensitivity. This inquiry, which continues the similar analysis provided in Chapters 5 and 6 above, will build on the distinction between denying liability on the alternative grounds of lack of duty or lack of breach of the required standard.

I. Negligence and Alternative Responses to Discrimination

While discriminatory behaviour of public authorities is not permitted, there is no general principle not permitting discrimination between private actors. Nonetheless, the common law has developed categories of activities in which discrimination is not permitted. These categories are characterized by the public nature of the service provided by private actors such as common callings (such as innkeepers and common carriers), public utilities (such as water suppliers) and businesses affected with public interest.[1] Indeed, the more public the setting in which the private actor operates, the greater the chances that discriminatory behaviour is prohibited by statute.[2] Anti-discrimination laws almost universally prohibit discrimination in the workplace, as well as discrimination by those offering services to the public. Many also prohibit housing and educational discrimination.[3] In addition to specific

---

1 For summary see Amnon Reichman, 'Professional Status and the Freedom to Contract: Toward a Common Law Duty of Non-Discrimination', 14 *Can JL & Juris* (2001) 79, pp. 90–99.

2 'Public nature' means that the service or product is offered to many and is impersonal in nature. This should not be confused with the identity of the defendant as a public authority.

3 See, e.g., Sex Discrimination Act 1975, Ch. 65, ss. 6, 29, 30–31, 22 (UK) (SDA) respectively; Race Relations Act, 1976, Ch. 74, ss. 4, 20, 21–4, 17 (UK) respectively; 42 USC ss. 2000e–2000e-17 (employment); ss. 2000a–2000a-6 (services); ss. 3601–19 (housing); ss. 2000d–2000d-7 (education) (2006); Human Rights Code, RSO 1990, c. H.19, ss. 1, 3 (services and contracts), 2, 21 (accommodation), 5 (employment), (Ontario) (OHRC). The

legislation, tort law could respond to the problem of discrimination by developing an independent tort of discrimination,[4] by using specific torts, such as intentional (or negligent) infliction of emotional distress, to combat discrimination,[5] or by treating discriminatory behaviour as negligent.[6]

The following discussion will focus on this last option. At the outset it will be useful to notice the similarity between discrimination law and negligence law. Discrimination law balances victims' claims for dignity and positive liberty with defendants' claims for negative liberty. Negligence similarly balances victims' claims for dignity and security with defendants' claims for negative liberty. This similarity suggests that perhaps negligence can become one of the legal responses to combat discrimination. The following discussion examines the promise and difficulties involved in such an avenue, and highlights the main issues that have to be addressed from institutional, conceptual and normative perspectives.

II. The Institutional Inquiry

Anti-discrimination legislation is widespread in modern common-law jurisdictions. One should therefore ask what should be the role, if any, of judicial responses to instances of discrimination that are not covered by the relevant legislation. Four preliminary points should be noticed. First, this chapter suggests using the tort of negligence to combat discrimination as a supplement to anti-discrimination legislation and not as a substitute for it. Society will thus enjoy the advantages of both responses.[7] Second, this institutional inquiry has broader implications than the possible existence of a negligence-based response to discrimination. Indeed, while there are almost no modern cases imposing liability for discrimination based on the tort of negligence, the discussion of the role of the judiciary in combating discrimination is a well developed topic.[8] In Canada, for example, judicial activism

---

chapter focuses on the obligation of an individual not to discriminate against the plaintiff. It does not deal with the state's obligation not to discriminate, or with its obligation not to let another individual discriminate against the plaintiff. Accordingly, the analysis covers neither ECHR decisions with respect to Article 14 of the European Convention on Human Rights, nor litigation controlled by domestic anti-discrimination public law norms.

4 Such possibility was rejected by the Canadian Supreme Court, on grounds of legislative pre-emption, in *Seneca Coll. of Applied & Tech. Bd. of Governors v Bhadauria* [1981] 2 SCR 181 (Can), *rev's* (1979) 27 OR (2d) 142; Cf., *Amin v Entry Clearance Officer, Bombay* [1983] 2 AC 818 (HL).

5 Compare, e.g., *Wiggs v Courshon*, 355 F Supp 206 (1973) (imposing liability for a racial epithet) and *Hall v Gus Construction Co.*, 842 F 2d 1010 (8th Cir 1988) (imposing liability for a series of sexist slurs), with *Logan v Sears, Roebuck & Co.*, 466 So 2d 121 (Ala 1985) (not imposing liability for a sexual-orientation slur) and *Bradshaw v Swagerty*, 563 P 2d 511 (Kan Ct App 1977) (not imposing liability for a racial epithet).

6 See CC (Tel-Aviv) 15/97 *Shamsian v Ganey Rosmary*, 14 *Dinim Shalom* 402 (Israel).

7 For example, in terms of proving discrimination, anti-discrimination legislation seems to be more favourable to plaintiffs than negligence.

8 See, e.g., Sandra Fredman, *Discrimination Law* (Oxford, 2002), pp. 67–8; Andrew Koppelman, *Antidiscrimination Law and Social Equality* (New Haven, 1996), pp. 19, 39,

was ultimately rejected in one context and endorsed in another. In *Bhadauria*,[9] the Supreme Court overruled the lower court's recognition of an independent anti-discrimination intentional tort, based on notions of legislative pre-emption. In *Vriend v Alberta*,[10] the Supreme Court read into Alberta's Individual Rights Protection Act[11] a prohibition against discrimination on the ground of sexual orientation.

Third, as *Bhadauria* exemplifies, the scope left for the operation of negligence law is partially determined by the extent to which the relevant legislation pre-empts the common law. One should distinguish between two issues here: whether negligence as a cause of action can exist when no statutory cause of action does; and whether the two causes of action can coexist. Since this book does not concern itself with issues of positive statutory interpretation and constitutional analysis, it will concentrate on the normative analysis of this question. Fourth, from a normative perspective, the institutional inquiry parallels to a great extent that offered in Chapter 3 above, especially with respect to the claims of illegitimacy and loss of liberty.[12] From a policy perspective, the main question that has to be answered is whether the advantages from allowing the judiciary to expand the scope of statutory-based liability for discrimination outweigh the disadvantages.

A. Advantages

1. Flexibility: Responsiveness to Shifting Social Conditions A major advantage of using negligence to combat discrimination is flexibility and responsiveness to changing social patterns. The case for using negligence law as a complementary device is based on the following facts: (1) the legislative process is lengthy and complicated; (2) new and unexpected forms of interactions (with their potential for discriminatory behaviour) are constantly being created; (3) legislative responses to such interactions are unlikely both before and after such interactions come into existence. Before, because they are not necessarily foreseeable. After, because, given the relative infrequency of such interactions, the costs associated with creating a rule regulating such interactions might be too high. The economic literature dealing with the choice between rules and standards suggests that since creation of rules is costly, as is the implementation of standards, when the relevant behaviour is frequent the use of rules is to be preferred, and vice versa.[13] There is a case, then, for applying the tort of negligence to new emerging paradigms, in addition to the regulation of established categories through anti-discrimination

---

46, 109–10, 118–19, 261; Nicholas Bamforth, 'Conceptions of Anti-Discrimination Law', 24 *Oxford J Legal Stud* (2004) 693, pp. 701–3.

9 *Bhadauria*, *supra* note 4.

10 *Vriend v Alberta* [1998] 1 SCR 493 (Can).

11 Alberta's Individual Rights Protection Act, RSA 1980, c. I-2.

12 Ch. 3.I, III.A above. By contrast, other claims, such as lack of effectiveness, randomness, and inefficiency, are less relevant.

13 See Louis Kaplow, 'Rules Versus Standards: An Economic Analysis', 42 *Duke LJ* (1992) 557, pp. 562–4.

legislation. Moreover, when a new discriminatory paradigm emerges, negligence law can provide an interim response until legislation is enacted.

2. Flexibility: Nuanced, Context-Dependent Response to Borderline Cases Another advantage of flexibility is the sensitivity of the negligence standard to the facts of the case. Rules suffer from over- and under-inclusiveness, while standards allow a result that fits the rationale underlying the legal rule.[14] In the grey zones of discriminatory behaviour – cases in the penumbra rather than at the core – an all-or-nothing approach to liability is inappropriate. For example, many human rights codes prohibiting discrimination in housing, create an exemption with respect to owners who live on the premises and rent out part of it.[15] While one can understand why a general rule prohibiting such behaviour was not adopted, one might still believe that some cases deserve to be sanctioned as negligent while others are not. The cultural context, the profiles of the two individuals, the way the property is arranged, the motives of the owner and the potential lessors, and their histories and upbringing might be relevant in order to evaluate whether we would like to prohibit such behaviour or to excuse it (and in extreme cases perhaps even to justify it). While an attempt to regulate all this 'soft' data in legislation or regulation is impossible, such an attempt to examine the concrete cases *ex post* might be desirable. Thus, for example, a refusal based on the preference of the owner to walk around his house in his underwear without feeling constrained (the 'shy owner') is in fact reasonable and should not be sanctioned, while a refusal based on a reasoning that women are stupid and hysterical (the 'Neanderthal owner') should be.

3. Symbolic Message: Empowering Victims and Concentrating on Discriminators' Fault There is a symbolic advantage in conceptualizing discriminatory behaviour as negligent. Finding the behaviour in question as negligent necessarily condemns the targeted behaviour. By contrast, anti-discrimination legislation might be understood to be based on strict liability standard,[16] and to be motivated by an aspiration to protect a disadvantaged group, or by distributive motivations.[17]

---

14 See, e.g., Frederick Schauer, 'Rules and the Rule of Law', 14 *Harv JL & Pub Pol'y* (1991) 645, pp. 646–9.

15 See, e.g., SDA, *supra* note 3, ss. 31(2), 32; 42 USC s. 3603(b) (2006); OHRC, *supra* note 3, s. 21(1).

16 On the disparate impact doctrine viewed as based on strict liability see e.g., Alfred W. Blumrosen, 'Strangers in Paradise: Griggs v. Duke Power Co. and the Concept of Employment Discrimination', *71 Mich L Rev* (1972) 59, p. 67; Andrew Morris, 'On the Normative Foundations of Indirect Discrimination Law: Understanding the Competing Models of Discrimination Law as Aristotelian Forms of Justice', 15 *Oxford J Legal Stud* (1995) 199. For a critique see Denise G. Réaume, 'Harm and Fault in Discrimination Law: The Transition from Intentional to Adverse Effect Discrimination', 2 *Theoretical Inq L* (2001) 349. Similarly, courts impose strict liability on employers for *quid pro quo* sexual harassment. See David B. Oppenheimer, 'Exacerbating the Exasperating: Title VII Liability of Employers for Sexual Harassment Committed by Their Supervisors', 81 *Cornell L Rev* (1995) 66, p. 71.

17 See, e.g., Samuel Issacharoff & Justin Nelson, 'Discrimination with a Difference: Can Employment Law Accommodate the Americans with Disabilities Act?', 79 *NCL Rev*

Therefore, the use of negligence law is more empowering to the victims of discrimination, and might have a greater potential to modify the behaviour of potential discriminators. Anti-discrimination legislation is more likely than negligence-based liability to trigger the costs involved in protectionist measures,[18] and unlike negligence-based liability, it does not necessitate a conclusion that the discriminatory behaviour is wrongful.

4. Progressiveness of the Judiciary as a Safe Harbour Another important advantage of using negligence law is that 'since one of the reasons for providing protection for particular groups is their political powerlessness, it is counter-productive to rely on the majority to enact anti-discrimination laws through the political process'.[19] Given the fact that the use of tort law is supplementary and not an alternative to anti-discrimination legislation, even those who are more suspicious of the belief that courts might be relatively more progressive than the legislature would find it hard to oppose a negligence-based response to discrimination. Since the relative progressiveness of the institutions might change with time, developing a jurisprudence that allows courts to combat discrimination through the tort of negligence is a prudent investment from an egalitarian perspective, even if currently anti-discrimination legislation is comprehensive and robust. In this respect, the responses to the illegitimacy claim, and in particular the complement thesis, as well as the ability of legislatures to respond to rulings they disfavour, are relevant.

5. Uncertain Scope of Liability as an Effective Deterrent Another possible advantage is the flip-side of a disadvantage to be discussed – uncertainty and curtailing liberty. Assuming that uncertainty exists with respect to the scope of liability for negligent discrimination,[20] then for as long as such uncertainty exists,[21] such behaviour might be better deterred under negligence law, complemented by anti-discrimination legislation, than under such legislation alone. This can be viewed as a justified trade-off, of the liberty of the 'haves' (by increasing deterrence due to uncertainty) for the better attainment of equality, security and dignity of the disadvantaged (by better combating discrimination). While *ex post*, uncertainty is likely to have a regressive effect, *ex ante*, under the assumption that the legal rule

(2001) 307, pp. 309–10; Hugh Collins, 'Social Inclusion: A Better Approach to Equality Issues', 14 *Transnat'l L & Contemp Probs* (2005) 897.

18 Arguably this argument is problematic by buying into right wing claims about the weakening nature of anti-discrimination legislation. The response to this critique is based on a pragmatic bent. Part of the symbolic aspect of law is a social construct. Therefore, it might be that anti-discrimination legislation has in fact a weakening effect even if ideally we think it should not have.

19 Fredman, *supra* note 8, p. 67.

20 The degree of uncertainty will be affected in part by the doctrinal choice between standard and duty of care as mechanism to curtail liability. See Part III.A below.

21 With time, precedents will accrue that will reduce the level of uncertainty with respect to the scope of liability in negligence for discrimination.

is going to affect more the behaviour of the potential discriminator than that of the victim, the uncertainty yields a progressive deterrent effect.

B. Disadvantages

The main arguments against the use of negligence to combat discrimination are tied to the arguments mounted against the use of tort law in order to advance more egalitarian distribution of entitlements. These arguments, which are based on the institutional characteristics of tort law and the courts, were marshalled at length above and will not be repeated here. Rather, the application of these arguments to this context will be briefly commented upon.

1. No Problem of Randomness The argument of randomness is irrelevant here, since the purpose of the cause of action is not to redistribute wealth but rather to prevent the defendant from impinging upon the right of the plaintiff not to be discriminated against. Therefore the use of the tort does not suffer from under-inclusiveness, over-inclusiveness or a gap between the result required by an ideal distributive scheme and that achieved by the tort. In other words, a corrective justice challenge against inserting a distributive motive to the operation of the tort is unwarranted here.

2. Illegitimacy The main challenge against the use of the tort is a combination of the excessive encroachment on liberty, lack of predictability and circumventing the balance of interests set by the legislature, which is an illegitimacy claim. As a matter of statutory interpretation, the court has to examine whether or not the omission of a given discriminatory behaviour from the anti-discrimination legislation is intentional. If it is, there is a strong case for not imposing a duty in negligence, although even in such a case an argument can be made that the legislature can always overrule such a development by immunizing the conduct in question from triggering tort liability. When the omission is unintended, there is a need to balance the competing interests of liberty and equality. It is important to note that while such a balance is difficult to strike, courts are not at disadvantage, from an institutional perspective, in engaging in such a task compared to the other two branches. Indeed, such a balance between the competing claims of two individuals is at the core of courts' capacity and private law subject matter. It was the common law's individualistic bent, rather than its lack of institutional capacity, that prevented development of judicially-crafted anti-discrimination norms.

3. Unpredictability and Excessive Encroachment on Liberty We are left with the argument that the unpredictability of negligence liability is undesirable. On the one hand, it will lead to costly litigation and achieve dubious deterrent effect due to the uncertainty of the result. On the other hand, it might lead to over-deterrence – excessive encroachment on liberty – for fear of liability. There are three answers to this concern. First, the fear of uncertainty should not be exaggerated. The extent of the uncertainty depends on the way the courts demarcate the scope of liability.[22]

22 Part III.A3, 4 below.

Moreover, with time, when a body of decisions is accumulated, the degree of uncertainty will decrease. Second, there is no fear of under-deterrence since the proposed solution will add tort liability for discrimination to the existing anti-discrimination legislation, rather than replace the latter with the former.

The third and main response to the fear of unpredictability deals with the fear of over-deterrence. Such fear is based either on a chilling effect rationale or on a fear of judicial error in setting the required standard of care and the scope of duty. Both fears are unconvincing for two reasons: the distributive effect of the possible error and the low value of the chilled activity. *The distributive effect of the possible error*: an error (real or imagined) to the detriment of potential discriminators threatens a relatively strong group and hence is less likely to happen, and, if it does, should concern us less than an error in the opposite direction. *The low value of the chilled activity*: the devaluation of potential discriminators' interests is based also on the fact that defendants' liberty interest protects undesirable behaviour that should not be condoned. Note that when liability for discriminatory behaviour is not imposed this is (often) due to a rationale of excuse rather than justification. Therefore, the benefits of potential tort liability are likely to outweigh its costs. The benefits consist of deterring discriminatory behaviour in appropriate cases which were not covered by existing legislation; the costs consist of the chilling effect of behaviour which either (1) does not amount to discrimination, although it borders on it, or (2) despite being discriminatory, is excused from triggering liability due to concerns for liberty. Since the value of these activities (and especially of the latter) is low, and since to begin with the possibility of chilling effect and judicial error to the detriment of the better-off is speculative, the interest of the 'haves' in liberty should not prevent the existence of an avenue to impose liability in appropriate cases.

There are two answers to a specific kind of a chilling effect that enhanced duty will cause the 'haves' to avoid contact with the disadvantaged. First, such behaviour is often already forbidden by anti-discrimination legislation. Second, the chilling effect should convince us to oppose liability, only if the *ex ante* segregation effect controls the *ex post* prevention of discrimination effect.[23] The benefits to the 'haves' from having contact with the disadvantaged – cheap labour, to take one example – make a wholesale avoidance strategy unlikely.

* * *

There is not much to be added with respect to the question of whether a concurrent negligence-based liability is desirable or not. To the extent that the potential remedies available in a tort suit are more significant, the advantages are clear. In addition, the symbolic advantage of a finding of negligence is especially relevant with respect to alternative bases of liability. However, it remains to be explored whether it is desirable to circumvent the remedial scheme set by the relevant act. Analogous questions arise with respect to other advantages accruing from a negligence action (such as circumventing a short period of limitation).[24] Moreover, given the significant costs

23 See Ch. 3.IV.B2(b) above.

24 Cf., in the context of sexual assault, *Stubbings v Webb* [1993] AC 498 (HL).

of negligence litigation, it is not clear that the advantages of allowing a concurrent cause of action are sufficient to justify such a result. In any event, the answer to this question should be derived in part from the relevant jurisdiction's jurisprudence with respect to the question of the possible existence of concurrent causes of action.[25] Doctrinally, a result of refusing to allow a concurrent negligence cause of action could be achieved either by way of statutory interpretation, that is, determining that the cause of action is pre-empted by the statute, or by negating the duty of care, given the existence of an alternative cause of action.

III. The Conceptual and Normative Inquiries

Imposing liability for discrimination based on negligence necessitates proving all three elements of the tort: duty, breach and causally related damage. The discussion begins with an analysis of the ramifications of negating liability based on the alternative grounds of lack of duty or lack of breach (Section A). Then, it examines the problems in establishing breach (Section B) and duty (Section C) and, finally, it briefly comments upon the element of damages (Section D).

A. Implications of the Choice between Duty and Standard for Denying Liability

Since the imposition of liability for discrimination infringes upon the liberty of the potential discriminator, few would dispute that not all instances of discrimination should trigger a legal response (refusing to consider marrying someone, based on their different religious identity is one obvious example). For now, the analysis leaves aside the important question where one should draw the line separating between discrimination which should and which should not trigger civil liability. Rather, the analysis examines – with respect to instances in which liability is unwarranted – what are the ramifications of negating liability based on lack of duty or lack of breach. The different rationales for negating liability should be translated into lack of duty and lack of breach reasoning.

Denying liability for conduct that has harmed another person can be based on one of two alternative grounds: that the behaviour was reasonable or that, despite the fact it was not, the defendant did not owe a duty to the plaintiff.[26] A duty is denied when either the injury to the plaintiff is not reasonably foreseeable or when there are

25 To use Dworkin's framework, an answer to the question should be given based not only on considerations of justification but also on considerations of fit. See Ronald Dworkin, *Law's Empire* (Cambridge, 1986), pp. 225–58.

26 Liability can be denied where both the behaviour was reasonable and there was no duty. Moreover, at times liability can be denied when the plaintiff has not proven that the defendant was negligent. In fact, courts have at least five alternative rationales for denying liability (not counting lack of causal connection or lack of damage): (1) defendant [D)] acted reasonably and there was no duty, (2) D acted reasonably and therefore there is no need to decide whether a duty exists, (3) a duty existed but D acted reasonably, (4) D acted negligently but there was no duty, and (5) there was no duty and therefore there is no need to decide whether D acted reasonably.

good policy considerations to deny liability. The choice between lack of duty and lack of breach as alternative bases for denying liability should be influenced by three factors which will be discussed in Sections 1–3. Sections 4 and 5 will suggest how to balance these considerations.

1. Stigmatizing and Educating Classifying discriminatory behaviour as negligent stigmatizes the defendant and makes the point that discriminatory behaviour is unreasonable. This message is lost if liability is denied on the ground that the conduct in question was not proved to be unreasonable. Therefore, in order to send the message that discriminatory behaviour is unacceptable, it is better to deny liability based on lack of duty, while stating that the behaviour was nevertheless unreasonable. Classifying a given behaviour as either reasonable or negligent utilizes the behaviour-guiding capacity of a negligence regime and advances the developments of clear norms. The greater the tendency of courts to deny liability based on lack of duty without clarifying whether the behaviour in question was unreasonable or not, the less this guiding potential will be materialized.

The advantages in sending a clear normative message relate to the law's expressivity. One should distinguish between a (contested) consequentialist claim and a claim regarding the intrinsic value of the law's meaning and its symbolic message.

The consequentialist claim is based on the assumption that law has to some extent the capacity to mould a person's values. This can happen either due to the internalization of the law's values by the law's addressees, or due to the fact that the relevant actor expects a social reward from others for abiding by the legal rule, and fears a social sanction for violating it. Accordingly, the argument goes, even if the defendant is not found liable due to the absence of a duty, there is support on consequentialist grounds for denouncing the act of discrimination as unreasonable, in that the defendant (and others) might internalize the undesirability of the conduct, or they might change their behaviour for fear of being stigmatized as persons whose conduct is unreasonable, with the possible ensuing social and economic losses.

To be sure, the extent to which either phenomenon (internalization or stigmatization) exists and is significant is debated in the literature.[27] Both phenomena require that the court should be perceived by the defendant and the community as legitimate and prestigious. Moreover, the argument hinges on the non-trivial assumption that despite the fact that the defendant is not liable, the decision will result in a negative social meaning being ascribed to the defendant's behaviour. Among other things, the stigmatizing effect necessitates that the decision be publicized, and that those who are exposed to the decision are sufficiently informed and sophisticated to understand that the court denounces the defendant's behaviour, despite the court finding the defendant not liable. These assumptions are far from trivial. However, the potential high visibility of a negligence-discrimination suit

27 For the debate see Ch. 3.III.B3 above. Both effects probably exist to some extent, and their significance is contingent. Defending this assumption goes well beyond the scope of this chapter.

might deter discriminatory behaviour even if liability is denied, and help broadcast the desired normative message.

In any event, even if the consequentialist claim is unconvincing, or deemed too speculative and optimistic, sending the right symbolic message and backing the result with an appropriate reasoning has an intrinsic value. As humanist jurists, we have to account for the law's coercion by justifying the law's norms in the best way possible. It is important to state clearly the desirable norms and the reasons for imposing liability (or not), even if the law is in fact incapable of guiding behaviour or affecting one's values. [28]

2. Concern for Liberty as an Excuse Typically,[29] when discriminatory behaviour is lawful, the reason is not that it is perceived as legitimate or socially desirable. Rather, it is the concern for liberty that overrides. Indeed, classic theories of rights insist that the essence of rights is to entitle the right-bearer to do that which one should not.[30] Analytically, the duty requirement is the proper place to host such considerations, according to which a decision to exculpate discriminatory behaviour from liability is based not on the idea that such behaviour is acceptable, but rather that responding to it by legally prohibiting it is undesirable.

3. Creating a Zone of Immunity Not recognizing a duty creates a zone of immunity. Within the scope of that immunity – for instance, no duty of landlords who reside on the property to avoid discriminating against potential tenants – no discriminatory behaviour, however unreasonable, triggers liability. By contrast, when a duty is recognized, denying liability has to be done in each suit in which the reasonableness of such discriminatory behaviour is litigated. The zone of immunity has both advantages and disadvantages. On the advantage side, having clear guidance as to the scope of permitted behaviour is recommended both in terms of predictability and in terms of efficiency. It helps both potential plaintiffs and potential defendants to know their rights and duties. The certainty increases the liberty of the defendant, who is not subjected to *ex post* scrutiny of his behaviour by the court. The certainty also avoids encouraging the plaintiff to believe that she might have a right not to be discriminated against. Bear in mind, that the assumption underlying this part of the discussion is that liability should not be imposed. If this is the case, why mislead the plaintiff into thinking that she might have a cause of action only to tell her, a few

28 Reasonable minds can differ with respect to the relative weight that should be given to the law's expressive function (from either intrinsic or consequential perspectives). Those who concentrate on the law's material incentives will accord minimal significance to the ground on which a negligence claim should be denied. If the expressive function is to be taken seriously, it follows that courts should carefully choose the ground for denying liability under negligence claims in all settings, not only in the context of discrimination. Indeed, such an approach warrants careful deliberation of the choice between alternative reasoning leading to the same practical result in all areas of law.

29 But not always. See Part III.B3 below.

30 Joseph Raz, 'A Right to dissent? I. Civil Disobedience', *The Authority of Law* (Oxford, 1979), pp. 262, 266–7.

years later, that she does not?[31] Finally, the certainty reduces litigation costs since a clear no-duty rule reduces the number of suits filed.

There are three disadvantages to creating a zone of immunity by denying duty. One is that the spectre of liability existing under a regime imposing duty will better deter discriminatory behaviour.[32] A second possible disadvantage of denying a duty is that the litigation itself might have a therapeutic value to the plaintiff, even if she is doomed to lose the case on the ground of lack of unreasonableness. This however seems unlikely. A third disadvantage of a zone of immunity pertains to its symbolic message. It connotes, as is generally the case with the absence of duty, an atomistic, individualistic and self-centred conception of social relationships between individuals in society. Moreover, the free hand to discriminate that is given by the legal system in the zone of immunity is undesirable in itself, and not merely due to its effect in reducing deterrence.

4. Differences Should Not Be Overstated The differences between the two alternatives of denying liability should not be overstated, however. The narrower the determination regarding the lack of duty, the more such a decision resembles a finding that the behaviour in question was reasonable. To illustrate, the court can determine that there is no duty of a landlord who lives on the property toward a potential tenant not to discriminate based on sex, when such discrimination was motivated by religious beliefs held in good faith. Such a result is similar, in terms of its effect on predictability, liberty, deterrence, litigation costs and meeting reasonable expectations, to a decision recognizing a duty but deciding that under the circumstances the behaviour was reasonable. (The main difference which remains between the two alternatives is the symbolic message.) Similarly, a broad holding that any kind of group-based discrimination by such a landlord against a potential tenant is reasonable, is nearly equivalent to a holding denying a duty of such landlords not to discriminate. To conclude: The degree of uncertainty in the two methods of dismissing suits is similar. In both cases the uncertainty decreases when the exact scope of the duty is demarcated as a result of the accumulation of decided cases.

5. The Suggested Solution Bearing the above analysis in mind, the decision between dismissing a suit on the alternative grounds of lack of duty or lack of breach should hinge on an evaluation of the reasonableness of the defendant's behaviour. A conclusion that there was nothing wrong in it calls for a decision that no breach has occurred. A conclusion that despite the wrongfulness of defendant's behaviour it is better not to impose liability on him, calls for a decision that no duty inheres. Whenever the court is satisfied that the behaviour was undesirable it should state so, even if no duty inheres. The opposite is equally true. Whenever the court is satisfied

31 Cf., Ariel Porat, 'Negligence Law in the Supreme Court: Search for the Underline Theory', 3 *Yearbook on Israeli Law* (1996) 373, pp. 391–2 (duty is denied when it is clear that there is no negligence). For a somewhat different approach see *Barrett v Enfield London Borough Council* [2001] 2 AC 550, 557–8, 575 (HL) (undesirability of striking claims arising in uncertain and developing areas of the law without full exploration of the facts).

32 See, e.g., *Barrett*, ibid., pp. 568, 575.

that the behaviour was reasonable it should state so, even though liability could be denied also based on lack of duty.[33]

In deciding on what grounds to dismiss a suit, the symbolic meaning of either alternative should, for normative, analytical and practical reasons, be accorded priority over other considerations. Normatively, it is important that the court stigmatize discriminatory behaviour as unreasonable whenever such a conclusion is merited. Analytically, it is important not to blur the division of labour between duty and standard. Practically, given the possibility of drafting either broad or narrow holdings with respect to both duty and standard, the practical implications of choosing either alternative to dismiss the case are not as significant as one might at first think. When the behaviour is unwarranted, it is better to bear the social costs involved in denying a duty in order to clarify the unreasonableness of the defendant's behaviour.[34]

One might think that using the tort system in order to send this message is a waste of public and private resources. This is not the case. Plaintiffs who insist on trying to persuade courts that the defendant was negligent in cases in which it seems that liability should not be imposed, should be allowed to do so, and, along the way, to reap the benefit of stigmatizing the defendant. The fact that these plaintiffs spend (or waste) their own resources in doing so, is their own business. The use of public resources in litigating the claim is a price society should be willing to pay in order to promote equality. Not only is the number of cases brought that have no likelihood of success not likely to be overwhelming, the plaintiff's suit also serves the public by reinforcing the desirable standard of conduct and by clarifying that a given behaviour is unworthy, even if it does not lead to liability. Finally, while this section has concentrated on instances in which we assume that liability should be denied, one should recall that in other instances tort liability will be an appropriate response to discrimination that is not prohibited under existing legislation.

B. Standard

1. Discrimination as Unreasonable Behaviour Breach of duty means a conduct that a reasonable person of ordinary prudence would not undertake under the circumstances, and while the standard is objective it is normative and not empirical. Courts (or juries) do not engage in an inquiry as to how the average person would have acted, but rather they set the standard that seems to them required. There is almost no conceptual or analytical difficulty in viewing discriminatory behaviour as unreasonable according to this standard. A reasonable person is one who behaves according to acceptable social standards. Since bigotry and discrimination are generally unacceptable, there is no reason not to see discriminatory behaviour

33 When it is clear that no duty exists, defendants would usually be able to get a summary judgment in their favour. Since in such proceedings any factual doubt is resolved to the benefit of the plaintiff, courts should use the opportunity to state that the defendant's behaviour, as presented by the plaintiff, is unreasonable.

34 These costs can be reduced by a narrow holding with respect to the scope of the immunity

as unreasonable. In making determinations of reasonableness, courts balance the interests of defendants against those of foreseeable potential victims. In practice, this is done mainly by some sort of cost-benefit analysis (albeit one which cannot be reduced to an efficiency analysis). Courts weigh the respective burden to the parties of engaging in the conflicting activities or abstaining from them according to the social value of these activities. Accordingly, a conclusion that the benefits derived by the discrimination (which are socially devalued) are outweighed by its costs is almost straightforward. This conclusion can draw support from, but does not hinge upon accepting, the analysis suggested in Chapter 5 above. According to this analysis, the fact that (almost by definition) those injured by discrimination are disadvantaged necessitates a conclusion that their disutility from being discriminated against is significant. Even if one ignores this point, the fact that the injury from discrimination is significant while the value of discriminatory behaviour is low, calls for a conclusion that discriminatory behaviour is unreasonable. Note, that classifying the interest of the defendant in discriminating as low-valued is also derived to a great extent from an egalitarian commitment to promote the interests of the disadvantaged.

2. Deliberate and Unintentional Discrimination The paradigmatic case of discrimination is deliberate behaviour (often, but not always, motivated by bigotry). Such behaviour is easy to characterize as unreasonable, as demonstrated above. Doing so, however, necessitates a preliminary conceptualization of deliberate behaviour as negligent. For reasons mentioned above, this hurdle should be crossed without hesitation. If negligent behaviour is one that a reasonable person would not do, and if such behaviour is one that is socially unacceptable, why not view deliberate behaviour as unreasonable? Does the reasonable person attack another, attempt to run over her, sexually harass her or discriminate against her? The answer should clearly be in the negative. There is nothing in the concept of the standard of care that justifies limiting it only to unintentional behaviour. Moreover, since a deliberate infliction of harm is more blameworthy than an unintentional one, exculpating the latter from liability is absurd. The modern tendency in common law jurisdictions is to view intentional behaviour as deviation from the relevant standard of care.[35]

Discrimination law has moved away from a requirement of intent to discriminate as a condition for imposing liability.[36] Indeed, research shows that in many instances the discrimination is not only unintended but is also unreflective.[37] Negligence law is, on its face, an appropriate instrument to deal with unintended discrimination. Unintended discrimination for purposes of the present argument includes instances

35 See Peter Cane, 'Mens Rea in Tort Law', 20 *Oxford J Legal Stud* (2000) 533; *Reeves v Commissioner of Police of the Metropolis* [2000] 1 AC 360 (HL); *A v Bottrill* [2003] AC 449 (PC 2002); *Non-Marine Underwriters, Lloyd's of London v Scalera* (2000) 185 DLR (4th) 1 (Can). The difficulty of bypassing the scope of liability set by intentional tort pertains to the concept of duty. See note 24 above and Parts II above, III.C below.

36 See note 16 above.

37 See, e.g., David B. Oppenheimer, 'Negligent Discrimination', 141 *U Pa L Rev* (1993) 899, pp. 899–915. For references to secondary literature on the matter see Michelle A. Travis, 'Perceived Disabilities, Social Cognition, and "Innocent Mistakes" ', 55 *Vand L Rev* (2002) 481, p. 489 n.35.

in which a hidden bias by the defendant negatively affects the plaintiff due to the latter's group affiliation. It does not include instances in which structural factors (such as exclusion due to poverty) negatively affect the plaintiff. While these structural factors should be taken into account by tort law (as the discussion in Chapter 5 demonstrates) they should not be considered as an unintentional discrimination by the defendant.

A finding of negligence hinges on the claim that failing to take steps that will reduce the chance of unintended discrimination is unreasonable. In this set of cases, the difficulty of treating an intentional act as negligent does not arise. Interestingly, most of the meagre literature dealing with the possibility of using negligence as a response to discrimination deals with unintended discrimination. However, the debate revolves mainly around statutory interpretation – whether according to the relevant statute negligent discrimination gives rise to a cause of action – rather than exploring the independent use of common law negligence to combat discrimination.[38]

Scholars debate whether a negligence-based response to unintended discrimination is a good idea or not. Some answer in the negative, based on fear of over-deterrence and the defendant's inability to eradicate effectively the phenomenon.[39] Others answer in the affirmative stressing the institutional aspect: in the labour market, in which the debate has arisen, the employing institution should take measures to counter the tendency of supervisors to discriminate unintentionally.[40] The following discussion will add to this debate by tying it both to the accident proneness theory and to the objective standard debate.

Seemingly, the support for viewing unintended discrimination as negligent should be limited to institutional settings. Indeed, Fleming James and John Dickinson, who believe in the somewhat deterministic accident proneness thesis,[41] draw doctrinal conclusions from the limited ability of tort sanctions to change the behaviour of individuals, in contrast to the ability of organizations to respond to the threat of liability.[42] This scepticism regarding the ability of individuals to better themselves if proper incentives are given lies at the heart of the debate regarding the justification of adopting an objective standard of care.[43] If negligence connotes undesirable

38 See Oppenheimer, ibid.; Jessie Allen, 'A Possible Remedy for Unthinking Discrimination', 61 *Brooklyn L Rev* (1995) 1299; Amy L. Wax, 'Discrimination as Accident', 74 *Ind LJ* (1999) 1129; Michael Selmi, 'Discrimination as Accident: Old Whine, New Bottle', 74 *Ind. L.J.* (1999) 1233; Marc R. Poirier, 'Is Cognitive Bias at Work a Dangerous Condition on Land?', 7 *Employee Rts & Emp Pol'y J* (2003) 459.

39 See Wax, ibid. Cf., Allen, ibid. (opposing a negligence response, yet supporting adoption of an objective standard which does not hinge on subjective intent).

40 Poirier, *supra* note 38, Oppenheimer, *supra* note 37.

41 This thesis is based on the statistical observation that a disproportionate share of the accidents that occur in society can be attributed to a small number of people, implying that a greater propensity to cause an accident stems from some personality trait or other characteristic of the given individual. See James Reason, *Human Error* (Cambridge, 1990), pp. 198–9.

42 See Fleming James, Jr & John J. Dickinson, 'Accident Proneness and Accident Law', 63 *Harv L Rev* (1950) 769, pp. 779–81 (suggesting a shift to strict liability).

43 For few classic treatments see Oliver Wendell Holmes, Jr, *The Common Law* (Boston, 1881), p. 108; Tony Honoré, 'Responsibility and Luck', 104 *LQ Rev* (1988) 530, pp. 530–37.

behaviour, how can we impose liability on those unable to reach that standard, or those for whom meeting the standard imposes a much more onerous burden than for the average person? Examining the justification of the objective standard goes beyond the scope of this section. Two comments will suffice.

First, assuming that the objective standard is binding upon those who cannot meet it, and for as long as this is the case, the fact that it is hard for the defendant not to discriminate unintentionally should not make failure to do so reasonable. Given the fact that the standard is normative – meaning that it sets a standard that the judge or jury decides is appropriate to demand as a minimum – the fact that many defendants are socially constructed in a way that makes them behave unintentionally in a discriminatory way should not serve as a sufficient defence.[44] Since in making evaluations of reasonableness courts should and do weigh the social utility of the interests involved, the burden to defendants from the need not to discriminate unintentionally should be discounted. (Similarly, the benefits from intended discrimination, however significant subjectively, should be accorded low objective value, if not ignored altogether for the purpose of balancing them against the interests of the plaintiffs.)

Second, it is often argued against the objective standard that it is unfair on distributive grounds since it 'discriminates' against the weak who cannot meet the required standard.[45] Indeed, the argument presented in Chapter 5 in favour of taking into account the effective burden on the parties given their prior holdings goes along that path. The context of negligent discrimination exemplifies a situation in which holding defendants to an objective standard – arguably one which they cannot meet – results in a progressive distributive result.[46] The distributive effect of viewing unreflective bias as negligent discrimination is that between two parties neither of whom can prevent the injury effectively, the better off bears the burden. Given the fact that the objective standard usually works to the detriment of the disadvantaged, it would be most unfair not to apply the standard in the cases in which it happens to work to their benefit.[47] Therefore, at least as long as the objective standard governs negligence law in general, it should justify a finding of unintended discrimination as unreasonable, even if we accept the assumption that the defendant can do little to avoid it.

3. Reasonable Discrimination? It has been suggested that a drawback of the use of negligence to combat discrimination is the problematic symbolic message of the existence of reasonable discrimination.[48] This claim is unconvincing for three reasons. First, the alternative, according to which a broad set of activities would not

44 The approach presented here, therefore, differs from Poirier, *supra* note 38, p. 464 who calls for imposing liability on the employer but not on the employee who acts based on unreflective discrimination.

45 For awareness of the problem yet a support of the objective standard see Holmes, *supra* note 43.

46 The analysis in the text draws of course on an assumption that those who are discriminated against are, at least on average, weaker than those who discriminate.

47 Cf. Ch. 6 above, notes 62, 80 and accompanying text.

48 Allen, *supra* note 38, p. 1324.

be subject to negligence scrutiny, and accordingly would be deemed by implication to be reasonable, is even more troubling. In fact, one of the advantages of the use of the tort is that it enables labelling discriminatory behaviour as unreasonable, even if liability is denied based on lack of duty. Second, in most cases in which liability would be denied, the result would hinge on lack of duty and not on lack of breach. Third, in rare cases, a finding of reasonable discrimination might be justified on the merits. When a disparate treatment is based on a relevant distinction, it should not be considered as discriminatory.[49] More generally, since unreasonableness is understood to be the improper balancing of one's self-interest with the interests of others, it follows that when the burden on the defendant of abstaining from seemingly discriminatory conduct is significant (according to an objective standard), while the burden on the plaintiff of being discriminated against is relatively insignificant, the conduct in question might be reasonable. Relevant parameters for evaluation (according to an objective standard) include the motive for the discrimination, the degree of offensiveness of the behaviour, the significance of the interests involved to both parties, and the degree of the intrusion caused to victims' interests by defendants' behaviour, and to defendants' interests by imposing liability.

To illustrate the nature of evaluations about reasonableness of allegedly discriminatory behaviour, consider the following nine examples: (1) the shy owner; (2) the Neanderthal owner;[50] (3) the Tutsi landowner – a Tutsi whose parents were murdered by Hutus, refuses to lease her place to a Hutu; (4) the silent tourist – an Austrian tourist refuses to travel to the Ivory Coast due to racial bigotry; (5) the loud tourist – the same tourist explains to a person from the Ivory Coast that he will not visit that country because he despises Africans; (6) the silent Israeli – a Jewish Israeli, descendant of holocaust survivors, refuses to visit Germany; (7) the loud Israeli – the same tourist explains to a German youth her reasons for not visiting Germany; (8) the Chinese scholarship fund – a Chinese foundation, funded by Chinese philanthropists, offers scholarships only to students of Chinese origin; (9) the non-Pakistani scholarship fund – a scholarship funded by a Caucasian Canadian philanthropist offers scholarships to all needy students except those of Pakistani origin.

It is submitted that the defendants in examples 1, 3, 6 and 7 acted reasonably, while the rest have not.[51] The relevance of motive and degree of offensiveness in the behaviour is illustrated by the difference between examples 1 and 2.[52] In example 1, the preference not to share accommodation with a woman is not based on sexist motives, but rather on notions of convenience and respect for one's own privacy. This also makes the damage to the interests of the plaintiff less significant – it injures her dignity and self-worth to a lesser extent. A secondary test for these criteria –

---

49 However, even then, the disparate impact serves as an independent factor weighing against the adoption of the policy leading to such a result.

50 For both examples see Part II.A2 above.

51 Recall that for the latter group, liability would hinge on the existence of duty. See Section C below.

52 A similar analysis can be applied to Examples 4 and 5 as opposed to Example 6, and to Example 7 as opposed to Example 8.

motive and offensiveness – is the distinction between preference for one's group and exclusion of another. Examples 8 and 9 exemplify this point. The behaviour in the former is less offensive, since it is based on notions of affiliation rather than on those of exclusion. Hence, the former is likely to be reasonable while the latter is likely not to be. A discriminatory motive that is not based on an assumption of the inferiority of the plaintiff is likely to be more reasonable.

The importance of the victim's interest and the degree of harm to that interest is illustrated by the distinction between examples 4 and 6 on the one hand, and examples 5 and 7 on the other. The interest of a citizen of the Ivory Coast in not having a potential tourist avoid visiting her country because of his bigotry is much less significant than the interest not to be humiliated by being directly exposed to racist views. In example 5, which is paradigmatic of intentional infliction of emotional distress cases, the burden to the plaintiff is significant (feelings of humiliation and anger) while the burden to the defendant (abstaining from communicating bigoted views) is not. The unreasonable behaviour is manifested in revealing the bigotry to the plaintiff (as distinct from having the bigotry in the first place and acting upon it). While the conclusion in terms of the existence of breach in examples 4 and 5 and its absence in examples 6 and 7 is the same, one should still appreciate the difference in the relative weight of the competing interests.

The relevance of the objective evaluation of the interests is illustrated by examples 4 and 6. From a subjective perspective, the burden on a racist from not acting upon his prejudice is probably more significant than the burden on the Ivory Coast plaintiff from not enjoying (or rather 'enjoying') the visit of the tourist. However, according to an objective standard, the burden on the racist should be discounted, so that from a social perspective the defendant's choice should be deemed unreasonable (as we will see below, the reason for not imposing liability in this example is ingrained in notions of duty). By contrast, in example 6 (as well as 7 and 3) the victim's interest not to interact with countrymen of her tormentors should be accorded value from a social perspective. Put differently, a bigotry which can be explained based on the personal history of the defendant dwells on the fine line between being excused and justified. A Tutsi whose parents were murdered by Hutus, can arguably be regarded as reasonable in refusing to lease her property to a Hutu. Granted, such behaviour unjustly visits the iniquity of the perpetrators upon their countrymen. However, the determination of unreasonableness should set the *minimum* baseline for behaviour and not the highest one. Meeting the reasonableness standard does not mean that the course of action is necessarily desirable, laudable or optimal. Denouncing such behaviour – judged against the history of the defendant – as unreasonable, sets too high a standard. A person in similar circumstances can be understood to be acting like this, even if we commend her if she found it in her heart to act differently.

C. Duty

Whether the law should prohibit discrimination in a given setting should be resolved by balancing the interests of potential defendants in negative liberty and plaintiffs' interests in dignity, positive liberty and equality. The task of balancing remains the same, whether it is done by means of anti-discrimination statute or the common law of negligence. Since there is voluminous discrimination literature on this subject the discussion will be brief. The scales should tilt toward imposing liability when the defendant's behaviour significantly undermines the plaintiffs' interests. By contrast, liability should be denied when the duty not to discriminate threatens significantly the liberty interest of the defendants while only lightly impinges upon the plaintiff's interests. When the actual burden on the defendant, measured by a subjective standard, is significant, a case arises for excusing him from liability, despite the fact that from an objective perspective his interests are devalued so that his behaviour is not deemed reasonable.[53]

Parameters for deciding whether the relationship between the plaintiff and defendant is close enough to justify recognizing a duty, include: whether the duty affects the defendant's private sphere or not, the intensity of the interaction between the parties, its concreteness and the extent to which it is unique, the degree of intrusion upon the interests of the victim, and the power gap between typical plaintiffs and defendants.

To illustrate these parameters, recall the nine examples brought in Section B above. Only in examples 4 and 6 (the silent tourist and the Israeli tourist refusing to visit Germany) no duty should inhere. However, in examples 8 and 9 (scholarships by private funders) reasonable minds can differ with respect to the existence of duty. When the examination of reasonableness is added to the analysis, the conclusion is that liability should be imposed in examples 2, 5 and 9 (the Neanderthal owner, the loud tourist and the non-Pakistani scholarship fund); in these cases duty exists and breach has occurred.

As regards the first parameter, the more the relevant conduct pertains to the private spheres of the defendant, the more immune it should be from being subject to a duty not to discriminate. Therefore, a person who discriminates against another on grounds of ethnic origin or race in the context of choosing a candidate for marriage or companionship should not be subject to liability, despite the fact that using such criteria is highly likely to be unreasonable. This is an example of both the quantitative and the qualitative aspects of preserving liberty. The quantitative aspect relates to the fact that the decision whom to choose as a partner affects numerous aspects of one's life for a long period of time. The qualitative aspect of liberty stems from the fact that choice of partner pertains to one's identity and to intimate spheres with respect to which there is a relative consensus that the law should not attempt to regulate.[54] In a similar vein, albeit to a lesser degree, one's decision where to spend one's leisure time can be understood as private. One might argue that a distinction should be drawn between examples 8 and 9. In the former, a decision to spend private funding on a group with which the spender has some kind of affiliation, makes the decision not only

53 This approach is supported by needs as a criterion for distribution. See Ch. 5.II.B1 above.

54 The modern tendency of enacting Heart Balm statutes, which abolish the common law cause of action for breach of promise to marry, reflects the same approach. See e.g., The Law Reform (Miscellaneous Provisions) Act 1970, Ch. 33, s.1 (UK); Marriage Act, RSO 1990, c. M.3, s. 32 (Ontario).

reasonable but also private, so there is no duty towards all other excluded persons. By contrast, once there is a decision to use private funding for a scholarship that is not based on special affiliation, the interaction becomes less private and hence is capable of forming a duty towards potential beneficiaries of the scholarship.

The existence of duty in examples 5 and 7 and its absence in examples 4 and 6 exemplify the following parameters: the intensity of the interaction between the parties, its concreteness, the extent to which it is unique and the degree of intrusion upon the interests of the victim. No concrete, unique and intense harm to an important interest of any victim can be established in examples 5 and 7. The expectation of citizens of a country that tourists will come is not sufficiently strong to establish a duty. In these cases, the spectre of unlimited liability with its effects on defendants' liberty and the creation of significant litigation costs, as well as the fact that the harm to any potential plaintiff is relatively small, all point to the same direction of denying duty. By contrast, the interest of an individual not to be directly exposed to bigoted views expressed against her identity are concrete, unique and intense enough in order to justify a duty.

More generally, the number of potential defendants affected by the discrimination is a consideration which can work in either direction. On the one hand, it makes the discrimination more potentially significant from a practical perspective, and therefore suggests that it should be eradicated. On the other hand, symbolically, when a large number of people are discriminated against, the relative disadvantage for each is smaller, and so is likely to be the symbolic aspect of the discrimination (to illustrate, compare 'no people from Africa are allowed in this party' with 'no people who are not from the Americas are allowed in this party'). Moreover, the larger the number of potential plaintiffs, the more significant is the exposure of the defendant to liability, and hence the threat to his liberty.[55]

From the plaintiff's perspective, the more (1) disadvantaged she is, (2) significant the harm from the discrimination or (3) offensive the ground for discrimination, the stronger the case for imposing a duty. The distinction between examples 4 and 5, 6 and 7 and possibly 8 and 9 exemplifies these points.

To conclude: when the discrimination causes significant injury to the plaintiff, the case for imposing duty becomes stronger. When either side would suffer a significant loss from an adverse legal rule, considerations of fault should allocate the loss to the faulty partner. In short, the extent to which the interaction in question is central to the well-being and the identity of both parties should be evaluated for purposes of determining the existence of duty.

Finally, a common consideration against imposing duty is that in the long run it might harm the interests of those for whose benefit the duty is imposed.[56] This should be taken into account, although this argument should not be accepted too easily in the context of discrimination.

---

55 What is relevant for the analysis is not only the number of potential plaintiffs but also (and mainly) the frequency of the interaction.

56 *Dobson v Dobson* [1999] 2 SCR 753, 779–80 (Can).

D. Damages

Discrimination harms many people at different levels. The person discriminated against may suffer from direct consequential loss (for example, the extra expense involved in not finding suitable accommodation easily), loss of dignity (feelings of humiliation, worthlessness and anger), loss to reputation (to the extent that third persons internalize the negative view of the person who discriminates) and indirect consequential losses (failure to climb the social ladder, given the harm to dignity and reputation). The members of the same group as the person discriminated against may suffer similar losses due to the self-perpetuating effect discrimination has, and they too may feel anger and humiliation. Moreover, members of other groups may also feel outraged by the defendant's discriminatory behaviour. While it is unwise to recognize a duty toward anyone who may have been injured by discrimination, for the purposes of evaluating both whether the behaviour was reasonable and whether duty should inhere, all these social costs of discrimination (to the extent they are foreseeable) should be taken into account.

Whether the plaintiff – the direct victim of discrimination – should be compensated for all losses caused by the discrimination is a separate matter. There are two conceptual difficulties and a practical one. Conceptually, some of the injuries caused to the direct victim may be too remote. Even more problematic are injuries caused to third parties, given the traditional compensatory principle, according to which damages in torts are designed to eliminate the *victim's* losses resulting from the tort. The discussion above has expressed unease with the principle of *restitutio ad integrum*.[57] Here as well it is called for a departure from this principle. From a deterrence perspective, leaving all those injuries uncompensated is undesirable. As for justice considerations, while the victim does not have a strong corrective justice claim for this amount, from a distributive perspective it is better that she will enjoy the windfall than that the defendant will. The defendant's claim for this amount is even weaker compared to the victim's. Not only is the defendant's claim not supported by desert, but it is also negated by notions of retribution. Moreover, assuming that typically those who are discriminated against are weaker than those carrying out the discriminatory acts, awarding the plaintiff this amount results in a progressive distribution of wealth.

Here, however, the concern for the defendant's liberty might kick in. The total amount of damages to all the direct and indirect social harm caused by his conduct could be significant. This leads us to the practical concern. Many of these harms are speculative, and in any event hard to measure, to verify and to quantify. It is therefore tentatively suggested that courts should award the plaintiff an amount reflecting the social costs of the discrimination to third parties without proving this concrete damage. This could be made in the form of punitive damages. Such an award would be determined on the basis of a judicial assessment. The parameters for its size would be the degree of offensiveness of the defendant's conduct and the estimated magnitude of the injury to third parties (which would be determined in part by the extent to which the discrimination was given publicity). Defending in full and developing this novel suggestion, however, will have to await future research.

---

57 Ch. 4.I.A above. See also Ch. 8 below.

Chapter 8

Conclusion

The gist of the argument advanced in this book is that tort law can and should strive to incorporate an egalitarian sensitivity as one of its goals. Such sensitivity can work either in the direction of limiting the liability of the disadvantaged in torts, or in the direction of expanding liability toward the disadvantaged. Egalitarian considerations can either work directly – a reason to expand/curtail liability is simply the positive/negative equality effect of the rule – or indirectly, by changing the moral evaluation and social meaning of one's acts and omissions, hence reformulating notions of corrective justice, desert, fault, fairness and efficiency. Chapter 5 demonstrated the latter point.

An egalitarian approach can entail two kinds of duties: the major one is the duty of policy-makers and lawmakers to create and implement tort rules that will have the desired equality effect. To this at times is added a second duty that is placed on potential defendants to act in a way that will promote the equality of the disadvantaged. Chapter 7 demonstrated the latter point, as did the discussion in Chapter 5 regarding the disputes over frozen ova. Situations giving rise to the second duty implicate necessarily also the first duty, since they involve the need to impose tort-based liability on defendants. While there is no bright line dividing the two categories, a starting point would be that in the latter category the defendant's failure to take equality into account is the basis for his being found liable in tort, while in the former category the equality effects of the tort response to the defendant's conduct should influence the scope of liability.

An egalitarian approach can tackle different kinds of inequality. In particular, tort law can tackle both issues of recognition and redistribution. Chapter 6 focused on gender inequality, Chapter 7 focused mainly on issues of recognition, and Chapter 5, while focusing on material inequality (Examples 1–5, 8 and 9), dealt also with issues of gender injustice (Examples 6, 7 and 10).

Egalitarian considerations emerge in a host of different settings that could be classified according to many criteria, such as (1) the degree of intimacy between the interacting parties,[1] (2) the existence of a contractual relationship,[2] (3) the interest affected and the head of damages involved,[3] and (4) whether or not the defendant

1 Contrast, for example, maternal prenatal duty (Ch. 6 above) with a driver's duty towards another to install safety mechanisms (Ch. 5, Example 4 above). Cf. Ch. 4.V.E2(c) above.

2 Contrast, for example, disputes over frozen ova (Ch. 5, Example 7 above) with a physician's duty towards the patient's partner (Ch. 6 above) or the lawyer's duty towards the other party (Ch. 5, Example 6 above).

3 For the following interests: bodily integrity, economic loss, lost earnings, pain and suffering, loss of autonomy, property loss, harm to dignity in libel suits see respectively Ch.

is a repeat player.[4] These and other distinctions affect the policy analysis. Thus, the level of intimacy might affect the parties' expectations of altruistic and egalitarian behaviour, and the weight that should be given to the promotion of equality. The existence of a contractual relationship affects the potential of circumventing the desired distributive result. When the defendant is a repeat player, the rule should take into account that party's greater ability to pass on the cost (a fact that implicates to a greater degree intra-group justice), the increased likelihood of achieving deterrence, and the fact that the power gap between the litigating parties will often be greater.[5]

A major distinction in the analysis is between the equality effects of liability and compensation rules. The discussion has concentrated on the former. In what follows there is an attempt to sketch some possible reforms to compensation rules in order to make them more egalitarian. The root of the current inegalitarian compensation rules is the principle of *restitutio ad integrum* (RAI).[6] Accordingly, comprehensive solutions should consider the following: (1) standardizing awards; (2) using a means-based multiplier in order to increase or decrease damages, based on the classification of either or both defendant and plaintiff as poor or rich; (3) giving judges the discretion to reduce damages based on the defendant's means; (4) abolishing compensation for negligent property damage (and perhaps even physical injury) while channelling victims to first-party insurance. The merits of first solution were briefly discussed above,[7] and that of the second solution elsewhere;[8] the third solution is adopted in Scandinavia;[9] the fourth solution has been suggested by, among others, by Richard Abel, Patrick Atiyah and Stephen Sugarman.[10]

Even if one is reluctant to adopt such radical solutions across the board, partial steps in this direction could be taken. One could, for example, standardize the awards for non-pecuniary damages.[11] If indeed currently the size of these awards is positively correlated to that of pecuniary damages,[12] standardization will

---

4.IV.A, Examples 7, 1, 5, Ch. 3, note 129, Ch. 4.IV.A, Example 6, Ch. 5, Example 4, Ch. 4.III. B2 above.

4 Contrast negligent parental supervision (Ch. 5, Example 8 above) with liability of public authorities (Ch. 5, Examples 9 & 10).

5 For other observations see the discussion of the four questions posed in Ch. 1 above.

6 See Ch. 4.I.A above.

7 Ch. 3 above, note 100 and accompanying text.

8 Tsachi Keren-Paz, 'Private Law Redistribution, Predictability and Liberty', 50 *McGill LJ* (2005) 327, pp. 336, 339–40.

9 See Ch. 5 above, note 53 and accompanying text.

10 See Stephen D. Sugarman, 'Doing Away with Tort Law', 73 *Cal L Rev* (1985) 555; Patrick S. Atiyah, *The Damages Lottery* (1997); Richard L. Abel, 'Should Tort Law Protect Property Against Accidental Loss?', 23 *San Diego L Rev* (1986) 79; Richard Abel, 'General Damages Are Incoherent, Incalculable, Incommensurable, And Inegalitarian (But Otherwise A Great Idea)', 55 *DePaul L. Rev.* (2006) 253, pp. 323–4 (abolishing monetary awards for pain and suffering, and equalizing special damages by setting income replacement at median).

11 Abel, ibid., p. 326.

12 Ibid., p. 312 n.495; Gregory T. Miller, 'Behind the Battle Lines: A Comparative Analysis of the Necessity to Enact Comprehensive Federal Products Liability Reforms', 45 *Buffalo L Rev* (1997) 241, p. 273.

eliminate an important component of what makes tort law regressive. Second, an egalitarian approach also casts doubt on the desirability of compensating victims for loss of earning capacity in the 'lost years'.[13] It is doubtful whether the part of the award which exceeds the loss of the dependants is a real loss at all, and awarding compensation for lost years exacerbates the regressive cross-subsidy. Third, in cases of claims by minors for lost earnings, an egalitarian approach supports applying a unified lost-earning index which does not take into account the plaintiff's gender or socio-demographic status.[14] As shown elsewhere, such a solution is not problematic on grounds of randomness.[15] To that analysis the following could be added. If the unified index is based on the average earnings index of both men and women (as opposed to an index based solely on men's earnings), as I have tentatively suggested that it should,[16] and if courts apply the unified index, as they should, to claims of boys as well, the argument against the suggested solution is rooted in intra- rather than inter-group justice. On average, defendants will pay the same amount of damages (and hence premiums). However, the distribution of the damages will be different. Under a gendered index, injured boys receive more compensation than injured girls. The losers from a shift to a unified index will therefore be injured boys, rather than defendants. The argument of these boys against adopting a unified index, however, is weak, as it is based on the expectation that the patriarchal order, which accounts for the gender-gap in earnings, will be perpetuated by courts' damages decisions.

If men's lost-earnings index is used to compensate all injured minors, including girls, then the justice claim against such a solution is that of defendants who arguably pay more than the real damage they create. But in such a case it is defendants who base their claim on the expectation that the patriarchal order, which holds women's salaries down, will be perpetuated by the courts. In addition, as Elizabeth Adjin-Tettey has argued, women's lower earning capacity is based on under-valuation of their real contribution to society.[17] Using men's index rectifies this under-valuation and in this way partial justice is achieved.

Fourth, an egalitarian approach seems to support awarding compensation in cases involving the loss of autonomy by patients who did not give informed consent but who would have, had it not been for the violation of their autonomy.[18]

---

13 Ch. 4.IV.B above.

14 Such an approach was taken recently by the Israeli Supreme Court. See CA 10064/02 *Migdal v Abu Hanna*, Takdin-Elyon 2005(03) 3932 (Israel). For a review of the opposite tendency in the United States and Canada See Tsachi Keren-Paz, 'An Inquiry into the Merits of Redistribution through Tort Law: Rejecting the Claim of Randomness', 16 *Can JL & Jur* (2003) 91, p. 122. But see *Greyhound Lines, Inc. v Sutton*, 765 So 2d 1269 (Miss 2000).

15 Keren-Paz, ibid., pp. 121–6.

16 Ibid., pp. 122 n.94, 124 n.103 and accompanying text. For another view see Elizabeth Adjin-Tettey, 'Replicating and Perpetuating Inequalities in Personal Injury Claims Through Female-Specific Contingencies', 49 *McGill LJ* (2004) 309.

17 Adjin-Tettey, ibid., p. 314 n.6.

18 See Ch. 4.IV.A, Example 6 above.

For the fifth application of an egalitarian approach to tort damages consider the following example.[19] A plaintiff was seriously injured and, due to his lack of funds, was placed in a nursing home, where he suffered from the effects of isolation and was at risk of eventual mental degradation. The courts had to grapple with the question whether the principle of RAI required that the defendant bear the (much higher) cost of accommodating the plaintiff in his own home. The trial court answered this question in the negative, but the Supreme Court reversed and remanded for a determination of damages. It ruled, however, that the higher amount was to be paid only as of the date on which the plaintiff would return home. An egalitarian approach would insist that the higher amount should be paid as of the date on which the defendant was medically fit to be moved home. On the assumption that the principle of RAI gives the plaintiff a right to be kept at home, it is unfair that this right should be denied because of lack of funds. Since it is reasonable to assume that, had the plaintiff had sufficient funds to be kept at home before the litigation ended he would have received full reimbursement of these costs, denying the impecunious plaintiff the same amount treats him disfavourably due to his poverty. Another reasoning leading to the same conclusion is that the plaintiff should be at liberty to live in an institution and spend (or save) the difference between the cost of living at home (to which he is entitled) or in the nursing home. This right derives from the victim's autonomy, which should be especially respected given the devastating loss of autonomy that serious injuries entail. However, even if one is reluctant to respect such a choice (based perhaps on paternalistic and rehabilitative considerations), surely the plaintiff cannot be denied the difference between these two amounts when he did not make this choice and when his staying at the institution was the result of the defendant's tort and plaintiff's lack of means.

This point can be generalized. The dilemma that arises from the previous example is this: who should bear the collateral loss resulting from the plaintiff's lack of means, the victim or the tortfeasor? The common law has traditionally allocated this loss to the victim, viewing it as too remote to be attributable to the tortfeasor. Recently, however, this attitude has been changing. In *The Edison*,[20] the court did not award the plaintiffs compensation for the full cost of hiring a replacement for their dredger which was sunk due to defendants' fault, when these costs significantly exceeded the cost of purchasing a replacement dredger, despite the fact that they were unable to purchase a replacement due to liquidity problems. Lord Wright treated the plaintiffs' lack of means as an independent cause of the loss, and as an extraneous matter which could not be compared to physical delicacy or high earning capacity.

An egalitarian approach would impose liability for the plaintiffs' loss in *The Edison*, and would perhaps curtail liability for the loss of high earning capacity. In both scenarios the damaged suffered is a combination of the defendants' tortious act and the plaintiffs' status. In the first case, the injury is greater than expected

19 It is based on the facts of CA 2934/93 *Soroka v Hababo*, PD 50(1) 675 (Israel). For a critical treatment see Tsachi Keren-Paz 'How Does Compensation Law Render the Poor Even Poorer? (And Why Does the Supreme Court Give Inconsistent Interpretation to the Compensation to Victims of Road Accidents Act?)', 28 *Tel-Aviv ULR* (2004) 299.

20 *Liesbosch v Edison* [1933] AC 449 (HL).

due to the plaintiffs' poverty; in the second case, it is so due to the plaintiffs' wealth. It is hard to justify the liability of the defendants in the latter but not in the former case, especially given that the loss is not more foreseeable in one case than in the other, and that the disutility to the rich plaintiffs is likely be lesser than the disutility to the poor plaintiffs. If one is content with the idea that the defendant should take plaintiff as he finds her, why should the poor plaintiff be treated unfavourably? And why should not the plaintiff's poverty be viewed as just one kind of sensitivity which increases the plaintiff's injury, such that the defendant would be required to compensate the plaintiff in full under the eggshell skull doctrine? Surely the poor plaintiff is no more at fault for being poor than the rich plaintiff is at fault for being rich.

If, alternatively, one is dissatisfied with the lottery-like nature of tort law, then the particular harm caused to both rich and poor plaintiffs, which results in each case from their financial status, should be ignored. Yet an egalitarian approach can be asymmetrical as well (although it would tilt to the opposite direction than *The Edison* did). It would require compensating the poor for the collateral loss caused by their poverty, but not for compensating the rich for the full extent of their loss.[21] Such an approach can be defended either on the grounds that tort law should take into account the disutility to the uncompensated plaintiff of bearing a loss, or on notions of the plaintiff's ability to prevent the collateral injury. Under the first approach, the disutility to the poor would be more significant than the disutility to the rich. Under the second approach, the poor have limited ability to prevent or mitigate the collateral loss in case of injury, while the rich can purchase income or property insurance that exceeds the average (or reasonably expected) loss. Accordingly, the defendant will be liable in full to the poor plaintiff, but will be liable to the rich plaintiff only for the average loss caused by the injury. The rich plaintiff would bear the risk of loss with respect to the difference between the actual and the average damage, and would be able to insure himself against such risk.

In *Lagden v O'Connor*[22] the House of Lords overturned *The Edison* (whose holding had previously been narrowed), ruling that the plaintiff's lack of funds should be taken into account if reasonably foreseeable. The court's holding, by a 3 to 2 majority, was that impecunious plaintiffs could be compensated for the more expensive credit hire agreement for replacing a car when they were unable to afford commercial hire charges. While this decision is an important step in the right direction, it does not create a clear-cut rule that reasonable financing costs are recoverable. Thus, at least according to Lord Hope, who wrote the main speech, it seems that those who have to rely on an overdraft facility in order to finance their car hire charges will not be able to recover the additional cost of this method of financing.[23] Similarly, in the context of special accommodation expenses, the interest paid for the difference in value of the adapted accommodation over the value of the

21 For discussion of similar asymmetric solutions, see Ch. 5, Examples 5 & 9 above.

22 *Lagden v O'Connor* [2004] 1 All ER 277 (HL).

23 Ibid., p. 290 (access to credit or debit card as dividing line). Cf. pp. 302–3 per Lord Scott dissenting (no basis for distinguishing between those with no access to credit and those who can overdraw).

pre-accident accommodation is not set according to the rate of borrowing.[24] This of course disadvantages those who do not have available funds.

This study merely touched upon issues regarding causation. An egalitarian approach might support the relaxation of traditional notions of factual causality and a move towards doctrines such as market share liability and compensation for lost chance.[25] To the extent that the latter doctrine gives lower compensation to a greater number of people, it might be supported based on notions of diminishing marginal utility of money.[26] To the extent that these doctrines help the typically small, unorganized disenfranchised consumer against giant profit-motivated corporations, they might be justified as a matter of inter-group justice. However, full analysis has to take into account the downside of increasing liability from thc perspective of intra-group justice, due to the problem of regressive cross-subsidy.[27]

It is appropriate to end this book by offering a new frontier for an egalitarian reformulation of tort law, which combines issues of both liability and compensation: trafficking in persons.[28] There is an extensive legal academic and advocacy-based discussion of this horrible form of modern slavery. Most of it, however, focuses on aspects such as human rights, criminal and international law,[29] and little has been written on private law responses to this problem. This is unfortunate, since tort law and unjust enrichment law are important potential tools for combating trafficking. The advantages of using tort law in this battle are the following: first, tort law is more focused than criminal law on compensating the victims of trafficking for the horrible violations that they have been subjected to. Second, trafficking involves huge profits to traffickers, and one cannot combat the phenomenon without targeting these profits.[30] Tort law and unjust enrichment law, by cutting deep into these profits, will hopefully reduce somewhat both the incentive to traffic and the extent of trafficking. While profits can be targeted through forfeiture legislation, a private law response

24 See *Roberts v Johnstone* [1989] QB 878 (Eng. CA); Harvey McGregor, *McGregor on Damages* (17th edn, London, 2003), pp. 1263–6.

25 See *Barker v Corus* [2006] UKHL 20 (whose ruling was effectively abolished by s. 3 of the Compensation Act 2006, Ch. 29 (UK); *Hymowitz v Eli Lilly & Co*, 539 NE 2d 1069 (NY Ct App 1989).

26 Ch. 4.I.A above. In addition, a lost chance doctrine might be supported by notions of needs, as well as another understanding of equality, namely, that people with equal needs should get the same amount of compensation regardless of the cause of their injury. This is so, since under the lost chance doctrine, those injured by natural causes are subsidized by tort victims. Such doctrine can be supported by considerations of deterrence and some understanding of corrective justice. See Ariel Porat & Alex Stein, 'Liability for Uncertainty: Making Evidential Damage Actionable', 18 *Cardozo L Rev* (1997) 1891.

27 For an analysis of the same tension in a similar context, see Ch. 4 above, notes 26, 53 and accompanying text.

28 The discussion concentrates on trafficking for purposes of sex enslavement, although other kinds of trafficking exist. Part of the framework, but not all, applies to other kinds of trafficking.

29 See Mohamed Y. Mattar, 'Trafficking in Persons: An Annotated Legal Bibliography', 96 *Law Libr J* (2004) 669.

30 Susan W. Tiefenbrun, 'Sex Sells but Drugs Don't Talk: Trafficking of Women, Sex Workers and an Economic Solution', 24 *T Jefferson L Rev* (2002) 161.

– and this is the third advantage – could add effectiveness by not being limited by the higher procedural guarantees that govern the criminal process. Finally, a tort response might be appropriate with respect to parties, such as clients and state agencies, who contribute to the exploitation through their actions and omissions, in those situations where a criminal response might deemed to be too harsh.

With respect to traffickers, liability as such does not involve conceptual problems. However, given evidentiary problems, important changes should be made to compensation rules in order to facilitate gain-based recovery.[31] A more contested battleground is the possible tort liability of clients and of the state.[32] Such liability involves difficult normative, conceptual, evidentiary and practical hurdles, and it should await a separate inquiry.[33] A tort response that might reduce trafficking and that provides partial redress to the victims against the perpetrators reveals the humane, empowering, and practical nature of egalitarian tort law, its importance, and essentiality.

31 See Nomi Levenkron, 'Civil Suits of Victims of Trafficking Against the Traffickers: And Yet, It Does Move', in Guy Mundlak & Mimi Ajzenstadt (eds), *Law, Society & Culture: Empowerment* (forthcoming, 2007); two recent lower court decisions in Israel granted compensation to victims: L (Be'er-Sheva) 4634/03 *M v Salsarevski*, Takdin-Avoda 2005(03) 97 (Israel); CC (Tel-Aviv) 2191/02 *K v Eagor*, Takdin-Mehozi 2006(1) 7885 (Israel). While both decisions include problematic theoretical and practical aspects, the direction they were taking is laudable.

32 At the time of this writing, Adv. Nomi Levenkron, Head of the Legal Department of the Hotline for Migrant Workers, is working on filing a suit against the state demanding that restitution be provided to victims from the confiscated profits of traffickers, based on claims of unjust enrichment and negligence.

33 Among the questions that will have to be addressed are the following: What is the basis for liability? Should it require knowledge of the trafficking? Is an objective standard sufficient? Can a strict liability regime be defended, and if so on what ground? For what damage is the client responsible? Is the creation of the demand a sufficient ground? Can a rationale of a failure to rescue justify liability for harm occurring after the encounter? How can liability be established, given evidentiary problems? Is a tort response against clients practical? How will a tort response affect women being trafficked, both current and potential?

Table of Cases

A v Bottrill [2003] AC 449 (PC 2002) 173
Adarand Constructors v Pena, 115 S Ct 2097 (1995) 56
Amin v Entry Clearance Officer, Bombay [1983] 2 AC 818 (H.L) 162
Avellone v St John's Hosp., 135 NE 2d 410 (Ohio 1956) 129
Barclays Bank plc v O'Brien [1994] 1 AC 180 (H.L) 115
Barker v Corus [2006] UKHL 20 186
Barrett v Enfield London Borough Council [2001] 2 AC 550 (H.L) 171
Bittner v Tait-Gibson Optometetrists Ltd (1964) 44 DLR (2d) 113 (On CA) 127
Blyth v Birmingham Waterworks Co. (1856) 11 Ex 781 126
Bolam v Friern Hosp. Management Comm. [1957] 1 WLR 582 (QB) 130
Bonte v Bonte, 616 A.2d 464 (NH 1992) 136, 138
Boomer v Atlantic Cement Co. Inc., 257 NE 2d 870, 873 (NY Ct App 1970) 75
Bowditch v McEwan and Ors [2002] QCA 172 138
Bradshaw v Swagerty, 563 P 2d 511 (Kan Ct App 1977) 162
British Railways Board v Herrington [1972] AC 877, 899 (HL) 127
Brown v Board of Education, 349 US 483 (1954) 25
Bruttig v Olsen, 453 NW 2d 153 (Wis Ct App 1989) 52
Caparo Industries Plc. v Dickman [1990] 2 AC 605 (HL) 94, 117
Caradori v Fitch, 263 NW 2d 649 (Neb 1978) 130
Cashman v Reider's Stop-N-Shop Supermarket, 504 NE 2d 487 (Ohio Ct App 1986) 52
Chenault v Huie, 989 SW 2d 474 (Tex Ct App 1999) 137, 138, 151, 158
Chester v Afshar [2004] 4 All ER 587 (HL) 77
Daaka v Carmel Hospital, CA 2781/93 PD 53(4) 526 (Israel) 77
Dabron v Bath Tramways Ltd [1946] 2 All ER 333 (CA) 88
Daly v Liverpool Corp. [1939] 2 All ER 142 (KBD) 130
Davis v Davis, 842 SW 2d 588 (Tenn 1992) 116, 121
Dean v Allin & Watts [2001] 2 Lloyd's Rep 249 (CA) 115
Doe v Board of Commissioners of Police (1998) 39 OR 3d 487 (Gen Div) 124, 131
Dobson v Dobson (1997) 148 DLR (4th) 332 (NBCA) 136
Dobson v Dobson [1999] 2 SCR 753 (Can) 137, 138, 139, 140, 141, 146, 154, 158, 159, 179
Donovan v Fiumara, 442 SE 2d 572, 580 (NC Ct App 1994) 75
East Suffolk Rivers Catchment Bd v Kent [1941] AC 74 (HL) 127
Escola v Coca Cola Bottling Co., 150 P 2d 436 (Cal 1944) 93, 129
Evans v Amicus Healthcare Ltd [2004] EWCA Civ 727 (CA), *aff'm* [2003] 4 All ER 903 (Fam) 116
Evans v UK, 6339/05 [2006] 1 FCR 585 (ECHR) 116, 120

Fletcher v City of Aberdeen, 338 P 2d 743 (Wash 1959) 130
Fuller v Studer, 833 P 2d 109 (Idaho 1992) 122
Gabay v Luzon, CA 64/89 PD 48(4) 673 (Israel) 131
Gissen v Goodwill, 80 So 2d 701 (Fla 1955) 122
Glasgow Corporation v Muir [1943] AC 448 (HL) 126
Goldman v Hargrave [1967] 1 AC 645 (PC) 127
Goodwill v British Pregnancy Advisory Service [1996] 2 All ER 161 (CA) 77, 135
Gough v Thorne [1966] 3 All ER 398 (CA) 130
Granville Savings & Mortgage Corp. v Slevin [1993] 4 SCR 279 (Can) 115
Greyhound Lines, Inc. v Sutton, 765 So 2d 1269 (Miss 2000) 183
Grodin v Grodin, 301 NW 2d 869 (Mich Ct App. 1980) 138, 147
Groobner v Municipality of Haifa, CA 343/74 PD 30(1) 141, 158 (Israel) 88, 123
Haley v London Elec. Bd [1965] AC 778 (HL) 130
Hall v Gus Construction Co., 842 F 2d 1010 (8th Cir 1988) 162
Hamed v State of Israel, CA 5604/94 PD 58(2) 498, 518–21 (Israel) 126, 127
Hammond v Wabana (1998) 44 CCLT (2d) 101 (Nfld CA) 127
Hamstra v BC Rugby Union [1997] 1 SCR 1092 (Can) 130
Hatfield v Gracen, 567 P 2d 546 (Or 1977) 88
Heath v Swift Wings, Inc., 252 SE 2d 256 (NC App 1979) 130
Hercules Managements Ltd v Ernst & Young [1997] 2 SCR 165 (Can) 94
Hymowitz v Eli Lilly & Co., 539 NE 2d 1069 (NY Ct App 1989) 186
Jerusalem Chevra Kadisha v Kestenbaum, CA 294/91 PD 46(2) 464, 530 (Israel) 131
Jordan v Duff & Phelps, Inc., 815 F 2d 429 (7th Cir 1987) 44
K v Eagor, CC (Tel-Aviv) 2191/02 Takdin-Mehozi 2006(1) 7885 (Israel) 187
Killip's Television Service Ltd. v Stony Plain [2000] 3 WWR 702 (Alta QB) 127
Lagden v O'Connor, [2004] 1 All ER 277 (HL) 185
Liesbosch v Edison [1933] AC 449 (HL) 184
Lister v Romford Ice & Cold Storage Co. Ltd [1957] 1 All ER 125 (HL) 130
Logan v Sears, Roebuck & Co., 466 So 2d 121 (Ala 1985) 162
Lynch v Lynch (1991) 25 NSWLR 411 138
M v Salsarevski, L (Be'er-Sheva) 4634/03 Takdin-Avoda 2005(03) 97 (Israel) 187
McConville v State Farm Mut. Auto. Ins. Co., 113 NW 2d 14 (Wis 1962) 129
Matthews v Amberwood Associates Ltd Partnership, Inc., 719 A 2d 119 (Md Ct App 1998) 129
Meyers v Robb, 267 NW 2d 450 (Mich Ct App 1978) 88
Migdal v Abu Hanna, CA 10064/02 Takdin-Elyon 2005(03) 3932 (Israel) 52, 129, 183
M'Kibbon v Glasgow Corp., 1920 Sess Cas 590 (Scot 2nd Div) 130
Montgomery v National Convoy & Trucking Co., 195 SE 247 (SC 1938) 117
Montreal Tramways Co. v Leveille [1933] SCR 456 (Can) 136
Mullin v Richards [1998] 1 All ER 920 (CA) 130
Municipality of Haifa v Moskovitz, CA 283/89 PD 47(2) 718, 725 (Israel) 88, 145
Murphy v Brentwood District Council [1990] 2 All ER 908 (HL) 136
Nahmani v Nahmani, CFH2401/95 50(4) PD 661 (Israel) 56, 116, 118, 119
Nahmani v Nahmani, OM (Haifa) 599/92 PM 1994(1) 142, (Israel) 119, 120

Nahum v Dorenbaum, CA 2625/02 PD 58(3) 385 (Israel) 115, 128, 129, 135
De Nartini v Alexsander Sanitarium, 13 Cal Rptr 564 (Ct App 1961) 130
National Casualty Company v Northern Trust Bank of Florida, 807 So 2d 86 (Fla Ct App 2002) 138
Nelson v Nationwide Mortgage Corp., 659 F Supp 611 (DDC 1987) 115
Non-Marine Underwriters, Lloyd's of London v Scalera (2000) 185 DLR (4th) 1 (Can) 173
Paris v Stepney Borough Council [1951] 1 All ER 32 (HL) 127
Parmiter v Coupland (1840) 6 M & W 105 75
Payton v Abbott Labs, 437 NE 2d 171 (Mass 1982) 136
Pickett v British Rail Engineering Ltd, [1979] 1 All ER 774 (HL) 78
Priestman v Colangelo [1959] SCR 615 127
Reeves v Commissioner of Police of the Metropolis [2000] 1 AC 360 (HL) 173
Reilly v United States, 665 F Supp 976, 997 (RI 1987), *aff'd,* 863 F 2d 149 (1st Cir 1988) 131
Remi v MacDonald, 801 NE 2d 260 (Mass 2004) 137
Robbins of Putney Ltd v Meek [1971] RTR 345 118
Roberts v Johnstone [1989] QB 878 (Eng CA) 186
Seneca Coll. of Applied & Tech. Bd of Governors v Bhadauria [1981] 2 SCR 181 (Can) 162, 163
Shamsian v Ganey Rosmary, CC (Tel-Aviv) 15/97 14 Dinim Shalom 402 (Israel) 162
Shows v Shoney's, Inc., 738 So 2d 724 (La App 1st Cir 1999) 131
Snider v Henniger (1992) 96 DLR (4th) 367 77
Soroka v Hababo, CA 2934/93 PD 50(1) 675 (Israel) 184
Stallman v Youngquist, 531 NE 2d 355 (Ill 1988) 137, 151
Stubbings v Webb [1993] AC 498 (HL) 167
Sun Mountain Prod., Inc. v Pierre, 929 P 2d 494 (Wash Ct App Div 1 1997) 122
Transco Plc v Stockport Metropolitan Borough Council [2004] 1 All ER 589 130
Turpin v Sortini, 643 P 2d 954, 965 (Cal 1982) 145
Ultramares Corp. v Touche, 174 NE 441 (NY Ct App 1931) 94, 134
United States v Carrol Towing Co., 159 F 2d. 169 (2d Cir 1947) 87
Viasystems (Tyneside) Ltd v Thermal Transfer (Northern) [2005] 4 All ER 1181 (CA) 73
Vriend v Alberta [1998] 1 SCR 493 (Can) 163
Watt v Hertfordshire County Council [1954] 2 All ER 368 (CA) 88
White v Jones [1995] 2 AC 207; [1995] 1 All ER 691(HL) 135
Wiggs v Courshon, 355 F Supp 206 (1973) 162
Winnipeg Child and Family Services (Northwest Area) v DFG [1997] 3 SCR 925 (Can) 139, 140, 151, 155
Wright v Lodge [1993] 4 All ER 299 (CA) 117
Young v Bella [2006] SCC 3 128

Table of Legislation

Act of Tort Ch. 2 -4 (Finland) 113
Alberta's Individual Rights Protection Act, RSA 1980, c. I-2 163
Compensation Act 2006, ch. 29 (UK) 186
Human Rights Code, RSO 1990, c. H.19 161, 164
The Law Reform (Miscellaneous Provisions) Act, 1970, ch. 33, s. 1 (UK) 178
Marriage Act, RSO 1990, c. M.3, s. 32 (Ontario) 178
Sex Discrimination Act 1975, ch. 65 (UK) 161, 164
Sv. Prop. 1975:12, at 177 (Sweden) 113
Race Relations Act 1976, Ch.74 (UK) 161
42 USC ss. 2000e–2000e-17, 2000a–2000a-6, 3601–19, 2000d–2000d-7, (2006) (US) 161, 164

Bibliography

Books

Aristotle, *Nicomachean Ethics* (trans. Martin Ostwald, Book Five, New York, 1962).
—— *Ethica Nicomachea* (trans. William D. Ross, Book V.3, Oxford, 1925).
Atiyah, Patrick S., *The Damages Lottery* (Oxford, 1997).
—— *An Introduction to the Law of Contract* (5th edn, Oxford, 1995).
—— *Vicarious Liability in the Law of Torts* (London, 1967).
Atwood, Margaret E., *The Handmaid's Tale* (New York, 1986).
Barak, Aharon, *Interpretation in Law* (vol. 3, Jerusalem, 1994).
Beale, Hugh G. (ed.), *Chitty on Contracts* (29th edn, vol. 1, London, 2004).
Bowie, Norman E., *Towards a New Theory of Distributive Justice* (Amherst, 1971).
Braybrooke, David, *Meeting Needs* (Princeton, 1987).
Buckley, Richard A., *The Modern Law of Negligence* (3rd edn, London, 1999).
Calabresi, Guido, *The Costs of Accidents* (New Haven, 1970).
Cane, Peter, *Atiyah's Accidents, Compensation and the Law* (London, 1993).
Card, David & Krueger Alan .B., *Myth and Measurement: The New Economics of the Minimum Wage* (Princeton NJ, 1995).
Chin, Audrey & Peterson Mark A., *The Rand Corporation, Deep Pockets, Empty Pockets: Who Wins in Cook County Jury Trials?* (Santa Monica, 1985).
Coleman, Jules L., *Risks and Wrongs* (Cambridge, 1992).
Conaghan, Joanne & Mansell Wade, *The Wrongs of Tort* (London, 1993).
Dagan, Hanoch, *Unjust Enrichment: A Study of Private Law and Public Values* (Cambridge, 1997).
Daniels, Cynthia R., *At Women's Expense: State Power and the Politics of Fetal Rights* (Cambridge, 1993).
Deakin, Simon F., Johnston Angus & Markesinis Basil, *Markesinis and Deakin's Tort Law* (5th edn, Oxford, 2003).
Dewees, Don, Duff David & Trebilcock Michael, *Exploring the Domain of Accident Law: Taking the Facts Seriously* (New York, 1996).
Dworkin Ronald, *Sovereign Virtue: The Theory and Practice of Equality* (Cambridge, 2000).
—— *Law's Empire* (Cambridge, 1986).
Ely, John H., *Democracy and Distrust* (Cambridge, 1980).
Englard, Izhak, *The Philosophy of Tort Law* (Aldershot, 1993).
Farber, Daniel A. & Frickey Philip P., *Law and Public Choice: A Critical Introduction* (Chicago, 1991).
Farnsworth, E. Allan, *Contracts* (3rd edn, New York, 1999).

Feldthusen, Bruce, *Economic Negligence* (4th edn, Toronto, 2000).
Fineman, Martha A., *The Illusion of Equality: The Rhetoric and Reality of Divorce Reform* (Chicago, 1991).
Fleming, John G., *The Law of Torts* (9th edn, Sydney, 1998).
Fletcher, George P., *Rethinking Criminal Law* (1978).
Fraser Nancy, *Justice Interruptus: Critical Reflections on the 'Postsocialist' Condition* (New York, 1997).
Fredman, Sandra, *Discrimination Law* (Oxford, 2002).
Fried, Charles, *Right and Wrong* (Cambridge, 1978).
Hans, Valerie P., *Business on Trial: The Civil Jury and Corporate Responsibility* (New Haven, 2000).
Harris, Donald, *Compensation and Support for Illness and Injury* (Oxford, 1984).
Hart, H.L.A., *The Concept of Law* (2nd edn, Oxford, 1994).
Heuston, R.F.V. & Buckley R.A.B., *Salmond & Heuston on the Law of Torts* (21st edn, London, 1996).
Hewlett, Sylvia A., *A Lesser Life: The Myth of Women's Liberation in America* (New York, 1986).
Holmes, Oliver Wendell Jr, *The Common Law* (Boston, 1881).
Horwitz, Morton, *The Transformation of American Law, 1780–1860* (Cambridge, 1977).
Hutchinson, Allan C., *It's All in the Game: A Nonfoundationalist Account of Law and Adjudication* (Durham, 2000).
—— *Waiting For Coraf: A Critique of Law and Rights* (1995).
Ison, Terence G., *The Forensic Lottery: A Critique on Tort Liability as a System of Personal Injury Compensation* (London, 1967).
Katz, Michael B., *The Undeserving Poor: From the War on Poverty to the War on Welfare* (New York, 1989).
Keeton, Page, *Prosser & Keeton on the Law of Torts* (5th edn, St Paul, 1984).
Kennedy, Duncan, *A Critique of Adjudication: Fin de Siècle* (Cambridge, 1997).
Koening, Thomas H. & Rusted Michael L., *In Defense of Tort Law* (New York, 2001).
Koppelman, Andrew, *Antidiscrimination Law and Social Equality* (New Haven, 1996).
Landes, William M. & Posner Richard A., *The Economic Structure of Tort Law* (Cambridge, 1987).
Lucas, John R., *On Justice* (Oxford, 1980).
McCormick, Charles T., *Handbook of the Law of Evidence* (1st edn, St Paul, 1954).
McGregor, Harvey, *McGregor on Damages* (17th edn, London, 2003).
MacKinnon, Catharine A., *Sexual Harassment of Working Women: A Case of Sex Discrimination* (New Haven, 1979).
Nozick, Robert, *Anarchy, State, and Utopia* (New York, 1974).
O'Connell, Jeffrey, *The Lawsuit Lottery: Only the Lawyers Win* (New York, 1979).
Olson, Mancur, *The Logic of Collective Action: Public Goods and the Theory of Groups* (Cambridge, 1965).
Pearce, David W. & Nash Christopher A., *The Social Appraisal of Projects: A Text in Cost-Benefit Analysis* (London, 1981).

Polinsky, A. Mitchell, *An Introduction to Law and Economics* (2nd edn, Boston, 1989).

Porat, Ariel & Stein Alex, *Tort Liability Under Uncertainty* (Oxford, 2001).

Posner, Eric A., *Law and Social Norms* (Cambridge, 2000).

Posner, Richard, *Overcoming Law* (Cambridge, 1995).

Prosser, William L., *Handbook of the Law of Torts* (4th edn, St Paul, 1971).

Rawls, John, *A Theory of Justice* (rev. edn, Cambridge, 1999).

Reason, James, *Human Error* (Cambridge, 1990).

Rogers, W.V.H., *Winfield and Jolowicz on Tort* (16th edn, London, 2002).

Sadurski, Wojciech, *Giving Desert Its Due: Social Justice and Legal Theory* (Dordrecht, 1985).

Schlozman, Kay L. & Tierney John T., *Organized Interests and American Democracy* (New York, 1986).

Shavell, Steven, *Economic Analysis of Accident Law* (Cambridge, 1987).

Sher, George, *Desert* (Princeton, 1987).

Summers, Robert S., *Instrumentalism and American Legal Theory* (Ithaca, 1982).

Trebilcock, Michael J., *The Limits of Freedom of Contract* (Cambridge, 1993).

Unger, Roberto M., *The Critical Legal Studies Movement* (Cambridge, 1986).

Walton, C.T., *Charlesworth & Percy on Negligence* (10th edn, London, 2001).

Walzer, Michael, *Spheres of Justice: A Defense of Pluralism and Equality* (Oxford, 1983).

Weinrib, Ernest J., *The Idea of Private Law* (Cambridge, 1995).

Wilhelmsson, Thomas, *Critical Studies in Private Law* (Dordrecht, 1992).

Chapters in Books

Anderson, Elizabeth, 'Compensation Within the Limits of Reliance Alone', in John W. Chapman (ed.), *Compensatory Justice Nomos XXXIII* (New York, 1991), p. 178.

Austin, John L., *A Plea for Excuses*, in James O. Urmson & Geoffrey J. Warnock (eds), *Philosophical Papers* (2nd edn, Oxford, 1970), p. 175.

Brickman, Phillip *et al.*, 'Microjustice and Macrojustice', in Melvin J. Lerner & Sally C. Lerner (eds), *The Justice Motive in Social Behavior* (New York, 1981), p. 173.

Cooper-Stephenson, Ken, 'Corrective Justice, Substantive Equality and Tort Law', in Ken Cooper-Stephenson & Elaine Gibson (eds), *Tort Theory* (Toronto, 1993), p. 48.

—— 'Economic Analysis, Substantive Equality and Tort Law', in Ken Cooper-Stephenson & Elaine Gibson (eds), *Tort Theory* (Toronto, 1993), p. 131.

Cullen, Bernard, 'Philosophical Theories of Justice', in Klaus R. Scherer (ed.), *Justice: Interdisciplinary Perspectives* (Cambridge, 1992), p. 15.

Friedman, Milton & Stigler George J., 'Roofs or Ceilings? The Current Housing Problem', in Walter Block & Edgar Olsen (eds), *Rent Control: Myth and Realities* (Canada, 1981), p. 87.

Goodin, Robert E., 'Compensation and Redistribution', in John W. Chapman (ed.), *Compensatory Justice Nomos XXXIII* (New York, 1991), p. 143.

Hartmann, Heidi, 'Capitalism, Patriarchy and Job Segregation by Sex', in Elizabeth Abel & Emily K. Abel (eds), *The Signs Reader: Women, Gender and Scholarship* (Chicago, 1983), p. 193.

Kennedy, Duncan, 'Law-and-Economics from the Perspective of Critical Legal Studies', in Peter Newman (ed.), *The New Palgrave Dictionary of Economics and the Law* (vol. 2, London, 1998), p. 465.

Levenkron, Nomi, 'Civil Suits of Victims of Trafficking Against the Traffickers: And Yet, It Does Move', in Guy Mundlak & Mimi Ajzenstadt (eds), *Law, Society & Culture: Empowerment* (forthcoming, 2007).

Martin, Sheilah L., 'The Control of Women through Gender-Biased Laws on Human Reproduction', in Richard F. Devlin (ed.), *Canadian Perspectives on Legal Theory* (Toronto, 1991), p. 291.

Posner, Richard A., 'Wealth Maximization and Tort Law: A Philosophical Inquiry', in David G. Owen (ed.), *Philosophical Foundations of Tort Law* (Oxford, 1995), p. 99.

Rawls, John, 'The Basic Structure as Subject', in Alvin I. Goldman & Jaegwon Kim (eds), *Values and Morals* (Dordrecht, 1978), p. 47.

Raz, Joseph, 'A Right to dissent? I. Civil Disobedience', *The Authority of Law* (Oxford, 1979).

Stapleton, Jane, 'Duty of Care Factors: A Selection from the Judicial Menus', in Peter Cane & Jane Stapleton (eds), *The Law of Obligations: Essays in Celebration of John Fleming* (Oxford, 1998), p. 59.

Sutherland, Kate, 'The New Equality Paradigm: The Impact of Charter Equality Principles on Private Law Decisions', in David Schneiderman & Kate Sutherland (eds), *Charting the Consequences* (Toronto, 1997), p. 245.

Taylor, Charles, 'The Nature and Scope of Distributive Justice', in *Philosophy and the Human Sciences* (Cambridge, 1985), p. 289.

Waldron, Jeremy, 'Moments of Carelessness and Massive Loss', in David G. Owen (ed.), *Philosophical Foundations of Tort Law* (Oxford, 1995), p. 387.

Wright, Richard W., 'Right, Justice and Tort Law', in David G. Owen (ed.), *Philosophical Foundations of Tort Law* (Oxford, 1995), p. 159.

—— 'The Standards of Care in Negligence Law', in David G. Owen (ed.), *Philosophical Foundations of Tort Law* (Oxford, 1995), p. 249.

Wiggins, David, 'Claims of Need', in Ted Honderich (ed.), *Morality and Objectivity: A Tribute to J.L. Mackie* (London, 1985), p. 149.

Articles

Abel, Richard L., 'General Damages are Incoherent, Incalculable, Incommensurable, and Inegalitarian (But Otherwise A Great Idea)', 55 *DePaul L Rev* (2006) 253.

—— 'A Critique of Torts', 37 *UCLA L Rev* (1990) 785.

—— 'Should Tort Law Protect Property Against Accidental Loss?', 23 *San Diego L Rev* (1986) 79.

Ackerman, Bruce A., 'Regulating Slum Housing Markets on Behalf of the Poor: Of Housing Codes, Housing Subsidies and Income Redistribution Policy', 80 *Yale LJ* (1971) 1093.

Adjin-Tettey, Elizabeth, 'Replicating and Perpetuating Inequalities in Personal Injury Claims Through Female-Specific Contingencies', 49 *McGill LJ* (2004) 309.

Adler, Matthew D. & Posner Eric A., 'Rethinking Cost-Benefit Analysis', 109 *Yale LJ* (1999) 165.

Allen, Jessie, 'A Possible Remedy for Unthinking Discrimination', 61 *Brooklyn L Rev* (1995) 1299.

Annas, George J., 'Pregnant Women as Fetal Containers', 16 *Hastings Cent Rep* (1986) 13.

Arend, Patrice S., 'Defamation in an Age of Political Correctness: Should a False Public Statement That a Person is Gay be Defamatory?', 18 *N Ill UL Rev* (1997) 99.

Avraham, Ronen, Fortus David & Logue Kyle, 'Revisiting the Roles of Legal Rules and Tax Rules in Income Redistribution: A Response to Kaplow & Shavell', 89 *Iowa L Rev* (2004) 1125.

Ayers, Ian & Gertner Robert, 'Filling Gaps in Incomplete Contracts: An Economic Theory of Default Rules', 99 *Yale LJ* (1989) 87.

Bamforth, Nicholas, 'Conceptions of Anti-Discrimination Law', 24 *Oxford J Legal Stud* (2004) 693.

Bender, Leslie, 'An Overview of Feminist Torts Scholarship', 78 *Cornell L Rev* (1993) 575.

—— 'A Lawyer's Primer on Feminist Theory and Tort', 38 *J Legal Educ* (1988) 3.

Bernstein, Lisa, 'Private Commercial Law in the Cotton Industry: Creating Cooperation through Rules, Norms, and Institutions', 99 *Mich L Rev* (2001) 1724.

—— 'Understanding the Limits of Court-Connected ADR: A Critique of Federal Court-Annexed Arbitration Programs', 141 *U Pa LR* (1993) 2169.

Bittker, Boris I., 'A "Comprehensive Tax Base" as a Goal of Income Tax Reform', 80 *Harv L Rev* (1967) 925.

Blumrosen, Alfred W., 'Strangers in Paradise: Griggs v. Duke Power Co. and the Concept of Employment Discrimination', *71 Mich L Rev* (1972) 59.

Brion, Denis. J., 'An Essay on LULU, NIMBY, and The Problem of Distributive Justice', 15 *BC Envtl Aff L Rev* (1988) 437.

Calabresi, Guido & Hirschoff Jon T., 'Toward a Test for Strict Liability in Tort', 81 *Yale LJ* (1972) 1055.

Calabresi, Guido & Klevorick Alvin K., 'Four Tests for Liability in Torts', 14 *J Legal Stud* (1985) 585.

Calnan, Alan L., 'Distributive and Corrective Justice Issues in Contemporary Tobacco Litigation', 27 *Sw UL Rev* (1998) 577.

Cane, Peter, 'Mens Rea in Tort Law', 20 *Oxford J Legal Stud* (2000) 533.

Chavkin, Wendy, 'Mandatory Treatment for Drug Use During Pregnancy', 266 *JAMA* (1991) 1556.

Chemerinsky, Erwin, 'The Supreme Court, 1988 Term-Foreword: The Vanishing Constitution', 103 *Harv L Rev* (1989) 43.

Coffey, Carolyn, 'Whither v. State: Aberrational Judicial Response or Wave of the Future for Maternal Substance Abuse Cases?', 14 *J Contemp Health L & Pol'y* (1997) 211.

Cohen, Morris R., 'Property and Sovereignty', 13 *Cornell LQ* (1927) 8.

Coleman, Jules & Ripstein Arthur, 'Mischief and Misfortune', 41 *McGill LJ* (1995) 91.

Collins, Hugh, 'Social Inclusion: A Better Approach to Equality Issues', 14 *Transnat'l L & Contemp Probs* (2005) 897.

Cooter, Robert, 'Prices and Sanctions', 84 *Colum L Rev* (1984) 1523.

Craswell, Richard, 'Passing on the Costs of Legal Rules: Efficiency and Distribution in Buyer-Seller Relationships', 43 *Stan L Rev* (1991) 361.

Cross, Frank B., 'The Judiciary and Public Choice', 50 *Hastings LJ* (1999) 355.

Dagan, Hanoch, 'The Craft of Property', 91 *Cal L Rev* (2003) 1517.

—— 'Just Compensation, Interests and Social Meanings', 99 *Mich L Rev* (2000) 134.

—— 'Takings and Distributive Justice', 85 *Va L Rev* (1999) 741.

Dagan, Hanoch & Heller Michael, 'The Liberal Commons', 110 *Yale LJ* (2001) 549.

Delgado, Richard, 'Affirmative Action as a Majoritarian Device: Or, Do You Really Want to Be a Role Model?', 89 *Mich L Rev* (1997) 1222.

—— ' "Rotten Social Background": Should the Criminal Law Recognize a Defense of Severe Environmental Deprivation?', 3 *L & Ineq J* (1985) 9.

Dotan, Yoav, 'The "Public", the "Private" and the Legal Norm of Equality', 20 *Can JL & Soc* (2005) 207.

Dworkin, Ronald, 'Darwin's New Bulldog', 111 *Harv L Rev* (1998) 1718.

—— 'Is Wealth a Value?', 9 *J Legal Stud* (1980) 191.

Elhauge, Einer R., 'Does Interest Group Theory Justify More Intrusive Judicial Review?', 101 *Yale LJ* (1991) 31.

Epstein, Richard A., 'The Social Consequences of Common Law Rules', 95 *Harv L Rev* (1982) 1717.

'Intentional Harms', 4 *J Legal Stud* (1975) 391, p. 441.

—— 'A Theory of Strict Liability', 2 *J Legal Stud* (1973) 151.

Eskridge, William N., Jr & Frickey Philip P., 'Statutory Interpretation as Practical Reasoning', 42 *Stan L Rev* (1990) 321.

Feliciano, Tanya, 'Davis v. Davis: What About Future Disputes?', *26 Conn L Rev* (1993) 305.

Fenrich, William J., 'Common Law Protection of Individuals' Rights in Personal Information', 65 *Fordham L Rev* (1996) 951.

Fletcher, George P., 'Fairness and Utility in Tort Theory', 85 *Harv L Rev* (1972) 537.

Galantar, Marc, 'Why the "Haves" Come Out Ahead: Speculations on the Limits of Social Change', 9 *Law & Soc'y Rev* (1974) 95.

Gallagher, Janet, 'Prenatal Invasions & Interventions: What's Wrong with Fetal Rights', 10 *Harv Women's LJ* (1987) 9.

Gilles, Stephen G., 'On Determining Negligence: Hand Formula Balancing, the Reasonable Person Standard, and the Jury', 54 *Vand L Rev* (2001) 813.

—— 'The Invisible Hand Formula', 80 *Va L Rev* (1994) 1015.

Gordon, Wendy J., 'On Owning Information: Intellectual Property and the Restitutionary Impulse', 78 *Va L Rev* (1992) 149.

Hale, Robert L., 'Coercion and Distribution in a Supposedly Non-coercive State', 38 *Pol Sci Q* (1923) 470.

Hammitt James K., 'Tort Standards and Jury Decisions', 14 *J Legal Stud* (1985) 751.

Hans, Valerie P., 'The Illusions And Realities of Jurors' Treatment of Corporate Defendants', 48 *DePaul L Rev* (1998) 327.

Henderson, James A., Jr & Twerski Aaron D., 'Consumer Expectations' Last Hope: A Response to Professor Kysar', 103 *Colum LR* (2003) 1791.

Hettinger, Edwin C., 'Justifying Intellectual Property', 18 *Phil & Pub Aff* (1989) 31.

Hogg, Peter W. & Bushell Allison A., 'The Charter Dialogue Between Courts and Legislatures', 35 *Osgoode Hall LJ* (1997) 75.

Honoré, Tony, 'Responsibility and Luck', 104 *LQ Rev* (1988) 530.

Howard, Rhoda, 'The Full-Belly Thesis: Should Economic Rights Take Priority Over Civil and Political Rights? Evidence from Sub-Saharan Africa', 5 *Hum Rts Q* (1983) 467.

Hutchinson, Allan C., 'Birth Rights: The Burden of Caring For Unwanted or Seriously Injured Children', 4(2) *National* (1995) 40.

—— 'Beyond Non-Fault', 73 *Cal L Rev* (1985) 755.

Issacharoff, Samuel & Nelson Justin, 'Discrimination with a Difference: Can Employment Law Accommodate the Americans with Disabilities Act?', 79 *NCL Rev* (2001) 307.

James, Fleming, Jr & Dickinson John J., 'Accident Proneness and Accident Law', 63 *Harv L Rev* (1950) 769.

Johnsen, Dawn E., 'The Creation of Fetal Rights: Conflicts with Women's Constitutional Rights to Liberty, Privacy, and Equal Protection', 95 *Yal*e *LJ* (1986) 599.

Jolls, Christine, 'Behavioral Economics Analysis of Redistributive Legal Rules', 51 *Vand L Rev* (1998) 1653.

Kahn, Douglas A. & Lehman Jefferey S., 'Tax Expenditure Budgets: A Critical View', 54 *Tax Notes* (1992) 1661.

Kahneman, Daniel, Knetsch Jack L. & Thaler Richard H., 'Anomalies: The Endowment Effect, Loss Aversion, and Status Quo Bias', 5 *J Econ Persp* (1991) 193.

Kaplow, Louis, 'Rules Versus Standards: An Economic Analysis', 42 *Duke LJ* (1992) 557.

Kaplow, Louis & Shavell Steven, 'Should Legal Rules Favor the Poor? Clarifying the Role of Legal Rules and the Income Tax in Redistributing Income', 29 *J Leg Stud* (2000) 821.

—— 'Why the Legal System is Less Efficient than the Income Tax in Redistributing Income', 23 *J Leg Stud* (1994) 667.

Keating, Gregory C., 'Distributive and Corrective Justice in the Tort Law of Accidents', 74 *S Cal L Rev* (2000) 193.

Kennedy, Duncan, 'Distributive and Paternalist Motives in Contract and Tort Law, with Special Reference to Compulsory Terms and Unequal Bargaining Power', 41 *Md L Rev* (1982) 563.

Keren-Paz, Tsachi, 'Compensating Injury to Autonomy: Normative Evaluation, Recent Developments and Future Tendencies', 11 *Colman LR* (forthcoming 2007).
—— 'Private Law Redistribution, Predictability and Liberty', 50 *McGill LJ* (2005) 327.
—— 'On Mothers, Babies and Bathwater: Tort Law, Distributive Justice and Prenatal Duties', 14 *Social & Legal Studies* (2005) 179.
—— ' "It Costs Me More": Rejecting the Arguments of Illegitimacy and Excessive Cost Brought against the Promotion of Equality in Private Law', 7 *Haifa ULR* (2004) 541.
—— 'How Does Compensation Law Render the Poor Even Poorer? (And Why Does the Supreme Court Give Inconsistent Interpretation to the Compensation to Victims of Road Accidents Act?)', 28 *Tel-Aviv ULR* (2004) 299.
—— 'Egalitarianism as Justification: Why and How Should Egalitarian Considerations Reshape the Standard of Care in Negligence Law', 4 *Theor Inq L* (2003) 275.
—— 'An Inquiry into the Merits of Redistribution through Tort Law: Rejecting the Claim of Randomness', 16 *Can JL & Jur* (2003) 91.
Kerr, Ian R., 'Pre-Natal Fictions and Post-Partum Actions', 20 *Dal LR* (1997) 237.
Kolder, Gallagher & Parsons, 'Court-Ordered Obstetrical Interventions', 316 *New Eng J Med* (1987) 1192.
Koropp, David E., 'Setting the Standard: A Mother's Duty During the Prenatal Period', 2 *U Ill L Rev* (1989) 493.
Kronman, Anthony T., 'Contract Law and Distributive Justice', 89 *Yale LJ* (1980) 472.
Kysar, Douglas A., 'The Expectations of Consumers', 103 *Colum LR* (2003) 1700.
Lee, Robert G., 'Rent Control – The Economic Impact of Social Legislation', 12 *Oxford J Legal Stud* (1992) 543.
Littleton, Christine A., 'Reconstructing Sexual Equality', 75 *Calif L Rev* (1987) 1279.
Llewellyn Karl, 'Some Realism About Realism: Responding to Dean Pound', 44 *Harv L Rev* (1931) 1222.
Logue, Kyle & Avraham Ronen, 'Redistributing Optimally: of Tax Rules, Legal Rules, and Insurance', 56 *Tax L Rev* (2003) 157.
McAdams, Richard H., 'The Origin, Development, and Regulation of Norms', 96 *Mich L Rev* (1997) 338.
Macaulay, Stewart, 'Law and Behavioral Sciences: Is There Any There There?', 6 *Law & Pol'y* (1984) 149.
McCann, Michael W., 'Reform Litigation on Trial', 17 *Law & Soc Inq* (1992) 715.
McGuire, Kevin T., 'Repeat Players in the Supreme Court: The Role of Experienced Lawyers in Litigation Success', 57 *J Pol* (1995) 187.
McIntyre, Sheila, 'Backlash Against Equality: The "Tyranny" of the "Politically Correct" ', 38 *McGill LJ* (1993) 1.
Macneil, Ian R., 'Contracts: Adjustment of Long-term Economic Relations Under Classical, Neoclassical and Relational Contract Law', 72 *Nw UL Rev* (1978) 854.
Mandel, Michael, 'Democracy and the New Constitutionalism in Israel', 33 *Isr L Rev* (1999) 259.

—— 'A Brief History of the New Constitutionalism, or "How We Changed Everything So That Everything Would Remain the Same" ', 32 *Isr LR* (1998) 250.

Martin, Robyn, 'A Feminist View of the Reasonable Man: An Alternative Approach to Liability in Negligence for Personal Injury', 23 *Anglo-Am L Rev* (1994) 334.

Martin, Sheilah & Coleman Murray, 'Judicial Intervention in Pregnancy', 40 *McGill LJ* (1995) 947.

Mattar, Mohamed Y., 'Trafficking in Persons: An Annotated Legal Bibliography', 96 *Law Libr J* (2004) 669.

Mautner, Menachem, ' "The Eternal Triangles of the Law:" Toward a Theory of Priorities in Conflicts Involving Remote Parties', 90 *Mich L Rev* (1991) 95.

Miller, David, 'Distributive Justice: What the People Think', 102 *Ethics* (1992) 555.

Miller, Gregory T., 'Behind the Battle Lines: A Comparative Analysis of the Necessity to Enact Comprehensive Federal Products Liability Reforms', 45 *Buffalo L Rev* (1997) 241.

Morris, Andrew, 'On the Normative Foundations of Indirect Discrimination Law: Understanding the Competing Models of Discrimination Law as Aristotelian Forms of Justice', 15 *Oxford J Legal Stud* (1995) 199.

Neilsen, Kai, 'Radical Egalitarian Justice: Justice as Equality', 5 *Soc Theory & Prac* (1979) 209.

Note, 'Distributive Liberty: A Relational Model of Freedom, Coercion, and Property Law', 107 *Harv L Rev* (1994) 859.

Note, 'The Impact of Medical Knowledge on the Law Relating to Prenatal Injuries', 110 *U Pa L Rev* (1962) 554.

Oppenheimer, David B., 'Exacerbating the Exasperating: Title VII Liability of Employers for Sexual Harassment Committed by Their Supervisors', 81 *Cornell L Rev* (1995) 66.

—— 'Negligent Discrimination', 141 *U Pa L Rev* (1993) 899.

Otsuka, Michael, 'Killing the Innocent in Self-Defense', 23 *Phil & Pub Aff* (1994) 74.

Page, Benjamin I. & Shapiro Robert Y., 'Effects of Public Opinion on Policy', 77 *Am J Pol Sci* (1983) 75.

Paltrow, Lynn M., 'Pregnant Drug Users, Fetal Persons, and the Threat to *Roe v. Wade*', 62 *Alb. L. Rev*. (1999) 999.

Panitch, Alise R., 'The Davis Dilemma: How to Prevent Battles over Frozen Embryos', 41 *Case W Res L Rev* (1991) 543.

Pape, Julie Barker, 'Physician Data Banks: The Public's Right To Know Versus The Physician's Right To Privacy', 66 *Fordham LR* (1997) 975.

Peck, Cornelius J., 'The Role of the Courts and Legislatures in the Reform of Tort Law', 48 *Minn L Rev* (1963) 265.

Perry, Stephen R., 'The Moral Foundations of Tort Law', 77 *Iowa L Rev* (1992) 449.

Poirier, Marc R., 'Is Cognitive Bias at Work a Dangerous Condition on Land?', 7 *Employee Rts & Emp Po"y J* (2003) 459.

Porat, Ariel, 'Negligence Law in the Supreme Court: Search for the Underline Theory', 3 *Yearbook on Israeli Law* (1996) 373.

Porat, Ariel & Stein Alex, 'Liability for Uncertainty: Making Evidential Damage Actionable', 18 *Cardozo L Rev* (1997) 1891.

Posner, Eric A., 'Economic Analysis of Contract Law After Three Decades: Success or Failure?', 112 *Yale LJ* (2003) 829.

Posner, Richard A., 'A Theory of Negligence', 1 *J Legal Stud* (1972) 29.

Priest, George L., 'The Current Insurance Crisis and Modern Tort Law', 96 *Yale LJ* (1987) 152.

Ramsay, Iain, 'Consumer Credit Law, Distributive Justice and the Welfare State', 15 *Oxford JL Stud* (1995) 177.

Réaume, Denise G., 'Harm and Fault in Discrimination Law: The Transition from Intentional to Adverse Effect Discrimination', 2 *Theoretical Inq L* (2001) 349.

Reichman, Amnon, 'Professional Status and the Freedom to Contract: Toward a Common Law Duty of Non-Discrimination', 14 *Can JL & Juris* (2001) 79.

Robertson, John A., 'Procreative Liberty and the Control of Conception, Pregnancy, and Childbirth', 69 *Va L Rev* (1983) 405.

Sanchirico, Chris W., 'Deconstructing the New Efficiency Rationale', 86 *Cornell L Rev* (2001) 1003.

—— 'Should Legal Rules be Used to Redistribute Wealth? Taxes Versus Legal Rules as Instruments for Equity: A More Equitable View', 29 *J Legal Stud* (2000) 797.

Schauer, Frederick, 'The Calculus of Distrust', 77 *Va L Rev* (1991) 653.

—— 'Rules and the Rule of Law', 14 *Harv JL & Pub Pol'y* (1991) 645.

Schroeder, Christopher H., 'Corrective Justice and Liability for Increasing Risks', 37 *UCLA L Rev* (1990) 439.

Schwartz, Alan, 'Products Liability and Judicial Wealth Redistributions', 51 *Ind LJ* (1976) 558.

Schwartz, Gary T., Mixed Theories of Tort Law: Affirming Both Deterrence And Corrective Justice', 75 *Tex L Rev* (1997) 1801.

—— 'Tort Law and the Economy in Nineteenth-Century America: A Reinterpretation', 90 *Yale LJ* (1981) 1717.

Scott, Robert E., 'The Legal Construction of Norms: The Limits of Behavioral Theories of Law and Social Norms', 86 *Va L Rev* (2000) 1603.

Segal, Jeffrey A., 'Separation-of-Powers Games in the Positive Theory of Congress and Courts', 91 *Am Pol Sci Rev* (1997) 28.

Selmi, Michael, 'Discrimination as Accident: Old Whine, New Bottle', 74 *Ind LJ* (1999) 1233.

Sheinbach, Donna M., 'Examining Disputes over Ownership Rights to Frozen Embryos: Will Prior Consent Documents Survive if Challenged by State Law and/or Constitutional Principles?', 48 *Cath UL Rev* (1999) 989.

Sherwin, Emily L., 'The Limits of Feminism', 9 *J Contemp Leg Issues* (1998) 249.

Simons, Kenneth. W., 'The Hand Formula in the Draft Restatement (Third) of Torts: Encompassing Fairness as Well as Efficiency Values', 54 *Vand L Rev* (2001) 901.

Stern, Paul, 'Citizenship, Community and Pluralism: The Current Dispute on Distributive Justice', 11 *Praxis-Int'l* (1991) 261.

Stigler, George J., 'The Economics of Minimum Wage Legislation', 36 *Am Econ Rev* (1946) 358, pp. 362–3.

Sugarman, Stephen D. 'Doing Away with Tort Law', 73 *Cal L Rev* (1985) 555.

Sunstein Cass R., 'On the Expressive Function of Law', 144 *U Pa LR* (1996) 2021.

—— 'Interest Groups in American Public Law', 38 *Stan L Rev* (1985) 29.

Tiefenbrun, Susan W., 'Sex Sells but Drugs Don't Talk: Trafficking of Women, Sex Workers and an Economic Solution', 24 *T Jefferson L Rev* (2002) 161.

Trakman, Leon E., 'Substantive Equality in Constitutional Jurisprudence: Meaning Within Meaning', 7 *Can JL & Jur* (1994) 27.

Travis, Michelle A., 'Perceived Disabilities, Social Cognition, and "Innocent Mistakes" ', 55 *Vand L Rev* (2002) 481.

Ursin, Edmund, 'Judicial Creativity and Tort Law', 49 *Geo Wash L Rev* (1981) 229.

Walter, Paula, 'His, Hers, or Theirs – Custody, Control, and Contracts: Allocating Decisional Authority Over Frozen Embryos', 29 *Seton Hall L Rev* (1999) 937.

Wax, Amy L., 'Discrimination as Accident', 74 *Ind LJ* (1999) 1129.

Weinrib, Ernest J., 'The Case for a Duty to Rescue', 90 *Yale LJ* (1980) 247.

Weiss Uri, 'The Regressive Effect of Legal Uncertainty', *Tel Aviv University Legal Working Paper Series. Tel Aviv University Law Faculty Papers;* Working Paper 30 (December 2005) <law.bepress.com/taulwps/fp/art30>.

Westen, Peter, 'The Empty Idea of Equality', 95 *Harv L Rev* (1982) 537.

Wise, Paul H., 'Child Beauty, Child Rights and the Devaluation of Women', 4(1) *Health and Human Rights* (1995) 470.

Wonnell, Christopher T., 'Replacing the Unitary Principle of Unjust Enrichment', 45 *Emory LJ* (1996) 153.

Woodall, Kevin, 'Private Law Liability of Public Authorities for Negligent Inspection and Regulation', 37 *McGill LJ* (1992) 83.

Yadlin, Omri, 'Judicial Activism and Judicial Discretion as a Strategic Game', 19 *Bar Ilan University L Rev* (2002) 665.

Young, Iris M., 'Unruly Categories: A Critique of Nancy Fraser's Dual Systems Theory', 222 *New Left Rev* (1997) 147.

Young, Robert, 'Egalitarianism and Personal Desert', 102 *Ethics* (1992) 319.

Zamir, Eyal, 'The Inverted Hierarchy of Contract Interpretation and Supplementation', 97 *Colum L Rev* (1997) 1710.

Other Sources

Keren-Paz, Tsachi, *Limits of Private Law* (DJur dissertation, York University, 2000).

Morris, Chris, 'Family Believes Ryan Forgotten', *The Toronto Sun* (10 July 1999).

Restatement (Second) of the Law of Torts (1965) (US).

Restatement (Third) of Torts: Products Liability (1998) (US).

Restatement (Second) of Contracts (1981) (US).

Royal Commission on New Reproductive Technologies, *Proceed with Care: Final Report* (vol. 2, Ottawa, 1993).

Tibbetts, Janice, 'Mother Attacks Pro-Choicers After Son Loses Foetal Rights Case: Expresses Anger in Letter Sent to Several Newspapers', *National Post* (15 July 1999) A5.

Index

Aristotle 5, 9

Calabresi, Guido 89
causation, *see also* remoteness
 factual causation 77, 186
 lost chance doctrine 186
 mass torts, in 77
 proximate cause 93
cognitive psychology
 cognitive bias 44–46, 63, 118
 endowment effect 49, 103, 105–106, 109
  — and progressive redistribution 63–64
 mental accounting 45–46
Cohen, Morris 25
compensation rules 182–186
 accommodation expenses 185–86
 adjustment rule, the 112–13
 consequential loss due to poverty 70, 184–86
 damages for discrimination 180
 disutility, and 52, 69, *see also* egalitarian approach, disutility of losses
 full compensation, *see restitutio ad integrum*
 home versus institutional care 77, 184
 lost years, the 78, 183
 pain and suffering 53
 progressive redistribution of wealth 180
 punitive damages 180
 restitutio ad integrum, see restitutio ad integrum
 retribution and 180
 standardized awards 40, 51–52, 78
  — to minor females 77–78, 131, 183
  — for non-pecuniary damages 182–83
complement thesis, the 35–36, 57–58, 165
contextual analysis 14–16, 44, 58, 60, 62, 65, 71, 80–81, 104, 181
 of criteria for distribution 8
 importance of 3
 and judicial discretion 15–16

corrective justice 1, 6, 24, 41, 59, 85–89, 96–101, 166, 180, 186
 and distributive justice 24, 59, 87–89, 95–96, 99, 113
 features of 87
Craswell, Richard 63
Cross, Frank 29–30
cross-subsidy
 adverse selection 148–49
 maternal prenatal duty 148–50
 negligence and strict liability 71
 progressive cross-subsidy 41, 61, 148–49
 regressive nature of 35, 41, 54, 61, 64, 69, 113, 149

damages *see* compensation rules
desert 7, 17, 72, 93, 96–101, 148–152, 180
deterrence 17, 165–67, 170–71, 182, 186
 administrative costs and 45, 52, 170–71
 cognitive biases and 44–6
 compensation rules and 51–52
 insurance and 43–44, 139, 149
 maternal prenatal duty and lack of 139–140, 146, 149
 other incentives to be cautious 15, 139
 scepticism about 44, 52
 self preservation and 15
 under compensation and 52
diminishing marginal utility of money 11, 69, 92, 94, 99, 105–106, 109–10, 123, 186, *see also* egalitarian approach, disutility of losses; insurance
discrimination *see* negligence, discrimination as, egalitarian approach and
distributive effects of legal rules, inevitability of 24–25, 46–47, 58
distributive justice 5–8, *see also* egalitarian approach; equality effect; intra-group justice; redistribution
 criteria for distribution 6–8, 90, 92–101
  — contextual approach to 8
  — desert 7, 17, 96–101, 180, *see* desert

— entitlement theory 6–7
— equality 7, 17
as an appropriate criterion for distribution 83, 90, 94–96
— merit 17
— needs 7, 17, 178, 186, *see also* needs
entitlements distributed by
— material 6
— opposite distributive results 76, 147–48
— symbolic 6, 17, 42
localized distributive justice 34
participants in 6, 34–35
pluralist theories of 8, 19–20
political nature of 23
duty of care 93, 168
cost-benefit analysis 134, 157
discriminate, not to 77, 168–72, 177–79
lawyer's liability 77, 114–15, 134–35
maternal prenatal duty *see* maternal prenatal duty
preventing a risk created by a third party 121
role of 133–36, 157, 177–79
subjective burden created by 178
vasectomy operations 77, 135

economic analysis 1, 42–54, 147 *see also* deterrence
efficiency *see* efficiency and egalitarianism; tort law, goals of
game theory 31–32
legal rules, guiding potential of 44, 62–63, 169–70
moral hazard 52, 147
public choice 28–31, 39, 57
— difference between tort law redistribution and judicial review 30–33
— easier to block phenomenon 30, 35–36, 58
risk aversion 147, 155
rules versus standards 163–64
wealth effects 51–52
efficiency and egalitarianism 42–54, 82, 104, 107–109, 170
congruence of efficiency and equality 52–53, 135, 143
equal distortion of incentive to work 44–46
equal effectiveness 46–51
pareto superior rule as improving the lot of the disadvantaged 63
trade-off between efficiency and equality 51–53, 78, 83, 114, 122–23
egalitarian approach 8–13, *see also* equality effect; distributive justice; intra-group justice; redistribution
accident proneness and 45, 54, 174–75
accountability of judges 23–33
ad hoc rules 59
— *ex ante/post* analysis 44, 63–64, 165, 167
— regressive effect of 59
andocentric bias 119
asymmetric solutions and 114, 122–23, 185
autonomous nature of 79
backlash 13, 61–65, 118, 182
barrier to comprehensive change, as 18–19, 159–60, *see also* egalitarian approach, complement thesis and; egalitarian approach, backlash
— excessive cost/randomness and 60
comparative institutional progressiveness 55–57
complement thesis and 35–36, 57–58, 165
concepts of equality 8–11, 94–96
contracts and 20, 53, 62–63, 115, 131
corrective justice and 59, 96–101
costs of endorsing inequality 36, 56, 58
courts' practice as consistent with 128–29
criterion in distributive justice, as 7
deep pockets 89, 93, 128–29
descriptive claims 20–21, 125–31
desert 17, 72, 96–101, 150–52
determinative, is not 80
difference principle, and the 7, 65, 76, 111–12
different levels of operation 12–13, 70–73
— desirability of specific torts and doctrines 73
— no-fault regime 71–72, 130
— tort law and alternative compensation schemes 70–71
disadvantage and 12, 19
discrimination 20, 47, 79–80, 161–180
disempowering, as 76, 144, 165
distinction between private and public 20
disutility of losses 52, 69, 89, 92–96, 99–100, 118, 120–4, 173, 185, *see also* compensation rules, disutility, and
— comparing disutility 105–113
efficiency and, *see* efficiency and egalitarianism
egalitarian ethos and 8, 56, 58, 130–31

empowering, as 46, 48–50, 101–103, 154, 164–65
equality effect, and the 12
excuse 8, 50, 94–96, 101–103, 134, 167, 170, 177
fairness and 71, 82, 90–91, 99, 104, 113, 122, 136, 149
gender equality and 25, 54, 60, 115–121, 122–23, 124–25, 131, 139–142, 144, 150, 158–59 *see also* frozen ova; intra-group justice; maternal prenatal duty; parents' liability for negligent supervision
group identity 6, 10, 12
illegitimacy 23–33, 57, 163, 166
immutable characteristics and 12–13, 39, 59, 73
ineffectiveness 55–65
insurance *see* insurance
intra-group justice 35, 39, 61–62, 63–65 *see also* intra-group justice
intrinsic value of 51, 169–170
juries 128
justification 96, 101–103, 167, 177
justification of the regressive result 83
liberty 41–42, 166–67, 170–71
limits of 19–21, 57
limits of private law and 20
loss-spreading 71, 82, 89, 93, 129
multiplicity of disadvantage 73–74
over- and under-inclusiveness 59–60, 82, 166
— randomness/excessive cost and 59, 159–160
parties' expectations 82–83
paternalism and 147–48, 152, 154
passing on 60–61, 75, 78, 82, 182
predictability 40–41, 59, 155, 166–67, 170–71
pricing 61–65
— homogenous/heterogeneous beneficiaries and 64, 74, 76
— redistribution and 63–64
private law, in 20, 117–18, 131
randomness 33–40, 57, 159, 166, 183
Rawls and 11, *see also* egalitarian approach, difference principle, and the; Rawls, John
reasonableness and 117–18
reciprocity and 142
recognition 10–11, 47–48
redistribution 10, *see also* redistribution; distributive justice
regressive results as an illegitimate exception 149, 156, 158, 175
relationship between judge's accountability and progressive outcomes 56–57, 58
relative advantage of the 'haves' in litigation and legislation 57–58
relative progressiveness of the judiciary 18–19, 55–57, 165
relevance of 79, 83, 124–25
risk of error and 167
status quo and 19, *see also* status quo
strength of other policy considerations 83–84
strong version of 12
third parties 61, 75, 120, 121–125, 135–36, 143
veto, should not serve merely as 80
weak version of 12, 46
weight accorded to 80–84
equality effect, *see also* egalitarian approach; distributive justice; intra-group justice; redistribution
balancing against other considerations 80–84, 135–36, 144, 148–49
conflicting dimensions of
— conflicting effects on different disadvantaged groups 76, 142–43
— conflicting effects on members of same group (intra-justice) 72
— conflicting effects on the same person 76, 147–48
— trade-off between symbolic and material results 76, 147–48
dimensions of 76, 81
expanding liability due to progressive effect 77–78, 175
factual and conceptual problems in determining 73–74
importance of overall effect 74–76, 142–43
limiting liability due to regressive effect 78
magnitude of 81
negligence and strict liability, of 71–72
particular versus general 13, 73
status of parties 81–82
symbolic effect of regressive result 83, 144, 147–48, 152–54, *see also* insurance; negligence; standard of care; tort law

third parties 60–61, 75, 143
unclear recommendations 78–79

Fraser, Nancy 10
frozen ova, disputes over 25, 77, 115–121
backlash 61–62, 118
negligent misrepresentation 115–17
promissory estoppel 116–17
reliance 118–120

Goodin, Robert 36–37

Hale, Robert 25
Hand formula, the 87–89, 91,
capable of including egalitarian considerations 126
regressive nature of 95, 97, 106–109
and the single owner test 98–99
Horwitz, Morton 72

informed consent, *see* tort law, informed consent
insurance
deterrence 43–44, 139
guaranteeing predictability, as 41
loss-spreading and 129–130, 148–49
maternal prenatal duty and 53, 76, 137–38, 140, 145–160
— creating unity of interests 145–47
— increasing autonomy 146
premiums collection 148–150, 156
premiums, sex based 54, 148–150
progressive cross-subsidy 54
regressive cross-subsidy 35, 69
response for partial participation in redistribution 35
symbolic meaning of liability, change of 154
instrumentalist approaches to law 1, 13–14
intra-group justice, *see also* distributive justice; egalitarian approach; equality effect; redistribution
backlash and 62, 64–65, 118
blurred distinction with inter-group justice 74
defendants, among 74, 78, 148–152
disadvantaged, among 37, 39–40
giving end, among the 35
'haves', among the 37, 39
homogenous/heterogeneous claimants 64, 72, 74
passing on 61
parents, among 78
plaintiffs, among 71, 73, 74, 78, 123–25, 186
— in standardized awards 183
potential victims of sexual assault, among 125
pregnant women, among 148–153
race and class 150–52
receiving end, among the 35
tension with inter-group justice 40, 72, 77, 83, 186
under-inclusiveness and 82
inter-group justice 35, 37, 39, 148–150, 152–53, 186
pricing and 62–63
tension with intra-group justice 40, 72, 77, 83, 186

judiciary, the
discretion in developing law 26
— value judgments, made by 15–16, 24, 25–26, 104
legislature, and the 26–27, 33
— legislature's ability to amend 31–32, 165

Kaplow, Louis 42–54
Keating, Gregory 90

legislature, the
status quo and the 26–27
judiciary, and the, *see* judiciary and the legislature
libertarianism 25, 48–49, 68

maternal prenatal duty 47, 80, 131, 136–160
abortion, right to 139–140
collusion 146, 158
compensation and 139
desert and 148–152
deterrence and 139, 149
egalitarianism and 150
— unconditional duty 141–42
efficiency and 53, 143
fairness and 149
injunctions 155–56
insurance and 53, 140, 145–160
lifestyle choices 136–37, 151, 156
limited liability 78
loss-spreading and 149–150, 152, 158
option, as an 154, 156

symbolic effects of denying duty 76, 83, 147–48, 154
symbolic effects of imposing duty 140, 142, 151–52, 152–54, 159
— as distinct from the underlying behaviour 153
— as empowering 154
third parties (men), effects on 75, 143

needs 7, 17, 92–94, 99–101, 129–131, 178, 186
negligence, *see also* compensation rules; standard of care; tort law
analytical structure of 157–58
balancing between liberty and security, as 97, 162
discrimination as 161–180
— advantages in 163–66
— excuse, and 170, 177–78
— flexible response to, negligence as 163–64
— justification, and 177
— role of duty and standard 168–172
— symbolic aspect of discrimination 179
duty of care, *see* duty of care
inter- and intra-group justice 74
maternal prenatal duty, *see* maternal prenatal duty
negligent misrepresentation 116, 135
negligent supervision by parents, *see* parents' liability
non-legal sanctions 50, *see also* tort law, non-legal sanctions
standard of care, *see* standard of care
standard, negligence as 163–64
strict liability regime as opposed to 71–72, 78–79

Olson, Mancur 28

parents' liability for negligent supervision 47–48, 122–23, 134
desirable scope of 78, 122–23
efficiency and 52–53, 122
egalitarian solution to 52
fairness and 122
limited liability 78
— and over- and under-inclusiveness 59
regressive nature of the common law rule 52–53, 122–23
symbolic effects of liability 52, 83, 122–23
Perry, Stephen 34
pluralist approaches
distributive justice and, *see* distributive justice
law and 1, 8, 41, 44
necessity of trade-off, and 8, 41, 44
Posner, Richard 21
procedural justice 27–31, 55, 57
majoritarianism and 28, 57
trade-off with substantive justice 32–33, 55
promissory estoppel 116–17
public authorities, liability of 20, 78, 83, 121, 123–25, 127, 129, 135–36, 161
sexual assault, failure to prevent 124–25
public/private divide 25
punitive damages 180

Rawls, John 11, 27
and the difference principle, *see* egalitarian approach, difference principle, and the
redistribution 28, 30, 33, *see also* distributive justice; egalitarian approach; equality effect
abstaining from, political nature of 25–26
anti-discrimination rules 175
crudeness of results 33–34, 38–40
entitlements other than wealth 10, 42, 46–48, 54, 63
— better effectiveness of private law redistribution 46–48
— judiciary, redistribution by as desirable 57
endowment effect and 63–64
ideal distributive scheme, the 33–34, 37–39, 82, 143, 166
— direction of deviation from 37, 39, 54
— magnitude of deviation from 37
liberty, of 42
partiality of participants 33–34, 37–38, 159–160
pricing and 63
pro-disadvantaged redistributive rules 39, 63
rectifying regressive redistribution created by the same rule 46, 48–51, 53–54
— egalitarian commitment should not be limited to 53–54
tort law, redistribution by
— contract law, in comparison to 20, 42, 49, 62–63, 67

— empowering, as 46, 48–51
— tax and transfer, in comparison to
accountability, *see* illegitimacy
administrative costs 42–43, 49
complementing methods of
redistribution 51, 162
efficiency 42–54
illegitimacy 23–33, 57
liberty 41–42
likelihood that tax-based
redistribution will be used
42, 49, 53–54
predictability 41
randomness 34, 36
social meaning of redistribution
46, 48–51
visibility of 45–46, 49
remoteness 93, 160
eggshell skull doctrine 185
victim's lack of means 184–86
restitutio ad integrum 160, *see also*
compensation rules
choice of liability regime and 71–72
deviation from 6
efficiency and 51–52
policy considerations and 51–52
regressive effect 51, 67–69, 112
— diminishing marginal utility of
money 69
— ideological level 67–68
— incentive to risk the poor 68, 71
— partial compensation in practice
68–69
— regressive cross-subsidy 69, 71
regressive exposure to risk 49
retribution and 180

Schwartz, Alan 24
Shavell, Steven 42–54
standard of care, *see also* negligence; tort law
accident proneness 174
activity levels 88
considerations in determining negligence
104
comparing absolute value of accident and
precaution costs is regressive 70
cost-benefit analysis 126–27, 173
courts' endorsement of egalitarian
considerations 127–28
courts' practice as reflecting egalitarian
considerations 128–29
definition 125–27
deliberate activity and 173
discrimination and 172–77
efficiency and 104
fairness and 104
Hand formula, the, *see* Hand formula
non-liability as justification 50, 177
objective 130, 174–75
preventing sexual assault by a third party
83, 124–25, 131
progressive shift of risk 78, 114, 123–24
reasonable person, the 126, 172–73
risk shifting 78, 83, 121–122, 123–124
subjective 53, 130
— pecuniary loss of average victim
test 106–108
— pecuniary loss of same status
plaintiff test 108–109
— proportion test 105–106
— remaining wealth test 106
— wealth-dependent 50, 62–63, 78,
105–125
symbolic aspects of liability 87, 164–65,
167, 169–170, 175–76
— absence of duty, the difference
from 169–170, 171–72
— intrinsic value 169–170
unintended discrimination as breach of
174–175
status quo, the 19, 26–27
false neutrality of 25–26, 67
importance in challenging 39
less just than partial progressive
redistribution 36–40
perpetuating inequalities, as 36
strict liability 71–72, 78–79, 82, 85, 99,
107, 108, 113–114, 123, 164, 174
anti-discrimination legislation as strict
liability 164

tort law, *see also* compensation rules;
negligence; standard of care; strict
liability
alternative compensation schemes, and
70–71
contracts, and the difference from 1, 20,
42, 49, 82
causation, *see* causation
causing regressive redistribution, *see*
redistribution; *restitutio ad integrum*
defamation 75, 78, 131

descriptive claims 20–21, 125–131
deterrence 16, *see also* deterrence
distributive justice and 19–20, 24–25
egalitarian approach and 17, 19
fairness and 17, 71, 90–91
foreseeability 110
goals of 1, 16–17, 19–20, 71, 85–101
— corrective justice 86–89, 180, 186, *see also* corrective justice
— desert 17, 92–93, 96–101, 151, 180, *see also* desert
— efficiency 87–89, 186, *see also* deterrence; economic analysis
— equality 94–96, 130–31, 186, *see also* egalitarian approach
— loss-spreading 17, 71, 89, 92–94, *see also* insurance; needs
— needs 92–94, 99–101, 129–130, 186, *see also* needs
— translation to criteria for distribution 17
informed consent 13, 77–78, 183
intentional infliction of emotional distress 131, 162, 177
maternal prenatal duty, *see* negligence
negligence, *see* negligence
NIMBYs and LULUs 68
non-legal sanctions 47, 169, *see also* negligence, non-legal sanctions
nuisance 75
political nature of 1
products liability 114, 129
public authorities, liability of, *see* public authorities, liability of
punitive damages 180
redistribution by, *see* redistribution
remoteness *see* remoteness
symbolic aspects of 17, 40, 42, 46–51, 75, 113, 153, 169, *see also* negligence; standard of care
trafficking in persons 186–187
trespass 59
vicarious liability 73, 129
welfare state and 17–19
— Finnish experience, the 18

Weinrib, Ernest 21, 24, 34, 38